ENGLISH LITERATURE ADVANCING THROUGH HISTORY 3
The Seventeenth Century

Literature Series: 03

ENGLISH LITERATURE ADVANCING THROUGH HISTORY 3

The Seventeenth Century

By Petru GOLBAN

Copyright © 2021 Transnational Press London

All rights reserved. This book or any portion thereof may not be reproduced or used in any manner whatsoever without the express written permission of the publisher except for the use of brief quotations in a book review or scholarly journal.

First Published in 2021 by TRANSNATIONAL PRESS LONDON in the United Kingdom, 13 Stamford Place, Sale, M33 3BT, UK.

www.tplondon.com

Transnational Press London® and the logo and its affiliated brands are registered trademarks.
Requests for permission to reproduce material from this work should be sent to: sales@tplondon.com

Paperback
ISBN: 978-1-80135-087-7
Digital
ISBN: 978-1-80135-088-4

Cover Design: Nihal Yazgan

Transnational Press London Ltd. is a company registered in England and Wales No. 8771684.

ENGLISH LITERATURE ADVANCING THROUGH HISTORY 3

The Seventeenth Century

WITH THEORETICAL INTRODUCTION AND PRELIMINARIES

Petru GOLBAN

TRANSNATIONAL PRESS LONDON

2021

CONTENTS

Preface   1

Introduction: 7
Approaching Literary Practice and Studying British Literature in History

Preliminaries: 41
Learning Literary Heritage through Critical Tradition or Back to Tynyanov

Genre Theory for Poetry   61

1. The Intellectual Background   85
    1.1 The Period and Its Historical, Social and Cultural Implications
    1.2 The Philosophical Advancement of Modernity
    1.2.1 Francis Bacon and the "New Method"
    1.2.2 The Advancement of Classicism: French Contribution
    1.2.3 The Social and Political Philosophy: Thomas Hobbes and
        Leviathan
    1.2.4 Rationalists and Empiricists
    1.3 The Idea of Literature as a Critical Concern in the Seventeenth
        Century
    1.3.1 The English "Battle of the Books" or "La Querelle des Anciens et
        des Modernes" in the European Context
    1.3.2 Restoration, John Dryden and Prescribing Neoclassicism

2. The Literary Background   109
    2.1 The British Seventeenth Century and Its Literary Practice
    2.2 Metaphysical Poetry, Its Alternatives and Aftermath
    2.3 The Puritan Period and Its Literary Expression
    2.4 The Restoration Period and Its Literature
    2.5 The Picaresque Tradition in European and English Literature

3. Major Literary Voices   133
    3.1 The Metaphysical Poets I: John Donne
    3.2 The Metaphysical Poets II: George Herbert
    3.3 The Metaphysical Poets III: Andrew Marvell
    3.4 John Milton: The Voice of the Century
    3.4.1 *L'Allegro* and *Il Penseroso*
    3.4.2 *Lycidas* and Sonnets
    3.4.3 *Paradise Lost* and the Epic of Puritanism
    3.5 John Dryden and His Critical Theory and Literary Practice

Conclusion: The Literature of a Turbulent Age	171
References and Suggestions for Further Reading	181
Index	189

PREFACE

The present book is third in a series of works which aim to expose the complexity and essence, power and extent of the major periods, movements, trends, genres, authors, and literary texts in the history of English literature. Following this aim, the series will consist of monographs which cover the most important ages and experiences of English literary history, including Anglo-Saxon or Old English period, the Middle Ages, the Renaissance, the Restoration, neoclassicism, romanticism, Victorian Age, and the twentieth-century and contemporary literary backgrounds. The reader of these volumes will acquire the knowledge of literary terminology along with the theoretical and critical perspectives on certain texts and textual typology belonging to different periods, movements, trends, and genres. The reader will also learn about the characteristics and conventions of these literary periods and movements, trends and genres, main writers and major works, and the literary interaction and continuity of the given periods. Apart from an important amount of reference to literary practice, some chapters on these periods include information on their philosophy, criticism, worldview, values, or episteme, in the Foucauldian sense, which means that even though the condition of the creative writing remains as the main concern, it is balanced by a focus on the condition of thought as well as theoretical and critical writing during a particular period.

Articulating the literary phenomenon are literary voices and mediating its comprehension in the consciousness of the public are critical voices. Diachronically, they have different statuses. Homer, Euripides, Cervantes, Dante, Shakespeare, Donne, Austen, Dickens, Dostoyevsky, Proust, Joyce are among those literary voices whom the public has continuously perceived with an unchanged high intensity of interest and admiration. It is only natural that the "voice of an authentic author passes easier through time and possesses more longevity and resonance than that of the critics" (Munteanu, *Metamorfozele* 9). Indeed, Sarasin, Bayle, Lessing, Johnson, Herder, Taine, Sainte-Beuve, Gautier, Stephen, Lubbock are among those critical voices that can hardly be considered to be our contemporaries, and, in spite of the value of their critical discourse, time has eroded their ideas to such an extent that they do not constitute a viable presence in the contemporary literary theory and criticism any longer. Apart from these two groups, there is a third one represented by those poets, novelists and playwrights who manifested both as writers and critics. Here as well, with a few exceptions like T. S. Eliot, who is, to the present day, acclaimed as both writer and critic, or Pater, who is nowadays remembered mainly as critic not writer, the literary history has proven the assumption that in the case of the writer-critics, their literary voice attracts a wider audience and is more persistent in time than their critical one.

It also appears that literary work possesses eternal temporal validity due to its autonomous aesthetic value, whereas criticism provides points of view having temporary and transitory significance; in other words, criticism represents historical version of a particular type of approach to literature. Despite such claims, the vector of methodology in our series of books, dealing with the history of English literature, relies on Viktor Shklovsky, T. S. Eliot, Mikhail Bakhtin, and especially Yuri Tynyanov. In this issue of diachronicity, criticism, similar to literature, attempts to acquire longevity, but, contrary to literary work, whose system remains relatively stable in time, and because literary work necessitates a continuous actualization, critical endeavour requires a permanent renewal of its material. Hence literary criticism is in a continuous developmental process which, being influenced by different factors, involves constant and rapid transformation of its typology, methodology, concerns, and, especially, its attitudes and viewpoints.

What is the developmental process of English literary practice; and how it has come to constitute a particular system comprising various other systems representing different periods, genres, individual literary activities, and so on; along with its interrelatedness with the critical thinking having embarked on its own process of development, represent the main concerns of our books in the series.

As critical writing emerges with the appearance of creative writing, our emphasis on this interrelationship between literature and criticism sparks from the awareness that, particularly before the twentieth century, it is quite impossible to render literary history apart from literary criticism and theory, to separate the text from the context, as if trying to forget that literary criticism has roots in literary practice and vice-versa, and that most of the critics are actually practitioners of literature, rightly called "writer-critics" and situated between critical theory and imaginative writing as authors of two related discourses; only in English literature: Philip Sidney, Ben Jonson, John Dryden, Alexander Pope, Henry Fielding, Samuel Johnson, William Wordsworth, Samuel Taylor Coleridge, Percy Bysshe Shelley, Matthew Arnold, Walter Pater, Oscar Wilde, John Ruskin, Henry James, Virginia Woolf, T. S. Eliot, David Lodge, and many others. This awareness represents the starting point of the present books. Our main concern is to ensure that literary production is viewed in relation to literary criticism and the works of imaginative writing are examined in the light of the critical theory which inspires their creation and shapes their thematic and structural context, and vice-versa, the literary works shaping the critical thinking.

One of the most important writer-critics of all times and the exponent of English modernism, T. S. Eliot gave, towards the end of his life, his own definition of the type of criticism he had practiced, which is a highly revelatory statement, including for our own line of reasoning: "the best of my literary criticism", Eliot claims, is "a by-product of my private poetry-workshop; or a prolongation of the thinking that went into the formation of my own verse".

Other writers would use, or rather materialise, their own artistic credo and literary theory in their literary texts, such as Wordsworth reifying his theory of the origin of poetry from the Preface to *Lyrical Ballads* in his poems *The Prelude* and *Tintern Abbey*, or Pater exemplifying the principles of aestheticism in his novel *Marius the Epicurean*. For some, like for Sidney and Shelley, criticism was a means of defending the aesthetic value of literature; for others, criticism represented the instrument to be used in an attempt to found a new genre, as it did for Fielding and his "comic novel", or even to introduce into the contemporary culture and to validate a whole new literary movement, as it was for Wordsworth and Coleridge.

The interrelationship between literature and critical theory can be seen all the way through the periods, including the twentieth century, where the field of literary theory and criticism reveals a threefold perspective of development. First, one may argue that the development of literary criticism is dependent on literary genres and movements which are dominant in different periods. This is the case of literary criticism especially for the periods until the twentieth century. Douwe Fokkema and Elrud Ibsch (1-2) exemplify this aspect by the theory of classicism which "should be understood as a generalization of the drama and epic of the time"; similarly, the biographical method in criticism is viewed as "one of the effects of Romanticism, which drew largely on autobiographical material"; another example would be the psychological novel which "is responsible for the psychological approach in literary criticism"; also, "the view has been defended that Russian Formalism is indebted to the ideals and slogans of futurism". Second, which is mainly the case of literary scholarship in the nineteenth and twentieth centuries, trends and schools in literary criticism are related to or rather determined by the new developments in science, philosophy, and society. Fokkema and Ibsch again claim: "[t]here is an unmistakable influence of Freudian psychology in psychologically-oriented literary criticism" and "Marxist literary criticism has been intertwined with particular political and sociological views"; also, the "search for a literary system or structure has certainly been inspired by *Gestalt* psychology. Russian Formalism is not only indebted to futurism, but also to new developments in linguistics". Third, these critics argue, where some trends in literary criticism "are closer to new trends in creative literature, [and] others are directly related to current developments in scholarship and society", there are also trends which "are somewhere in between" or they rather emerge, in particular some of the twentieth-century trends in criticism, from within the interpretative perspectives of the discipline of literary theory and criticism itself (for instance, narratology developed by structuralism).

In most general terms, with focus on art and, in this respect, on literature as one of the arts, it is art criticism that provides the analysis, study, and evaluation of individual works of art, as well as the formulation of general principles for the examination of such works. Literary theory and literary criticism are particular manifestations of art criticism developed and applied for the understanding and evaluation of literature; they constitute two distinct but interrelated disciplines which co-exist and are interrelated with a third one, the discipline of literary history, all three representing actually our instruments of approach to English literature which is conceived and constructed by us in its historical movement following the formalist, or rather neo-formalist, assumption that literature is a system of various central and peripheral elements – just as periods, movements, trends, genres, subgenres, and so on, are – and the advancement of literature through history is the substitution of systems.

Focusing on literary practice, applying critical theory and emerging from within our own teaching experience, the books in the present series, dealing with the history of English literature, are theoretical and surveyistic, like a monograph, whereas their more practical and text-oriented aspect should appeal as a student handbook for didactic purposes, in which certain literary texts or fragments from texts belonging to various writers from different periods are analysed and compared with regard to their source, form, thematic arrangements, message, ideas, motifs, character representation strategies, intertextual perspectives, structural or narrative techniques, and other aspects. Theoretical component apart, it is equally important to focus on particular literary works dealing with various concerns and building up different thematic perspectives, such as the process of growing up of the protagonist, because a particular theoretical contribution has no validity and efficiency unless it is well-rooted in the reality of the literary discourse which would eventually provide its practical argumentation. Thematic consideration of the text is indispensable from its structural analysis, be it a lyrical poem stimulating discussions on the use of figurative language for musical and pictorial effects, or a narrative text involving elements of formal organization such as narrator, narrative, narration, point of view, voice, or the principle of chronotope.

Chronos and *topos*, time and place, play a significant role as counterparts of one single mechanism of literary approach to the development of literature, in general, and of the image of its persona rendered in the work, in particular, and specifically in fiction. For Bakhtin, the chronotope is of several types, and, concerning literature, in the "literary artistic chronotope, spatial and temporal indicators are fused into one carefully thought-out, concrete whole. Time, as it were, thickens, takes on flesh, becomes artistically visible; likewise, space becomes charged and responsive to the movements of time, plot and history. This intersection of axes and fusion of indicators characterizes the artistic chronotope" (Bakhtin, "Forms of Time" 84). In Bakhtin dealing with the novel, the "chronotope" – the name (literally, "time space") being given to "the intrinsic connectedness of temporal and spatial relationships that are artistically expressed in literature" – is a key-element in his theoretical framework on genre (an important organ of memory and no less important vehicle of historicity) and, in particular, in his theory of the novel.

We still consider that an attempt to provide the learners of literature with a comprehensive and analytically structured insight into the movement of the literature of a nation or that of the world, in general, through history can be better achieved by drawing on theories of genre, system, and literary development. And we still believe that some of the most congenial theorizations, still valid and viable nowadays – emerging in the most recent books of literary scholarship, such as in those by Linda Hutcheon with her "system" and "constant", and Bran Nicol with the "dominant" – belong to Yuri Tynyanov, whose main reasoning would be that literature is a system of dominant, central and peripheral, marginalized elements – to us, "tradition" (centre) versus "innovation" (margin) engaged in a "battle" for supremacy, demarginalization, and the right to form a new literary system – and the development or historical advancement of literature is the substitution of systems.

The rise and development of genres represent an important aspect of our discussion, but our main concern is the diachronic movement of English literature through its main periods, movements, and trends which succeed each other, and each has its origin in certain precursors by rejecting some previous literary manifestations and continuing others – where innovation would reject what was before tradition and continue what was before innovation, and vice-versa – as well as being influenced by various contemporary developments and socio-cultural conditions. For this, we rely primarily on more traditional but established and recognized approaches to national literature, particularly on Tynyanov elaborating on system and formalism, on the whole, chiefly its emphasis on internal factors in literary historical movement and change, which, given their applicability nowadays through some changed perspectives of theoretical and critical consideration, may be viewed and labelled as "neo-formalism".

In viewing the literature produced in Britain as a literary system, we follow Tynyanov; in adding the historical dimension to the rise and development of an English – and not only – literature, we follow Tynyanov and Bakhtin again, among others, but more importantly is that our approach to the movement of English literature through history is conceived to go cyclically from theory (the existing theoretical categories of literary analysis) to practice (the direct approach to a number of literary works following the appropriate conceptions and points of concern according to specific features of the chosen texts), and then again to theory, or rather new theoretical arrangements which we hope would emerge in order to be used again in one's endeavours at practical, text-oriented criticism. In both theoretical and practical cases, the main purpose is to disclose and investigate the development and advancement of literary practice in relation to literary theory and criticism, and in this respect, the books focus diachronically on English literature from its beginnings in the Anglo-Saxon period to the present. By their interdisciplinary perspectives involving literary history, literary theory, and literary criticism, the present volumes should be useful to experts in literary studies, professional scholars of literary history and criticism, or to a more general readership, or anyone concerned with theoretical and practical consideration and understanding of literature, in general, and of English literary phenomenon, in particular, and whose knowledge on certain aspects of literature and literary thought in Britain might be enriched by reading these books.

The works represent an attempt of academic research in the field of literature but also meet the requirements of a teaching aid. The main target is student audience and the intention of the books regards the needs of students in their literature classes, aiming at introducing them to the domain of literary history. To students new in the field, at least, the books would supply insight into the historical study of literature; for them, these works would become an accompaniment to a course on literary history; and, we believe, by reading these books, they would secure a reliable grounding in major authors, texts, genres, subgenres, literary movements, trends, and periods. From the incompleteness and disembodiment of bibliographical assistance with regard to certain matters of concern, we believe to have progressed to certain interpretative modalities of our own, which consider the wholeness and complexity of the British literary history. These interpretative arrangements receive ultimate practical argumentation through direct approach to certain authors and their major texts, and they have been also validated by our teaching experience at universities in Turkey, Romania, and Moldova.

Our books are basically a survey tracing the development of British literature and literature related critical and theoretical thinking both as a unique experience and within the larger context of British and Western cultural and literary tradition. The first book in the series focuses diachronically on English literary phenomenon from its Anglo-Saxon beginnings to the end of the Middle Ages and covers the first two periods and experiences of English literary history, which are the Old English (Anglo-Saxon) and medieval ones. The second book considers the movement of English literature from the 1480s to the 1620s and covers the next periods and experiences of English literary history, namely the Renaissance, in general, and, in particular, Humanism, Reformation, and the Elizabethan Age. This third book is about the seventeenth century and offers insight into its main literary manifestations, including metaphysical poetry, Puritanism, and the Restoration. The fourth book considers the eighteenth century and covers some of the most important periods and experiences of the history of English literature in this long, complex and creatively potent age, namely neoclassicism, the rise of the English novel, and pre-romanticism. The fifth book in the series focuses on the period from the 1780s to the 1830s and covers one of the most important periods and experiences of English literary history, which is that of romanticism. The sixth book discloses the essence of the literary development in Britain from the 1830s to 1900 and focuses on other important periods and manifestations of English literary history, which are assigned together as the literature of the Victorian Age, in general, and, in particular, are known as post- and neo-romantic literature, realism, naturalism, and the avant-garde encompassing aestheticism, symbolism, and Pre-Raphaelite Brotherhood. The seventh book in the series is about the development of English literature in the twentieth century and focuses on the first half of the century with its Edwardian literature, the rise of modernism and experimental fiction, its poetry and drama, as well as the traditional literature of the period. The eighth book covers the second half of the twentieth century and offers an insight also into the contemporary literary background; its direct reference is to the post-war new realism of the Angry Young Men and other manifestations of the traditional novel versus a more visionary and philosophical continuation of the modernist and experimental trends, but the emphasis is on the postmodern theory along with postmodernism in its literary expression in fiction, poetry and drama, as well as on more recent alternatives to the postmodern thought and literary practice.

Before actually entering into the period or century in order to discuss its authors, works, movements, trends, culture, philosophy, critical thinking, and so on, our books contain an introductory part aimed to assist the reader to form an opinion on what is literature, what are the approaches to literature, and what are the major periods, movements, trends, authors and texts in the history of British and European literature. Coming after Introduction, the Preliminaries, relying on Yuri Tynyanov and others, would strengthen the understanding of literature as a system and the diachronic movement of literature as the substitution of systems whose central and marginal elements, tradition and innovation are in perpetual interaction and fight, rejection and continuation in order to build up – also as influenced by contemporary socio-cultural stimuli – new systems which we see as periods, movements, trends, genres, subgenres, and so on. Also, in three books in the series dealing with those periods in which a particular genre emerged to dominate the literary scene, there are chapters dedicated to the theoretical, methodological, terminological, and practical consideration of the narrative, lyrical, and dramatic genres. Namely, the theory of drama is explicated in the book on the Renaissance; lyrical genre is theoretically introduced and explained in the book on the seventeenth-century English literature; and, given the rise of the English novel in the eighteenth century, the book on this period contains a theoretical part on the narrative genre, including fiction, narrative poetry, categories and elements of narrative organization, and so on.

Apart from this, in every book of the series, the special emphasis is on those authors who manifested as important writers in the history of British literature, those who developed a national literary discourse making it a part of international cultural heritage. Their names need to be known, their main literary texts understood, and the historical order of events properly grasped in order to comprehend systemically and coherently the rise and development of English literature as a process, a diachronic advancement which encompasses periods, literary movements and trends, genres and subgenres, major authors and texts. Whether or not and to what extent this desideratum is likely to be accomplished by our endeavours, we shall see in the following.

INTRODUCTION

APPROACHING LITERARY PRACTICE AND STUDYING BRITISH LITERATURE IN HISTORY

> ***Keywords:*** literacy, popularity, consumerism, literature, literary system, communication, aesthetic value, approach to literature, literary history, literary criticism, literary theory, diachronic versus synchronic, objective versus subjective, substitution of systems, innovation versus tradition, centre versus margin, to follow, to continue, to reject, contemporary stimuli, period, movement, trend, genre, author, literary work, text, ancient period, medieval period, modern period, postmodern period, post-postmodern period

In terms of a media-culture perspective, the decline of literacy and the indefinite future of the imaginative writing are nowadays matters of general lament, as it is the fact that literature might have lost its primary role to satisfy the aesthetic and intellectual needs of the post-postmodern man. Facing a complexity of new cultural alternatives, our contemporaries display exaggerated confidence in television, cinema, computers, and Internet; they often watch television or surf the net web-pages instead of reading books, use compact discs for learning languages or getting acquainted with Dickens's novels. The books, then, would apparently survive a limited time in the human cultural store, and many of them are in danger of being forgotten in a remote corner of an old library.

The concept of literacy is an essential principle for the survival of the books, yet, besides literature, literacy refers to many other types of mass communications and theories of mass culture, and literature is not the only reliable vehicle for cultural communication, or improvement of modern thought, or acquisition of information. In some of these respects, one may argue, television and computer are much more reliable, practical, and resourceful tools than the whole of imaginative writing.

On the other hand, the invention of television and the computer has not decreased the printing of books; moreover, the computer screen, Internet, and communication through e-mail display more alphabetic letters than images. Also, as every human being has a novel inside, critics metaphorically claim, "web-fiction" and other forms of online writing have allowed imaginative flight of the people to increase and their creativity to flourish.

The problem is not to oppose visual and written types of cultural communication. It is that, though the whole of image-oriented culture and media attempts to reify a new form of literacy, the problem consists in a general illiteracy caused by the open exposure to a form of visual illiteracy of the media and the insufficient exposure to important and mind-appealing books. In vindicating the role of imaginative literature, "do not fight against false enemies", argues Umberto Eco, because, first of all,

> we know that books are not ways of making somebody else think in our place; on the contrary they are machines which provoke further thoughts. Secondly, if once upon a time people needed to train their memory in order to remember things,

after the invention of writing they had also to train their memory in order to remember books. Books challenge and improve memory. They do not narcotize it. This old debate is worth reflecting on every time one meets a new communicational tool which pretends or appears to replace books. (Eco, *Apocalypse Postponed* 89-90)

Drama, poetry, and fiction have a long developmental history starting in ancient period; they have continuously developed types, forms, concerns, and for this, they are free from the danger of not surviving for years and centuries in the human cultural depository, or of becoming a handful of dust in a remote corner of an old forgotten library. They focus on those issues and tackle those thematic perspectives which reflect the period, its culture, answer to the aesthetic needs of the reader as a form of entertainment or didactic principles, and are imaginatively disclosed and theoretically and critically scrutinized.

Another criterion of their and literature, in general, survival is popularity which is provided and determined by consumerist, public and market demand, and another one is their literacy, or aesthetic validity, which is assessed and supported by academic and critical evaluation.

Today both concepts – popularity and literacy as essential principles of their survival – comprise many types of mass communication and theories of mass culture. According to this media-culture perspective, during the last decades a number of worrying reports have been produced in Western countries on the decline of literary value and the future of imaginative literature. One reason, perhaps, would be the overconfidence in and reliance on technology, internet, cinema, and other forms of communication, of which some have become alternative forms of art and which, apart from traditional arts, including literature, are simultaneously our contemporary forms of art and our contemporary sources of *utile et dulce*.

In order to keep literature at least on the same level with the newly emerged forms of art, strengthen its status, show and defend its aesthetic validity, a repeated insight into the historical advancement of the literary phenomenon is still a valid matter of scholarly concern, and, to us, also a matter of didactic interest aimed to assist the students in their literature classes. In this respect, the following issues are to be answered in this introductory part of the book:

1. **What is Literature?**
2. **Approaches to Literature**
3. **The History of British and European Literature: Periods, Movements, Trends, Authors, and Texts**

In relation to our attempts to provide a concise surveyistic perspective of **3. The History of British and European Literature** in order to assist students better comprehend its major periods, movements, trends, authors, and texts, prior to this, questions such as

What is a literary period?
What is a literary movement?
What is a literary trend?
Are there any differences between movement and trend?

would help our endeavour.

Another issue – **4. Literary Genres** – is equally important in literary studies; in our series of books, for didactic purposes, this theoretical aspect is the concern not in this introductory part but in certain chapters in books on specific literary periods and movements: theory of drama in the book on the Renaissance, poetry in the book on the seventeenth century, and fiction in the book on the eighteenth-century English literature.

1. What is Literature?

As for the definition, literature, a cultural phenomenon, one of the arts, the verbal art, is in the simplest way defined as imaginative writing. Apart from the long established opinion that literature is "imaginative writing", literature is also "creative writing" since it "employs a special form of language, more evocative and "conative" than that used in other forms of writing" (Castle 6).

Based on a strong critical tradition, having its roots in Saussurean declaration of language to be a system of signs as well as in the formal, including formalist and structuralist, critical theory, literature is understood as a system of elements framed within the boundaries of a communicative situation. The term "literature" is therefore used to designate "a certain body of repeatable or recoverable acts of communication" (Scholes 18).

It should be agreed, however, that in literature, like in art in general, the purpose is not only the communication of fact but also a kind of aesthetic communication involving "the telling of a story (either wholly invented or given new life through invention) or the giving of pleasure through some use of the inventive imagination in the employment of words" (Daiches 4-5).

Being a kind of "writing", literature uses language in "peculiar ways", "offending" language and deviating from its ordinary use; literature "transforms and intensifies ordinary language, deviates systematically from everyday speech" (Eagleton 2). It seems that this peculiarity of every artistic endeavour – be it literary or musical – to "deviate", "offend", "destroy" in order to create – was long ago acknowledged by the artist himself or herself, as to remember just *A Musical Instrument* by Elizabeth Barrett Browning.

Because its material is language, made of words expressed in relation to creative imagination, and besides its aspect of communication, the second important function of literature is the aesthetic one. Both functions are interrelated and of equal importance. The object of literature is the subjective and objective universe, the inner and outer world, and the verbal matter which materialises this object forms the beauty, which is established under the sign of joy and integrity and is in this condition communicated to the public.

In linguistic terms, the six elements in communication, in general, as identified by Roman Jakobson in *Linguistics and Poetics* (1963), drawing on Tynyanov's and formalist basic term "system" of elements, are the following (Jakobson 34):

Addresser	Context Message Contact Code	Addressee	- the addresser (usually but not necessarily the same as the sender) - the addressee (usually but not necessarily the same as the receiver) - the message (the particular linguistic form) - the context (the referent or information, or more precisely, the contextual information on the world in which the message takes place; the social and historical framework in which the utterance is made; also, it refers to the circumstances or conditions relevant to a fact – a setting in which events occur; more recently, as prompted by Bakhtin, it is part of a text which determines its meaning, since the meaning cannot be understood outside the context) - the contact (the medium or channel; the physical channel and psychological connection between addresser and addressee) - the code (the language common to both addresser and addressee, which permits communication to occur)

In the same study, Jakobson shows that corresponding to each element in this taxonomy is a particular function of language:

Emotive	Referential Poetic Phatic Metalingual	Conative	- the emotive (to communicate inner feelings and states) - the conative (to attempt to determine/affect the behavior of the receiver) - the referential (to carry information in order to describe a situation, object, state) - the poetic (to focus on linguistic form) - the phatic (to open the channel for practical or social reasons) - the metalingual (to focus on language or dialect in order to clarify it or change it)

Literature as a system, the literary system, constitutes a literary discourse to be communicated to the reader; in other words, it is involved in a literary communicative situation. The structure, simple but relevant to any learner of literature, is provided by Guy Cook. He shows that the six elements in communication, as identified by Jacobson in *Linguistics and Poetics*, each having a corresponding function of language, receive in literary communication their equivalent counterparts: "addresser" or "sender" is the "author" or "writer", "message" is the "text", "addressee" or "receiver" is the "reader", and so on. They constitute the elements of the literary system. Guy Cook identifies and places these elements in a simple but comprehensive structure of the literary communicative situation (128):

		Society	
Author	Text	(Performer)	Reader
	Texts	Language	

Every literary work represents a text, written or oral; it is a particular individual verbal expression, the product of an author, known to us or anonymous. The literary work addresses a reader. Even if no one has yet read a given text, the author is its reader. The material and means of expression of the text is language. It is produced in relation to a certain social background; it is the result of the literary production of an epoch, country, region; it is the expression of the social relations which occur at a certain historical moment. The literary work always exists in relation to other texts, which represent previous literary traditions or the period which is contemporary to the given literary work, by which disclosing intertextual relations on the structural and, above all, thematic level.

2. Approaches to Literature

The consumption of literature and the apprehension of its aesthetic values and effects go hand in hand with the approach to literature. The approach to literature has shown itself as a modality capable enough to reassure and strengthen the role of imaginative writing as an agent able to satisfy the intellectual needs of the humans by its permanent re-evaluation of the past national and international literary heritage as well as by its study and evaluation of the contemporary literary practice, in the context of what Matthew Arnold, during Victorian times, defined and described literary criticism as a disinterested effort or endeavour to learn and propagate the best which is known and thought in the world.

This endeavour, the nineteenth-century scholar believes, is the "real estimate", the real approach to literature leading to its true understanding and to "a sense for the best, the really excellent, and of the strength and joy". These ideas seem nowadays superfluous and obsolete, being long ago rejected and replaced by the more scientific and methodological critical perspectives of formalism, structuralism, psychoanalysis, deconstruction, and other approaches developed by the twentieth-century literary theory and criticism.

In the most general terms, the previous and subsequent to Matthew Arnold periods have developed in the field of literary studies three major perspectives of approach to literature, three directions offering theoretical and practical possibilities to study and understand literature, and which are commonly referred to as critical, theoretical and historical.

The three approaches to literature – literary theory (the theory of literature), literary criticism, and literary history (the history of literature) – despite the huge debates over their functions and even necessity, represent three distinct scientific disciplines with their own definitions, characteristics, terminology, objects of study, and methodologies. They are interconnected, having obvious points of identification and separation.

Prior to the discussion of these disciplines either from a historical perspective or as looking at their contemporary status, it is necessary to clarify their definitions, concerns, aims, relation to diachronic and synchronic elements, and to subjectivity and objectivity, as well as their interrelationship, interdependence and usefulness in the understanding of the literary phenomenon.

The standard dictionary definition regards history of literature or literary history as the diachronic approach to literature which focuses on literary periods, movements, trends, doctrines, and writing practice (authors and works), all that represents the "objective facts of literary history" (Jauss, *Toward an Aesthetic of Reception* 51). Although in the contemporary state of terminology, "literary history" and "history of literature" are considered synonymous, it is also claimed that "history of literature gathers and classifies literary works, whereas literary history places and tries to explain these works by relating them to a series of historic, social, political, ideological, and cultural determinants" (Gengembre 4).

The modern "literary history was created in the Romantic age" (Perkins 338), with Herder in Germany as its founder, Madame de Staël and Chateaubriand in France, and in England with Robert Lowth, Thomas Percy, and especially Thomas Warton's *History of English Poetry* (1774-1781), which came to replace the older history of learning (*historia litterarum*) as promoted by Francis Bacon.

Literary criticism is the study, analysis, investigation, or approach to particular literary texts on both thematic and structural levels. Criticism interprets the text, discloses its meaning, and mediates between the text and the reader. If there are debates whether the average reader needs or not any help from criticism, concerning professional readers, academics and students, criticism has definitely acquired a solid position in the field of literary education, in which "criticism is both an end and a means, the natural culmination of study of an author and the instrument of literary training" (Culler, *Structuralist Poetics* vii).

In the process of critical interpretation, the complete meaning emerges out of the investigation of both content and form, thematic and structural dimensions of the text which are organically fused, since it is impossible to separate "what" is said in a literary work, or "what" is the text about, from "how" it is said, or the "way" in which the text is written.

The task of criticism as interpretation has a long history, from the medieval Biblical interpretation to "self-consciousness about the problem of textual meaning introduced by the Biblical hermeneutics associated with Schleiermacher at the beginning of the nineteenth century" (Collini 3-4) and then throughout the entire text and texts oriented theories of formalism, New Criticism, structuralism, and poststructuralism.

The theory and practice of interpretation range from the attempt to establish the exact meaning to Saussure's insistence on the arbitrariness of the signifier, Derrida's claim about the instability of all meaning in writing, and a more recent method by Umberto Eco of "interpreting the world and texts based on the individuation of the relationships of sympathy that link microcosm and macrocosm to one another" (Eco, "Overinterpreting texts" 45).

Literary theory looks at the nature of literature itself; it develops and offers terms, concepts, rules, criteria, categories, general strategies, methodologies and principles of research of the literary phenomena, including the text and other elements of the literary system. Theory "may connote a poetics or aesthetics concerned not with interpretation of texts but with theorising discourse in general" (Selden, "Introduction" 2).

Furthermore, theorizing within the field of literary studies "may have various objectives", but "the main aim has been to answer the question "What is literature?"" Discourses addressing this question have traditionally been called "poetics", more recently "theory of literature"" (Fowler 3). In short, literary theory is "the systemic account of the nature of literature and of the methods for analysing it" (Culler, *Literary*

Theory 1).

Concerning the concepts of "diachronic" versus "synchronic", if the first, historical approach or history of literature embarks on a diachronic perspective in literary studies and investigates the development of national and world literature, the second, literary criticism, is considered synchronic, and the third one, literary theory, is referred to as general and universal.

In matters of subjectivism and objectivism, literary history and, especially, literary theory are designated as sciences, requiring normative and methodological objectivism. Literary criticism is also required to be objective and to concentrate solely on text, not context: as seen by Stanley Fish in *Yet Once More*, the literary critic "is a specialist, defined and limited by the traditions of his craft, and it is a condition of his labours (...) that he remain distanced from any effort to work changes in the structure of society" (Machor and Goldstein 29). Literary criticism, however, "cannot avoid being partial and selective" (Lodge 63).

Literary criticism, indeed, allows subjectivism to intermingle with objective reasoning, art with science, fusing in one discourse the personal responses to literature and the scientific research, but what the critical discourse requires most is the accurate balance between the subjective and objective components.

The predominance of subjective element makes a certain type of criticism to be more "practical", "personal", or, as it is often called, "impressionistic criticism" in which, usually in the form of essay, "you wrote about your feelings, perhaps saying how moving you found a poem or how it reminded you of something in your own experience" (Peck and Coyle 177). The essay form is particularly popular among the Anglo-American critics and writer-critics, being the most "creative" critical writing. It is then only normal that the great writer-critics of the twentieth century T. S. Eliot and Virginia Woolf embraced this form, the latter, in particular, taking "full advantage of the liberties of the essay form, drawing her readers into playful digressions, allegorical fancies, unanswerable queries, and inconclusive reveries, inviting us through a collaborative "we" to join in an unchaperoned dance of impressions and ideas" (Baldick 257).

On the contrary, the reliance on theory rather than on personal impressions makes the critical text objective, neutral, at the same time "theoretical" or belonging to "academic criticism", which is "more analytic (...) commenting on the subject matter and method of the text" (Peck and Coyle 177). According to their methods and principles, in addition to practical, impressionistic, and theoretical, the critics are also categorized as formal, historical, moral, analytical, descriptive, affective, psychological, and so on.

The principle of separation within critical practice works on the more general level amid the three disciplines as well. There are many and influential voices that isolate literature and literary criticism from historical context and literary history, to mention just I. A. Richards and F. R. Leavis. There are even voices that separate criticism from theory, arguing that the theoretical account of literature "isn't useful in criticism, and will simplify, if attempted, encumber critics with "preconceived ideas" which will get between them and the text" (Barry 20).

> Where does the scientific/objective component in literary criticism come from? The answer is to be found in a more detailed presentation of the specificity of each of the three approaches to literature and in the explanation of the relationship of the three approaches to literature.

We have seen that literary history, or the history of literature, like literary theory and criticism, studies literature on the whole and the particular elements of the literary system.

> However, if the contemporary field of literary theory and criticism discusses the literary work as a synchronic phenomenon, removing the text from its temporal and spatial context, the history of literature performs a historical (diachronic) investigation of literature and studies the national and world literary development in relation to its periods, movements, trends, writers and works.

It is a critical, or rather metacritical, cliché in the Anglo-American academic world to start a book on literary theory and criticism by bringing into discussion Rene Wellek and his view (in *Concepts of Criticism*, 1963) of literary criticism as dealing with concrete works of art and that of literary theory as "the study of the principles of literature, its categories, criteria, and the like".

It is also a cliché to mention the name of Matthew Arnold and his definition of criticism as "a disinterested endeavour to learn and propagate the best that is known and thought in the world".

This definition is for many people a reason enough to claim that both literary theory and literary criticism should rely on science, objectivity, reason, method, and terminology, and reject creativity and imaginative flight. This opinion would contradict the claims by Raman Selden and Geoffrey Hartman that "critical and theoretical writing could assume a status equal to the literature it had once been thought to serve" (Stevenson 88-89). Likewise, in the twentieth century, Northrop Frye said that the "subject-matter of literary criticism is an art, and criticism is evidently something of an art too" (3).

Against Frye are those who consider literary criticism to be a science, among whom T. S. Eliot, who claims criticism to be scientific by focusing on technical analysis; also, Wellek and Warren, in the celebrated *Theory of Literature* (1949), call criticism "a species of knowledge or of learning"; and Roman Jakobson, who in *Linguistics and Poetics*, uses instead of "criticism" the term "poetics" or "literary study" and demands poetics to be an integral part of linguistics, since linguistics is the "global science of verbal structure".

Siding with Frye are those who view criticism as art, among whom Friedrich Schlegel and his famous statement on literary criticism: "Poetry can only be criticized by way of poetry. A critical judgement of an artistic production has no civil rights in the realm of art if it isn't itself a work of art". D. H. Lawrence, in *John Galsworthy*, calls criticism an art because it is too personal and based on emotion, not reason; Wilde, in *The Critic as Artist*, views criticism as full art emerging from the same imagination and creativity which are required by the literary work it criticises; whereas others see criticism "an art, although only a minor one" (Gardner 6). Theories are employed and methodologies and concepts are used, but most critics "have seen their profession not as a science but essentially an art, i.e., the art of commenting illuminatingly on literary works, of explaining and assessing them so as to increase our understanding and appreciation of literature" (Shusterman 213).

And it is the condition of the writer-critics to stand apart from other types of critics and be the first to promote criticism to the high sphere of creativity and imaginative flight, even against all threats of becoming subjective, defensive, combative, prescriptive, reflexive and slaves of literary practice.

The current critical theory, be it art or a scientific method of literary analysis, displays immense vitality and productivity, representing a complex phenomenon of theoretical diversity and intellectual collision, and being a true exponent of globalization and internationalization. This aspect is remarkably captured by the writer-critic David Lodge in his trilogy of campus novels; in his non-fictional works, Lodge also conceives highly of literary criticism, which is for him a "highly developed intellectual discipline" and "since its subject is human eloquence it has a responsibility to maintain as much continuity as possible with human discourse" (Lodge 41).

Leaving aside the debates on scientific/objective versus creative/subjective binary opposition in literary studies, it is more important to assume that literary theory, literary criticism, and literary history (history of literature) are interrelated and interdependent, and co-exist in the field of literary studies as bound by their major and common object of study, which is literary work.

Their interrelationship and interdependence form a permanent circular movement from the historically placed literary practice to literary criticism, from literary criticism to literary theory and from literary theory back to criticism.

The text – either produced recently or representing an earlier period in literary history – is subject to literary criticism whose concluding reflections (the necessary outcome of literary criticism), if generally accepted and proved valid in connection to other thematically and structurally similar literary texts, emerge into the domain of literary theory, become its general principles of approach to literature, and are applicable to the study of other particular texts and to the understanding of literature, in general.

This activity of the critic makes him or her expect to acquire a kind of eternal position in the critical discourse moving on "perpetually from one text to another": "the critic, having had a say about a particular text, hopes that later interpretations will assimilate that "say", incorporating it into an interpretative tradition" (Scholes 3).

Literary theory is fed and supported by the outcome of the practical action of criticism, but it often also "develops out of the application of a more general theory (of art, culture, language and linguistics, aesthetics, politics, history, psychology, economics, gender, and so on) to literary works in the interests of a specific critical aim", meaning that theory "grows out of this experimentation with concepts, terms, and paradigms taken from other spheres of intellectual activity" (Castle 9).

Literary criticism uses theory in practical matters of research whenever the study of particular literary works is required, adding to the objective theory the critic's individual response to the text. The expected result is, on one hand, the development of new or alternative theoretical perspectives, and, on the other hand, the change, promotion, discouragement, revival or, in some other ways, the influence upon the literary practice of its own historical period, and the influence upon the literary attitude of the reading audience concerning the contemporary and past literary tradition.

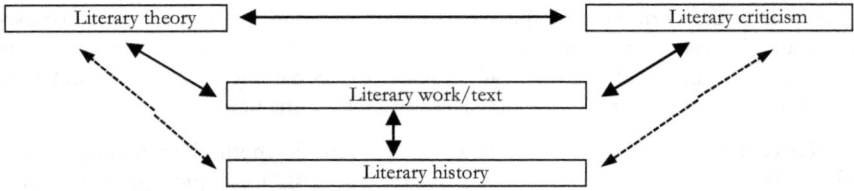

> Literary criticism is thus not to be regarded as just the analysis or evaluation of particular literary works, but also as the formulation of general principles of approach to such works.

Co-existing in the field of literary studies with literary history and literary theory, literary criticism combines the theoretical/scientific and practical levels of literary analysis. Criticism as science follows and applies the general principles and methods of research from literary theory, but it also reveals an artistic/creative aspect when the critic personalizes the discourse by his or her own opinions.

The true literary critic uses literary theory to evaluate the literary text and out of the synthesis of the borrowed theory with his or her personal views, the critic develops other theoretical perspectives while keeping the proper balance between the objective and subjective component, between the use of theory and personal contribution. Otherwise, the criticism would be meaningless, "talking about literature in a way that cannot help to build up a systematic structure of knowledge" (Frye 18).

Since the balance is hardly possible, there is this often-made distinction between "theoretical criticism" (with its heavy reliance on existing theories and the attempt to develop new ones) and "practical criticism" (also known as "impressionistic", "interpretive", or "applied criticism", which applies theories but its main concern is individual text which is studied through observation, close reading, analysis, determination of thematic and formal qualities, intertextuality, and so on).

In the circular movement from criticism to theory and vice-versa, primarily the "theoretical criticism" both uses literary theory and proposes to develop "an explicit theory of literature, in the sense of general principles, together with a set of term, distinctions, and categories, to be applied to identifying and analysing works of literature, as well as the criteria (the standards, or norms) by which these works and their writers are to be evaluated" (Abrams and Harpham 61).

The "practical criticism" focuses on individual texts and expresses personal responses which the texts evoke. As such, this type of criticism is less concerned with developing theory or applying theory, and "the theoretical principles controlling the analysis, interpretation, and evaluation are often left implicit, or brought in only as the occasion demands" (Abrams and Harpham 62).

Whatever its typology, literary criticism focuses on individual texts and is connected to theory and history, but apart from these two fields, in the study of literature, the critical discussion cannot be separated from the domain of language in which a certain literature is produced. Literary criticism relies here on other domains, namely linguistics and stylistics. Literature and language are interrelated and interdependent, in that "the literature cannot be examined in any depth apart from the language, any more than the language can be studied apart from the literature", and the study of language can become "a complement and aid to the study of literature" (G. N. Leech 1). Furthermore, concerning the critical practice, Geoffrey N. Leech argues that

> The type of critical activity known as "practical criticism" or "explication de texte" relies more heavily on linguistic evidence than others. In addition, much of the basic vocabulary of literary criticism ("metaphor", "figurative", "antithesis", "irony", rhythm", etc.) cannot be explained without recourse to linguistic notions. As a meeting-ground of linguistic and literary studies, stylistics is the field within which these basic questions lie. (1-2)

Likewise, David Lodge considers that all good criticism

> is a response to language – that it is good insofar as it is a sensitive response – whether or not there is any explicit reference to language in the way of quotation and analysis. This applies not only to the "structural" approach, but to the moral, mythical, historical, psycho-analytical and thematic approaches too; and it explains, I believe, why we can profit from criticism using radically different approaches from our own. (63)

Umberto Eco, combining semiotics, cultural philosophy and literary criticism in one scholarly personality, extends the implication of language in critical interpretation of the literary works to the more general context of culture and literary history:

> a text is produced not for a single addressee but for a community of readers – the author knows that he or she will be interpreted not according to his or her intentions but according to a complex strategy of interactions which also involves the readers, along with their competence in language as a social treasury. I mean by social treasury not only a given language as a set of grammatical rules, but also the whole encyclopaedia that the performances of that language have implemented, namely, the cultural conventions that that language has produced and the very history of the previous interpretations of many texts, comprehending the text that the reader is in the course of reading. ("Between author and text" 67-68)

The relationship of the three approaches to literature – criticism, theory, and history – suggests that literary history is more of a distinct discipline, standing apart, whereas literary theory and literary criticism are stronger connected, which is also based on the assumption that there is no non-theoretical literary criticism. Theoretical principles and implications "lurk behind even the most "practical" forms of criticism, even the most text-oriented interpretations and evaluations" (Harland xi), and even the most personal opinions on literature.

Hence theory and criticism are being considered by certain scholars as one discipline under the generic name of "**literary theory and criticism**" or "**critical theory**".

Others provide a clear delimitation between literary theory and literary criticism, naming them "theoretical criticism" and "practical criticism" (also labelled "applied criticism"), respectively. But the former is just another label given to literary theory, since it "formulates the theories, principles, and tenets of the nature and value of art"; the latter, only sharing the same name with I. A. Richards's and F. R. Leavis's method, corresponds to literary criticism and "applies the theories and tenets of theoretical criticism [i.e. literary theory] to a particular work" (Bressler 7).

The names may differ, it is clear, but the essence concerning the object of study and aims does not change. The actual problem affecting the disciplines considers their outcome and utility.

There are strong voices recurrently providing apocalyptic declarations about the death of historicity, including the history of literature or literary history, as well as about the uselessness of any theory or critical study since there are doubts about the possibility to achieve originality, to construct and impose a meaning, and to employ language to represent or reflect whatever is the creative interest.

There have always been numerous and repeated efforts to revive and provide a scientific substratum to the historical study of literature. Yuri Tynyanov and the formalist school, on the whole, attempt to renovate literary history through the view of literature as a system, the theorization of literary evolution, and the discussions on genres. Hans Robert Jauss warns that history of literature is being reduced to a mere gallery of biographies and becomes an obsolete object of study, whose existence would be determined only by a didactic purpose and the necessity of being traditionally included as a part of cultural information. If literary history is to be rejuvenated, argues Jauss, "the prejudices of historical objectivism must be removed and the traditional approach to literature must be replaced by an aesthetics of reception and impact" ("Literary History as a Challenge" 13).

Earlier, Rene Wellek and Austin Warren (in *Theory of Literature*) claimed that "a history of a national literature as a whole, is harder to envisage (...) histories of groups of literatures are even more distant ideals (...) Finally, a general history of the art of literature is still a far-distant ideal". Strongly bound to their Russian formalist origins, namely Tynyanov's theory of literary system, Wellek and Warren claim that literary history must be the study of the systems of "literary norms, standards, and conventions", and must be "the tracing of the changing from one system of norms to another" (264-268).

Wellek and Warren believe that the separation of criticism from the diachronic dimension of the literary history and its subsequent consolidation as a distinct domain were caused by the distinction between the consideration of literature as a simultaneous order and the view on literature as a line of works arranged chronologically and regarded as constituent parts of the historical process. But the practice of historical approach to literature replied to Wellek and other challengers of literary history by such masterworks as Erich Auerbach's *Mimesis: The Representation of Reality in Western Literature* (1946) or Ernst Robert Curtius's *European Literature and the Latin Middle Ages* (1948).

Neither the research of the text as a synchronic phenomenon nor the historicism of the literary experience are to be neglected, but in order to achieve the adequate comprehension of the literary works of different writers and periods, it is necessary to overcome the gap between literary criticism and literary history by fusing the synchronic and diachronic dimensions in literary analysis, and by strengthening the relationship between text and context.

> It is the task of literary criticism – apart from the thematic perspectives of approach – to involve the diachronic perspective in the study of the text.

Otherwise, without understanding literature with what literary history provides, which is essentially a scrutiny of the literary phenomenon in its growth, the relationship between tradition and innovation, the origins of literary work, the author as artist possessing distinct psychology and sensibility, and the social and cultural circumstances which make the production of the work possible and which are reflected in the work, the critic would scarcely offer competent judgement on the value of the text. The "method of historical reception is indispensable for the understanding of literature from the distant past", claims Jauss, and how then the text can be properly understood if "the author of a work is unknown, his intent undeclared, and his relationship to sources and models only indirectly accessible"? (*Toward an Aesthetic of Reception* 29)

> The perspective is reciprocal: it is also the task of literary history to remain a scientific discipline by involving in the study on the rise and development of literature the synchronic dimension of the literary criticism and the scientific principles of research offered by literary theory. The history of literature, in order to claim the status of a science, must be a rigorous system equipped with scientific methodology.

Moreover, the

gap between literature and history, between aesthetic and historical knowledge, can be bridged if literary history does not simply describe the process of general history in the reflection of its works one more time, but rather when it discovers in the course of "literary evolution" that properly socially formative function that belongs to literature as it competes with other arts and social forces in the emancipation of mankind from its natural, religious, and social bonds. (Jauss, *Toward an Aesthetic of Reception* 45)

The literary work is undoubtedly a phenomenon dated in time, and represents, as Romul Munteanu clearly states it in *Metamorphoses of the Modern European Criticism* (1988), the product of a historical time in which a human community develops a particular view on existence, a view which comes to be expressed by exceptional individuals, the producers of literary works, themselves exponents of a particular historical background.

In this respect, as stated above, the discipline of the history of literature performs a historical investigation of literature, and studies the national and world literary development in relation to its periods, movements, trends, genres, types of text, writers, and works, which are inscribed in a process of becoming to reveal the victory of historicism in modernity – weakened but still alive nowadays – and strengthen George Calinescu's claim that literary history resembles an epic scenario on a vast cultural scene.

Like philosophy and history, criticism was conceived as part of a process, a becoming, a diachronic phenomenon, and even as part of history and philosophy, although the aesthetic legitimacy of the work to be judged by critical criteria would not be among the primary aims of the literary history.

Since the Renaissance through the nineteenth century, with empiricist, rationalist and positivist thinking at power, the literary work came to be conceived as a constituent part of a nation's spiritual existence more than it would be viewed as an act of artistic creation whose value emerges from its aesthetic indicators. Literary history would provide evidence about the life and specificity of a nation and become a means of understanding the national psychology as well as advance the literary work as the product and reflection of the milieu and history (Taine); earlier, the romantics already promoted the historical and national along with the individual significance in literary practice and literary studies through an anteriority and posteriority dualism, which later becomes the cause and effect dichotomy.

Literary history having embarked on diachronic research, the dominant opinion was that this discipline is nothing than history (Gervinus) and necessitates no insight into the specificity of the literary phenomenon. Earlier, Friedrich Schlegel negates both literary history and literary criticism by reasoning that if art should be science and the scientific research ought to acquire an artistic nature – since philosophy and poetry constitute a unitary phenomenon – than poetry can be criticised only through poetry, the aesthetic judgement having value only in so far as it is legitimized as an work of art (Munteanu, *Introducere in literatura europeana* 9).

Prior to the twentieth century, this separation of literary history from aesthetic judgement, including literary criticism, conferred low esteem to the historical approach to literature and discredited its status; Tynyanov, among the first, at the beginning of the last century, and later Jauss and others pointed at the systemic and methodological discrepancy in the field of literary history and attempted to provide it with scientific rigour and relate it to literary theory and criticism.

Apart from the debates on the status and usefulness of the historical approach to literature, there are still voices that argue for the uselessness of literary criticism too, which is summarised by Umberto Eco as follows: "Some contemporary theories of criticism assert that the only reliable reading of a text is a misreading, that the only existence of a text is given by the chain of responses it elicits, and that, as maliciously suggested by Todorov (...), a text is only a picnic where the author brings the words and the readers bring the sense" ("Interpretation and History" 24).

Critical text is a metatext, a second degree text, they say, a valueless imitation of the original literary text emerging in the process of reading. Northrop Frye speaks about the conception, popular among artists, of the critic as a parasite and consequently literary criticism as a

> parasite form of literary expression, an art based on pre-existing art, a second hand imitation of creative power. On this theory critics are intellectuals who have a taste for art but lack both the power to produce it and the money to patronize it, and thus form a class of cultural middlemen, distributing culture to society at a profit to themselves while exploiting the artist and increasing the strain on his public. (3)

Even the critics themselves may suddenly decide "that the true subject of criticism is ineffable, and criticism, as a consequence, unnecessary", whereas others may confess "that one is too stupid, too unenlightened to understand a book reputedly philosophical" (Barthes 34). Even if this were true, literary criticism has proved to be an important and necessary domain for centuries, providing, among other things, the establishment of literary traditions, advancement of literary practice, expression of literary value, and mediation between art and its audience. The question is not about the necessity of criticism but about the professional validity of such critics. Barthes again:

> But if one fears or despises so much the philosophical foundations of a book, and if one demands so insistently the right to understand nothing about them and to say nothing on the subject, why become a critic? To understand, to enlighten, that is your profession, isn't it? You can of course judge philosophy according to common sense; the trouble is that while "common sense" and "feeling" understand nothing about philosophy, philosophy, on the other hand, understands them perfectly. (35)

If literary history and literary criticism may be considered, unjustly, of course, by some as useless and helpless, then the sole surviving and necessary domain for literary comprehension is literary theory, still valued, developed and conceived as the only real science of literature. When not considered useless in defining literature, the role of literary criticism is minimized and perceived in the context of a mere reading experience. According to this first assumption, literary criticism is an alternative way of reading the literary text.

Criticism is a common practice helping readers to avoid discrepancies and misunderstandings, or it remains just a practical approach in universities explaining the text and improving the students' competence. In this respect, the critics "tend to minimize textual problems as reading problems. Their concern is usually with evaluating a poet's work or with arguing for a particular reading, rather than overtly demonstrating interpretive goals and reading strategies" (Fairley 311).

Contrary to this first convention, which regards criticism as being secondary to literature, there is another which argues that literary criticism "can be seen as a means of constructing the body of writing and knowledge which it appears to take as its object of study; in other words, literature can be seen as a product of and dependent on criticism rather than the other way round" (Webster 7).

Be theory of literature the most important discipline, yet the relationship of co-existence and interdependence of the three approaches to literature emphasises that literary theory, literary criticism, and literary history are parts of a single written discourse about literature. They are parts of a single science, the science of literature, having as its object of study an art, namely the art of literature, or, in other words, the work of literary art, which is the text, and all the elements which construct and condition the work of literature, where the literary work, or text, from a formalist perspective, would constitute the centre of the system of literature surrounded by and interrelated with all the other elements of the literary system.

The notion of "system" and its theoretical premises are congenial and applicable for the three approaches to literature – history, criticism, and theory, which build up the science of literature – as well: like every science, the science of literature "has as its final aim the truth, which is revealed through notions, and as such it is created as a system that is generally applicable. Being a science that focuses its system on an art, the literary science constitutes a meta-art and follows the disclosure, from a unique perspective, of the infinite individual patterns" (Bomher 11).

> In addition, the relationship of the three approaches to literature points out that literary theory, literary criticism, and literary history are parts of a single cognitive system, a single discourse that assists the pragmatic function by its aim to form or facilitate a particular type of communication which involves the producer of literature and its receiver.

Interesting, comprehensive, systemic, and, above all, didactically useful for the learners of literature are the identification and explanation of the critical theories as provided by M. H. Abrams in his celebrated *The Mirror and the Lamp: Romantic Theory and the Critical Tradition* (1953).

According to him, in art, in general, four critical theories emerge and are dominant in different periods: "mimetic theory", "rhetorical" or "pragmatic theory", "expressive theory", and "objective theory". Abrams points out that all critical theories, as different as they could be, concentrate around four constituents, or major elements, which represent "the total situation of a work of art": (1) the "work", meaning the artistic product, the thing made by the maker; (2) the "artist", or the creator of the work; (3) the "universe", which is the world or nature which is imitated, where, when art is viewed as imitation, the materials of the real world and of the world of ideas become the substance of the work, out of which the work may be thought to take its subjects; and (4) the "audience", which is the receiver or addressee, to whom the work is addressed.

According to Abrams, the concern with one of these four elements results in a special critical theory on art. The critic that focuses exclusively on the "work" of art and views it as a self-contained entity, approaching art basically in its own terms, follows the so-called "objective theory". If art is discussed in relation to the "artist", the work being understood as the expression of the maker's own psychological and emotional states, the approach is called the "expressive theory". To view art in terms of "universe", which is in terms of what is imitated in the work of art, is to follow the "mimetic theory". Finally, to regard art in relation to the "audience", studying the effects of the work of art on the receiver, is to follow the "rhetorical" or "pragmatic theory".

Elements of art as a system	Corresponding critical theory
work	objective theory
artist	expressive theory
universe	mimetic theory
audience	pragmatic theory

Furthermore, Abrams believes, when viewed diachronically, the development of art and art criticism in the Western world reveals these theories to be dominant in different historical periods. In ancient classical age, the most characteristic theory was the mimetic theory, with Plato and Aristotle as its promoters. However, with Aristotle's *catharsis* as the effect of drama on audience and Horace's idea of art as *utile et dulce*, instruction and pleasure, the pragmatic theory emerged in ancient period as another dominant perspective to view art in critical terms. From Antiquity through the most of the eighteenth century, these two theories remain dominant, in particular the pragmatic theory with its focus on art's usefulness and its effects on audience, although in the Renaissance and, especially, in neoclassicism, the principle of imitation was also central to the evaluation of art.

The linearity of the aesthetic attitude of the Western world governed by the view of art as a major source of instruction mingled with delight and pleasure – and thus subject to normative prescriptions – and by the confidence in the imitative nature of art was broken by the romantic rejection of tradition and rules, by its claim of the freedom of artistic expression, the revival of innovative principle in art, and, especially, the emphasis on the artist's own emotional and psychological states.

Aristotle developed a kind of "reader-oriented" approach to literature, but with romanticism, the artist became the centre of attention, his or her power of imagination, creative flight, sensibility, subjective and psychological experience expressed in the work of art.

Thus the expressive theory – also known as the "expressive theory of authorship" – emerges as the most characteristic of the romantic attitudes towards art. Also, dominant in the nineteenth century and later in the twentieth century was the objective theory on art, based on the idea of art for its own sake, art *per se*, the work being viewed as a separate entity, complex enough in its thematic spectrum, range of symbols and imagery, along with its patterns of structure and form, to be a matter of critical concern in itself, as for the late nineteenth-century avant-garde (symbolism, aestheticism, decadence, and so on) and the twentieth-century formal approach to literature (Russian formalism, Anglo-American New Criticism, and French structuralism). However, the present diversity of approaches to art keeps the contemporary critic aware of all the four major theories in his or her endeavour to evaluate art, in general, and literature, in particular.

A closer look at the rise of the critical tradition in Britain reveals a process of development during certain periods or stages generally corresponding to periods and movements in English art and literature. British literary criticism, in particular, reveals some concerns with literature in the medieval period, but its actual beginnings are found in the Renaissance, and its development and consolidation occurred during the subsequent periods of the Restoration, neoclassicism, romanticism, and the Victorian Age, as to establish itself in the twentieth century as a scientific discipline, an objective, methodological and terminological domain developing and consisting of its own schools and trends of literary theory and criticism.

In order to understand better the whole range and complexity of the contemporary trends and schools in the theoretical and critical approach to literature, we may rely again on Tynyanov, Jakobson, and Cook with their grounding of the idea of system consisting of various interrelated elements.

Like with Abrams's distinction between four elements of the system of art and their corresponding critical theories, the literary work in itself and the different relations between the text and other elements of the literary system gave birth to different theories, trends and schools in modern literary theory and criticism. As a result, the contemporary literary critic faces a multitude of schools and theories which correspond to the categories from the structure of the literary system.

The methods of these critical trends compete with each other or conflict over the evaluation and interpretation of particular works, but they also complement each other, being united by the aim to provide an as much as possible comprehensive account of the literary work and to expose the total range of its meanings. But "there is no satisfactory total account of a work of literature except the work itself. It is only the work itself that presents all its meanings in the most significant and assimilable form" (Lodge 63). A writer cannot be asked to reveal the whole truth about life and likewise a critic cannot be expected to disclose the whole truth about a particular literary work.

Criticism cannot offer all the meanings of the work, since it does not and cannot reproduce the work of literature it discusses. Instead, criticism "sets beside this work another work – the critical essay – which is a kind of hybrid formed by the collaboration of the critic with the artist, and which, in this juxtaposition, makes the original yield up some of its secrets" (Lodge 63). Facing a large amount of contemporary critical theories, the question which naturally arises is whether an approach is better than any other. Instead of asking this question, one should "admit that any given method is justified by the use made of it by a particular critic" (Lodge 63). Also, instead of heavily borrowing ideas and providing quotations from the existing critical and theoretical studies, the critic may relate and apply them to his or her particular matters of concern. A more skilled critic considers the essence of different theories, modifying it according to the specificity of the research, and, by providing personal points of view and ideas, the critic progresses to certain interpretative modalities of his or her own.

Concerning the most important critical theories, trends and schools, and according to Guy Cook's literary communicative situation, corresponding to each category in his scheme are various types of critical theory. Thus, in the field of literary theory and criticism, the "author" is the matter of concern of literary scholarship and biography; "text" is studied by formalism, linguistics, linguistic criticism, and stylistics; "performer" by acting theory; "reader" by phenomenology, hermeneutics, reception theory, reader-oriented and reader-response theory, as well as by psychoanalysis, feminism, and poststructuralism; "society" by Marxist theories, cultural materialism, new historicism, and feminism; "texts" by structuralism, poststructuralism, and deconstruction; and corresponding to "language" are the theories of linguistics and stylistics.

author	literary scholarship and biography
text	formalism, linguistics, linguistic criticism, and stylistics
performer	acting theory
reader	phenomenology, hermeneutics, reception theory, reader-oriented theory, reader-response theory, psychoanalysis, feminism, and poststructuralism
society	Marxist theories, cultural materialism, new historicism, and feminism
texts	structuralism, poststructuralism, and deconstruction
language	linguistics and stylistics

Concerning intertextualism, themes, motives, influence, reception, and, in general, the different relations between the literary works, the initiative is that of comparative literature. The particular elements of the literary system and literature, on the whole, are also the matters of critical and theoretical concern of other theories and principles of research, such as those prompted by rhetoric, semiotics, Bakhtinian criticism, archetypal and myth criticism, folklore studies, ethnic literary studies, racial studies, colonial, postcolonial and transnational studies, cultural studies, environmentalism and ecocriticism, posthumanism, transhumanism, and other contemporary trends and schools in humanities and in literary theory and criticism.

These theories, trends and schools represent the twentieth century and the contemporary objective, scientific, and methodological literary theory and criticism. They also offer the picture of the science of literature as a large and chaotic domain concerning both the methods and aims of these types of literary criticism. In the celebrated *Nouveau dictionnaire encyclopedique des sciences du langage*, Oswald Ducrot and Jean-Marie Schaeffer reduce this diversity to five main directions: a) the evaluative criticism of the works; b) the historical and institutional analysis of literature; c) the interpretative disciplines; d) the theories of reading and reception; and e) all types of formal analysis (62-63).

Roman Jakobson's article *Linguistics and Poetics* has become a founding text of contemporary poetics and a point of reference for those critics who follow the formalist school and consider the applicability of linguistic methods in literary studies. Similar to literature, which represents a process of communication, literary criticism is a process of aesthetic reception, production and communication which involves the critic, author, and reader.

Jakobson's structure can, therefore, be applied to individualize both literary communication and critical communicative situation. Robert Scholes, for instance, adjusts Jakobson's diagram to describe the "reading of a literary text" and to arrange the active schools of critical theory "by their emphasis of particular features of this diagram" (8):

Author	Contexts Text Medium Codes	Reader

In his book on literary criticism, Raman Selden gives another interesting interpretation to Jakobson's view of communication, in general, as a system of elements and changes the structure according to the purpose of criticism (*A Reader's Guide* 3-4). Considering that "contact" can be omitted in discussing literature, "since contact is usually through the printed word (except in drama)", Selden rewrites the diagram as

Writer	Context Writing Code	Reader

and then places a number of critical theories according to their focus on a particular element in the diagram:

Romantic	Marxist Formalistic Structuralist	Reader-oriented

The long way of development of world literary theory and criticism has its origins in ancient period with its Greek and Latin critical theories, whereas concerning the rise and development of the theoretical and critical discourse on literature in Britain, one should consider the Renaissance and its subsequent periods until the rise of the formal approach to literature at the dawn of the last century.

In short, in the Western world, literary criticism starts its long developmental process in ancient Greece and Rome; it continues in the Middle Ages having a rather diminished status; the first modern methodological and analytical attempts at criticism based on the revived ancient tradition occurred at the beginning of the modern period in the Renaissance both in Britain and in Europe, in general.

Throughout the centuries, criticism developed within the context of the literary practice but gradually came to diversify its provenance, form, and category as to separate from the realm of literature in the nineteenth century and finally to flourish as an independent and scientific domain in the twentieth century and at the present time, which represent undoubtedly an age of criticism.

Throughout its history, criticism existed in a variety of forms, including dialogues, verse, essays, letters, prefaces, treaties, and books. Throughout its history, criticism belonged mainly to the domains of literature and philosophy.

Criticism has been continuously influenced by the literary process and has influenced in its turn this process. Criticism has been also continuously influenced by the new developments in thought as well as in natural and social sciences, art, culture, ideology, psychology, linguistics. As such, criticism has developed an impressive typology to which twentieth century and the present days have added a huge diversity of critical trends and schools.

Throughout its history, criticism has concerned first philosophers and later, to a much greater extent, artist-critics and writer-critics, especially poet-critics, as well as scholars from different fields (rhetoric, logic, mathematics, physics, sociology, psychology, linguistics, and so on), and finally reviewers, university academics, and just professional critics and theoreticians of literature, all those who are considered exponents of various contemporary schools and trends in literary theory and criticism representing a distinct scientific field of scholarly investigation into literature as a system with all its constituent elements.

3. The History of British and European Literature: Periods, Movements, Trends, Authors, and Texts

Before embarking on a surveyistic presentation of the historical advancement of literature, we should say a few words about a kind of rule of the development of literature, in general.

The place of literature in history is reified by the rise, development and consolidation of various literary periods, movements, trends, genres, writers, and literary works, which follow each other. Each of these is a particular literary system encompassing in its framework dominant (centre) and peripheral (margin) elements; the movement of these systems through history is their continuous development, change, or more precisely, substitution of systems.

Each of these is rooted in the previous ones, represents a continuation of the previous ones, and, at the same time, rejects the previous ones, attempting at suppressing them and taking their place in literary history. Also, each period, movement, trend, genre, etc., that is, every literary system, is determined by the contemporary developments in society, culture, philosophy, science, and so on.

Origins of the literary periods, movements, trends, genres, subgenres, and so on, each representing a literary system		
Relation to the past	1. **continuation**	of the previous periods, trends, etc., where innovation follows innovation, and tradition relies on tradition
	2. **rejection**	of the previous periods, trends, etc., where innovation reacts against tradition, and tradition marginalises innovation
Relation to the present	3. **contemporary**	socio-cultural stimuli

Each period, movement, trend, genre, subgenre, writer, and text is followed by another; each has its own rise, development, consolidation and decline, but not complete disappearance, as each one influences the next, gives its origins or is rejected by the next one, or the elements of its system are acknowledged in the systems of the subsequent periods, movements, trends, and literary works under different forms and functions. Each period, movement, trend, writer, and text represents one to another tradition and innovation, is placed one against the other, where a continuous "battle" takes place between their elements which are either central or peripheral within the structure of the literary system.

The place of literature in history is actually determined by the interrelationship, the "fight" between "**centre**" and "**margin**", "**tradition**" and "**innovation**", "**classical**" and "**modern**", "**conservative**" and "**experimental**", **dependence on rules** and the **freedom of artistic expression**. It is a correlation of two contrary factors whose interaction is the motor of change and development of literature, disclosing the **substitution of systems**.

In the history of literature, the concept of "**tradition**" is used to denote the ancient classical period, the revival of ancient classical tradition in the Renaissance, the eighteenth-century Age of Enlightenment (also referred to as classicism or neoclassicism), the nineteenth-century realism, and the twentieth-century and contemporary socially-concerned literature.

The term "**innovation**" denotes some literary experiences of the Renaissance period, metaphysical poetry, pre-romanticism, romanticism, the late nineteenth-century symbolism, aestheticism and other avant-garde trends, and the twentieth-century modernism in the first half of the century and postmodernism of the postmodern period, as well as other more recent experimental trends in literature.

The scholars and students of literature are familiar with the fight between **tradition and innovation** as the opposition and juxtaposition of **center and margin**; they also know this conflict between tradition and innovation under the name of "**the battle of the books**" or "la querelle des anciens et des modernes". Whatever the terms, it points again to the war between **innovation and tradition**, between **originality and authority**, between **classicism and modernism**.

The war started in Antiquity, was reinforced in the Renaissance, peaked in France and then throughout Europe at the turn of the seventeenth century and is still going on. In English culture, this conflict was remarkably captured by the neoclassical man of letters Jonathan Swift (1667-1745) in his satire on the battle between ancients and moderns known as *The Battle of the Books* (1704).

> In English literature advancing through history, just like in literature in general, innovation rejects tradition and innovation continues innovation or, better saying, **innovation continues as well as innovates the previous innovation.**

An example of the continuation of innovation, paralleled by the innovation of innovation occurring as an indispensable part of the literary development, would be romanticism, as innovation, assuming and changing, in order to advance further on the path of originality and experimentation, the innovation of pre-romanticism; in its turn, romanticism would be innovated by the nineteenth-century avant-garde which assumes some and change or totally reject other aspects of romanticism; likewise, Joyce and Woolf would adopt and innovate Pater's "impressions" placing them within the larger context of the abstract manifestations of the mind thematized in their modernist novels which focus on the psychological experience of the individual rendered by the stream of consciousness technique in the form of interior monologue.

The literary history studies the rise and development of a national literature and the world literary phenomena from its beginnings to the present day, and divides the historical process into literary periods, which may or may not correspond to the social or political ones.

Literary periods consist of literary movements and trends, which are represented by authors and their literary works and/or literary doctrine. The distinction made between movement and trend relies actually on the fact that a movement groups those writers who produce both literary works (which share similar thematic and structural features) and literary doctrine (texts of literary theory and criticism which share common ideas about their own type of literature) – romanticism, for example; whereas a trend is formed of the producers of only literary texts having common characteristics – the nineteenth-century realism, for example.

Literary periods are considered to refer to different sequences of time conceived in the temporal boundaries of an age, century, centuries, or years, but such an understating of the period may thwart any attempts at tracing clear demarcation lines between literary periods, movements and trends, or at clearly asserting them terminologically. The Renaissance, for instance, is certainly neither a movement nor a trend but a distinct period in the literary history. Metaphysical poetry, however, is first of all a trend which manifested itself only on the level of literary practice, but it is also a part of the larger period of the English Renaissance.

Romanticism represents a period: "Romantic Period", or the "Age of Romanticism", dated between the years of 1798 and 1824, or, in more general terms, between the last decades of the eighteenth century and the first decades of the nineteenth century. At the same time, romanticism is a literary movement: "Romantic Movement", consisting of both imaginative writing and the doctrine, literary texts (such as *Tintern Abbey* by Wordsworth, or *Kubla Khan* by Coleridge) and the critical ideas (from Wordsworth's *Preface to Lyrical Ballads*, for example, or Coleridge's *Biographia Literaria*) about these texts.

In British literature, neoclassicism is a period in literary history covering the last part of the seventeenth century throughout the eighteenth century; neoclassicism is a movement in literature with its poetic works and a strongly normative and prescriptive doctrine; and also neoclassicism is the creator of a particular trend in poetry, philosophical and satirical. Likewise, in both English and world literature, modernism is a period in the first half of the twentieth century, a complex artistic manifestation consisting of a number of distinct movements (futurism, for example) and developing a number of trends in the production of literary texts (for instance, the "stream-of-consciousness novel" of Marcel Proust and James Joyce).

In general, concerning both world and English literature, a diachronic perspective on literature in Britain reveals a historical process which follows the general European pattern, yet in some moments having its particular manifestations. A special problem here is the consideration of some more or less exact periods in the development of both British and world literature.

In most general terms, literature is regarded as passing through three major periods: ancient, medieval and modern, whereas since the middle of the twentieth century, humanity is in the postmodern period, a period claimed to represent the transition to globalization. The first period in European literature is the classical period of the ancient Greece and Rome, rejected and replaced by the Middle Ages.

Concerning British literature in the Middle Ages, historians have noticed the discrepancy between English and general world/European conditions: first, English literature does not have an ancient period to be claimed in relation to a particular civilization and culture, like Greece, Rome, Egypt, China, or India, and, second, its actual medieval period starts much later than the European one, which is the eleventh/twelfth century, for the simple reason that there was no English nation at all until that period.

It is hypothesized that until the sixth century BC, the British islands were inhabited by Iberians and from sixth/seventh century BC by Celts. The year of 55 BC is that of the Roman invasion, and the years between 410 AD and 441 AD date the period of the Roman retreat.

It was the fifth century AD which saw the invasion of the British islands by the Anglo-Saxon tribes coming from the Continent, which lasted for more than a century (449-600), and then the formation, the "becoming" of these people as English for more than four centuries, which marked a period called in the history of English nation, language and literature as "Anglo-Saxon" or "Old English" (449/600-1100/1200). Conquered in their turn by the Normans in the eleventh century (the starting point being the Hastings Battle of 1066), the newly formed English nation enters now "officially" into the Middle Ages which lasted for centuries until around 1500.

The medieval period is in its turn rejected and replaced by the age of Renaissance, which is considered either as the first part of the modern period – a view based on artistic line – which lasted until the middle of the twentieth century, or as a period of transition from the Middle Ages to modern period, now conceived as lasting from the seventeenth-century Enlightenment – a view linked to philosophical line – to the middle of the twentieth century.

The art and literature of the Renaissance already reveal two contradictory but co-existing aspects of "innovation" (for instance, sonnet in poetry) and "tradition" (the revival of ancient models, as, for example, in Renaissance tragedy), and a more detailed consideration agrees that henceforth the growth of literature displays a rather complex picture.

The emergence of the innovative spirit in literature continues after the Renaissance as the Baroque period (metaphysical poetry in English literature, also considered by some critics as the last manifestation of the British Renaissance), but this cultural extravaganza is rejected and suppressed by the much stronger and dominant traditional element which, based on the revival of ancient classical artistic doctrine and practice, becomes itself a period and dominates as Enlightenment (or neoclassicism, in England) the entire social as well as cultural and literary background of Europe for more than one hundred years starting with the middle of the seventeenth century.

By the middle of the eighteenth century, the doctrine of Enlightenment or neoclassicism is put into practice by the more pragmatic British mind, giving rise to Industrialisation and thus determining the decline and end of neoclassicism as a distinct period. It is also the eighteenth century that saw the rise of the novel in English literature, and by the middle of the period, the rise of the pre-romantic poetry. As a rejection of neoclassicism and the continuation of pre-romanticism, the romantic movement emerges at the end of the eighteenth century as reviving the innovative spirit in literature and breaking the linearity of literary development dominated for a long period after the Renaissance by the traditional and normative principles of the revived ancient classical doctrine. Romanticism ends as a regular trend by the middle of the nineteenth century, and henceforth in literature, "tradition" and "innovation" co-exist again under different names and in the framework of different movements and trends.

In the simplest consideration of the facts, romanticism gave, in the second half of the nineteenth century, symbolism, aestheticism, impressionism, expressionism, and other manifestations of the artistic avant-garde, which, in the first half of the twentieth century, continue into a more complex range of experimental and innovative trends and movements (surrealism, dadaism, cubism, "stream-of-consciousness" novel, etc.) assembled and assigned together as modernism, which in its turn continues in the second half of the twentieth century as the innovation and experimentation of postmodernism – this is the component of "**innovation**" in literary history, a line of development having its origins in the Renaissance, which continued in the Baroque, was suppressed by classical tradition but revived by romanticism, was developed by the late nineteenth century avant-garde trends and diversified by the twentieth-century modernism and postmodernism.

Some elements of the main "enemy" of romanticism, which is neoclassicism, re-appear in the second half of the nineteenth century in the system of the likewise conventional, normative and socially concerned realism, which emerges almost unchanged in its thematic and structural perspectives in the twentieth century, opposing with its traditional realistic concern the innovatory and experimental art – this is the component of "**tradition**" in literary history, a line of development having its origins in ancient period, which revived in the Renaissance, changed, developed and was institutionalised in the seventeenth and eighteenth century neoclassicism, was rejected and replaced by romanticism, but became present again on the literary scene as nineteenth-century realism, and continued and was diversified by the twentieth-century writers of social concern and realist interest.

> To summarise, every new literary period, movement, trend results in and rejects the previous ones on the basis of the opposition between normative tradition and experimental innovation. Tradition and innovation are parts of a single process of literary change and development, contrary but interrelated, emerging in different periods under different names and in the system of different movements, trends and literary works, rejecting and succeeding each other, but from the second half of the nineteenth century to the present day co-existing as two distinct dimensions of literature. Apart from rejection and continuation, every new literary period, movement, and trend is determined by the contemporary developments in thought, science, and other domains.

Concerning the major periods in the history of British literature, the standard opinion, originated in the nineteenth century in relation to the development of English language, regards four periods: the period between 449/700 and 1100/1200 is called "Old English (Anglo-Saxon) Literature"; "Middle Literature" between 1100/1200 and 1500; and the period from around 1500 till the second half of the twentieth century is "Modern British Literature", followed by the "Postmodern Period". A more suitable consideration divides British literature into (a) "Old English (Anglo-Saxon) Literature", (b) "The Middle Ages", (c) "The Renaissance", (d) "The Seventeenth Century", (e) "The Eighteenth Century", (f) "The Romantic Movement", (g) "The Victorian Age", (h) "The First Half of the Twentieth Century", and (i) "The Second Half of the Twentieth Century". A more recent consideration of the major periods in the history of British literature is provided by Andrew Sanders in *A Short Oxford History of English Literature* (2004), who divides English literary history into "Old English Literature" (447-1066), "Medieval Literature" (1066-1510), "Renaissance and Reformation" (1510-1620), "Revolution and Restoration" (1620-1690), "Eighteenth-Century Literature" (1690-1780), "The Literature of the Romantic Period" (1780-1830), "High Victorian Literature" (1830-1880), "Late Victorian and Edwardian Literature" (1880-1920), "Modernism and Its Alternatives" (1920-1945), and "Post-War and Post-Modern Literature" (1945-present).

Each of these periods – except, perhaps, the Old English period and romanticism – has its own particular stages which correspond to specific sub-periods, or movements, or trends, or just some major authors. Thus, the medieval period of British literature, preceded by the Anglo-Saxon age, covers Anglo-Norman literature, Geoffrey Chaucer and his epoch, and the fifteenth century. The Renaissance is divided into the period of humanism and that of the Elizabethan Age. The seventeenth century includes metaphysical trend in poetry, the Puritan period, and the Restoration period. The eighteenth century consists of neoclassicism, the rise of the English novel, and pre-romanticism. Neoclassicism, actually, lasting from 1660 to 1780s, is divided into three periods: its rise during the Restoration period (1660-1700), its climax and dominance during the Augustan Age (1700-1750), and its decline during the Age of Johnson (1750-1780s). Following the period of the Romantic Movement, the Victorian Age covers the literature of realism, post-and neo-romantic writing, the Pre-Raphaelite Movement or Brotherhood, and aestheticism ("art for art's sake" doctrine). The twentieth century includes, in the first half of the century, Edwardian period, modernism, and the new realist writing, and, in the second half of the century, the Angry Generation and other manifestations of the traditional realistic writing, and the postmodern and postmodernist literature.

---

1. <u>Old English (Anglo-Saxon) Period</u>
- dated 447-1066, or between 449/600 (invasion of Britain by Angles, Saxons, and Jutes) and 1100/1200 (establishment of the Norman rule)
- no trends or movements, but some major authors (Caedmon, Cynewulf, the Venerable Bede) and texts (chronicles, the anonymous epic *Beowulf*, and a number of poems such as *The Seafarer* and *The Wanderer*)

---

2. <u>Medieval English Literature</u>
- dated 1100/1200-1500, or, more precisely, between 1066 (Battle of Hastings and the beginning of the Norman Conquest) and 1509 (death of Henry VII and accession of Henry VIII)
- the actual medieval period of British literature with no particular trends or movements
- covers three periods:
    - the Anglo-Norman literature (1100/1200-1350s): includes chronicles, poetry, but the most important literary manifestation is the medieval romance (also referred to as chivalrous romance, Arthurian legend, metrical romance, or prose romance); for example, *Sir Gawain and the Green Knight*)
    - Geoffrey Chaucer and his epoch (1340-1400): includes the poem entitled *The Land of Cockaygne*, the famous alliterative poem *The Vision of William Concerning Piers the Plowman* ascribed to William Langland, *Voyages and Travels of Sir John Mandeville* by Sir John Mandeville, the works of John Gower, but the period is entirely governed by Geoffrey Chaucer (1340-1400) and his writings, in particular *The Canterbury Tales*
    - the fifteenth century: includes Sir Thomas Malory's prose romance *Morte d'Arthur*, the poetry of John Lydgate and Thomas Hoccleve, the popular ballads, but the most important literary manifestation is the rise of drama (with many forms, both religious and secular, of which the most important ones are "mystery play", "morality", and "interlude")

---

3. <u>Renaissance Literature</u>, or the period of "Renaissance and Reformation" in British literature
- very difficult to date precisely:
    - the sixteenth century in general
    - between 1510 and 1620
    - between 1500 and the Commonwealth Interregnum (1649-1660)
    - begins in 1485 (the accession of Henry VII and the establishment of the Tudor dynasty) or in 1509 (the accession of Henry VIII)
    - ends in the early seventeenth century in Europe, in general, and the year of 1616 (the death of Shakespeare) in England, or by the middle of the seventeenth century in Europe, in general, and the year of 1649 (the execution of Charles I) or the year of 1660 (the restoration of monarchy) in England
- <u>historically</u>, it consists of "Early Tudor Age" (c.1500-1557) and "Elizabethan Age" (1558-1603); it may also include "Jacobean Age" (1603-1625) and "Caroline Age" (1625-1649), if one would consider that the Renaissance lasted until the middle of the seventeenth century
- <u>concerning literature</u>, Renaissance is divided into the periods of
    - humanism (first half of the sixteenth century)
    - Elizabethan Age (second half of the sixteenth century)
    - baroque (metaphysical poetry) in the first part and middle of the seventeenth century, if one would consider that the Renaissance lasted until the 1650s
- no clearly defined literary trends or movements, except humanism and metaphysical poetry
- the former is considered within the fields of philosophy and politics, and the latter in the context of the baroque, which is said to have followed the Renaissance period as part of the seventeenth-century mannerism and cultural extravaganza
- major genres: sonnet and drama
- important writings: *Utopia* by Sir Thomas More; sonnets by Thomas Wyatt and Henry Howard; Edmund Spenser with *The Shepherd's Calendar*, *Amoretti* (88 sonnets), and *The Fairie Queene*; Sir Philip Sidney with 108 sonnets printed as *Astrophel and Stella*, a pastoral novel *Arcadia*, and *Apologie for Poetrie*; prose by Francis Bacon, John Lyly, Robert Greene, and Thomas Nashe
- the most important literary manifestation: the Elizabethan Drama
    - Pre-Shakespearian drama: anonymous plays and various authors such as Thomas Kyd, John

Lyly, Robert Greene, and Christopher Marlowe (famous for *The Tragical Historie of Doctor Faustus* and *Tamburlaine the Great*)
- William Shakespeare: poetry (sonnets) and drama (historical plays, comedies, and tragedies)

4. The Seventeenth Century, or the period of "Revolution and Restoration" in British Literature
- dated between 1620 and 1690, or between 1603 (the death of Elizabeth and the accession of James I) and 1714 (the inauguration of the Hanoverian Dynasty by George I)
- major historical events: the rise of Puritanism, the abolition of monarchy (the execution of Charles I) in 1649, the Commonwealth Interregnum led by Oliver Cromwell between 1649 and 1660, the restoration of monarchy (Charles II restored to throne) in 1660
- concerning literature, the period consists of
      - metaphysical poetry (or Baroque, 1620s to 1670s)
      - the Puritan period (1649-1660)
      - the Restoration period (1660-1700)
- includes already clearly defined literary trends, such as metaphysical trend in poetry and the "comedy of manners" in the Restoration drama
- major literary voices: metaphysical poets John Donne and Andrew Marvell, the great playwright Ben Jonson, the Puritan writer John Milton, and John Dryden as the most important representative of the Restoration literature

5. The Eighteenth-Century Literature (1700-1780s)
- the period of French Revolution, Agricultural Revolution, and Industrial Revolution
- in literature, the eighteenth century consists of
- neoclassicism (1660-1780s)
      - the rise of the English novel (throughout the century)
      - pre-romanticism (1750s-1780s)
- the neoclassical period is divided into three parts:
      - the "Restoration Age" (1660-1700), or the "Age of Dryden"
      - the "Augustan Age" (1700-1750s), or the "Age of Pope"
      - the "Age of Johnson" (1750s-1780s), or the decline of Neoclassicism
- major trends and movements include:
      - neoclassicism as a movement in literature with its poetic works (namely philosophical and satirical) and a strongly normative and prescriptive doctrine
      - pre-romantic trend in poetry
      - different trends in the genre of the novel, or rather types of the novel: picaresque novel, sentimental novel, epistolary novel, comic novel, moral novel, and others
- major literary voices representing:
      - neoclassicism: Alexander Pope and Dr Samuel Johnson
      - the rise of the English novel: Jonathan Swift, Daniel Defoe, Samuel Richardson, Henry Fielding, Laurence Sterne, Jane Austen
      - pre-romanticism: James Macpherson and Thomas Gray

6. Romantic Literature
    - dated between 1780s-1830s, or between 1798 (the publication of *Lyrical Ballads*) and 1824 (the death of Byron)
    - romanticism represents a period: "Romantic Period", or the "Age of Romanticism"
    - romanticism is a literary movement: "Romantic Movement", consisting of both imaginative writing and critical ideas
    - important for breaking the linearity of literary development dominated for centuries by the traditional classical spirit and for reviving the innovative spirit in arts and the proclamation of the freedom of artistic expression, individualism, nationalism, authorship, emotional experience, imagination, nature and rustic life, dualism of existence, and so on
    - important for its literary doctrine: major critical texts include Wordsworth's *Preface to Lyrical Ballads*, Coleridge's *Biographia Literaria*, and Shelley's *Defence of Poetry*
    - the genres and representatives of Romanticism:
        - poetry: the most important genre, represented by William Blake, William Wordsworth, Samuel

Taylor Coleridge, Robert Southey, Robert Burns, Percy Bysshe Shelley, George Gordon, Lord Byron, and John Keats
  - prose: the historical novel of Sir Walter Scott and the gothic fiction by Horace Walpole, Clara Reeve, Ann Radcliffe, and others
  - drama: Percy Bysshe Shelley and George Gordon, Lord Byron

7. The Victorian Literature
- dated 1830s-1900, or between 1837 (Victoria came to throne) and 1901 (the death of Queen Victoria)
- in ideology, politics, and society, the Victorian Age was a period of innovation, invention, progress, complexity, and change: democracy, feminism, unionization of workers, Newton's mechanics, Darwin's evolution, Comte's view of society, Marx's view of history, Taine's view of literature, Freud's view of human psyche, industrialization, steam power, railway, telephone, telegraph, photography, etc.
- in literature and other arts: the Victorians attempted to combine the romantic emphases upon self, emotion, and imagination with the neoclassical concern with the public role of art and responsibility of the artist
- hence the Victorian Age consisting of a great number of movements and trends co-existing during one period and as such revealing the co-existence of the traditional and innovative elements in literature
- "tradition" is represented by realism, a major literary trend which manifests in novel writing and which rejects romanticism and continues the neoclassical emphasis on rules and ethics, and the interest in the actual, immediate reality
- close to realism, but also different in many respects, is the trend called naturalism
- "innovation" is revived by the defiant spirit of the romantic writers, rejects tradition, rules and prescriptive doctrines, and manifests as a continuation of the romantic rebellious attitude in art
- the element of innovation represents the real source of literary complexity in Victorian period since it consists of a number of trends and movements
- the innovation in literature and arts growing out of romanticism has a twofold perspective:
    - first, innovation from romanticism, heavily influenced by the romantic attitude and comprising a great number of romantic characteristics
    - second, innovation out of romanticism, less influenced by the romantic attitude but still continuing a number of its features
- the first kind of innovation manifests as post- and neo-romantic trends, including most of the Victorian poetry as well as some of the fiction of the period, such as Emily Bronte's gothic novel and the later colonial prose of Kipling, Stevenson, Doyle, Wells, and Conrad
- the second type of innovation manifests as symbolism, aestheticism, impressionism, expressionism, Pre-Raphaelite Brotherhood, and other trends which represent the artistic avant-garde of the second half of the nineteenth century
- the dominant literary form is novel, then poetry, and to a lesser extent, drama
- the novel belongs mainly to realism and the realist novel is the main type of fiction
- there are some exceptions, like the gothic/post-romantic novel *Wuthering Heights* by Emily Bronte, or *The Picture of Dorian Gray* by Oscar Wilde which reflects aestheticism
- poetry in general continues the romantic tradition, but is also influenced by aestheticism and symbolism
- to summarise, the Victorian Age covers the literature of such literary trends and movements as realism, post-and neo-romantic writing, the Pre-Raphaelite Movement, aestheticism ("art for art's sake" doctrine), naturalism, and others
- main literary voices:
    - prose: Charles Dickens, William Makepeace Thackeray, Charlotte Bronte, Emily Bronte, George Eliot, Lewis Carroll, Oscar Wilde, Thomas Hardy
    - poetry: Alfred, Lord Tennyson, Robert Browning, Matthew Arnold, Gerald Manley Hopkins, Dante Gabriel Rossetti, William Morris, Charles Algernon Swinburne

8. English Literature in the First Half of the Twentieth Century, or the period of modernism and its alternatives (1900-1945)
- British literature in the first half of the twentieth-century consists of a wide range of movements and trends which can be grouped under two headings:
    - the first one includes the literary works which continue the nineteenth-century realistic texts, preserve unchanged the traditional and normative type of writing, and is referred to as realism, meaning realist, traditional, and conservative literature

- the second one rejects the traditional and conservative type of literature and consists of innovative, original, experimental and avant-garde trends which represent the literary dimensions of modernism
  - the first half of the twentieth century includes
    - the Edwardian period (1900-1910)
    - modernism (1910s-1930s)
    - realistic writing (throughout the period, although dominant in the first decade (the Edwardian period) and in the 1930s and 1940s)
  - modernism is a period in the first half of the twentieth century, an artistic movement, or rather a complex artistic manifestation consisting of a number of distinct movements and trends
  - in other words, it is more appropriate to use "modernism" as a generic term to be applied retrospectively to the wide range of experimental, avant-garde artistic and intellectual trends and movements of the first half of the twentieth century
  - the trends and movements of Modernism manifested in art in general, including painting, music, architecture, and literature
  - examples of modernist trends and movements: futurism, surrealism, cubism, dadaism, imagism, the stream-of-consciousness novel, and so on
  - composers such as Stravinsky and Schoenberg represent Modernism in music
  - the movements *les fauves*, cubism, and surrealism, and artists such as Picasso, Matisse, and Mondrian represent modernism in visual arts
  - in architecture and design, modernism is represented by Le Corbusier, Walter Gropius, and Mies van der Rohe
  - in literature, the leading figures of modernism are Guillaume Apollinaire, Louis Aragon, Jean Cocteau, Hilda Doolittle, William Faulkner, Ezra Pound, William Carlos Williams, Max Jacob, Federico Garcia Lorca, Franz Kafka, Marcel Proust, Gertrude Stein, Tristan Tzara, Paul Valery, and many others
  - in Britain, the major literary voices of modernism are James Joyce and Virginia Woolf in fiction (including the "stream-of-consciousness novel"), and T. S. Eliot and W. B. Yeats in poetry
  - other voice of Modernism in English fiction: D. H. Lawrence and Aldous Huxley
  - the realist literature of the first half of the twentieth century is represented by John Galsworthy, William Somerset Maugham, Graham Greene, George Orwell, George Bernard Shaw, and others

9. English Literature in the Second Half of the Twentieth Century, or "Post-War and Postmodern Literature" (1945-present)
- the second half of the twentieth century includes
    - the post-war literature (1940s and 1950s)
    - the postmodern literature (1960s to the present)
- the post-war literature is traditional and realist rather than experimental; the main trend is the Angry Young Generation (or Angry Young Men), whose representatives are Alan Sillitoe, John Wain, Kingsley Amis, and John Braine; however, the period also includes the visionary and philosophical writing of the 1950s and 1960s, which made possible the transition from realism of the post-war period to later flourishing of postmodernism, and which was at best represented by William Golding and Iris Murdoch
- the postmodern literature consists of two main parts:
    - realism, or the traditional realist writing, at best represented by Graham Greene, Evelyn Waugh, Charles Percy Snow, Sir Angus Wilson, Muriel Spark, Margaret Drabble, and others
    - postmodernism, or experimentation in art and literature
- like with modernism, postmodernism is a generic term used to name the wide range of contemporary experimental, innovative and original artistic and intellectual trends and movements of the second half of the twentieth century and of the first decades of the new millennium
- postmodernism in British literature can be divided in several trends and movements, among which:
    - the campus novel/global campus novel, at best represented by David Lodge
    - magical realism, at best represented by Angela Carter
    - historiographic metafiction, at best represented by Murial Spark, John Fowles, Graham Swift, and Ian McEwan
    - postcolonial writing, at best represented by Salman Rushdie and Monica Ali
- other postmodern and postmodernist voices in British literature: Julian Barnes and Peter Ackroyd in fiction; Ted Hughes, Dylan Thomas, Seamus Heaney, and Philip Larkin in poetry; John Osborne, Samuel Beckett, Harold Pinter, Tom Stoppard, and Caryl Churchill in drama

To summarise, with regard to the major literary trends and movements in English and general European literature, the students may consider the following:

humanism (Renaissance)
metaphysical poetry (baroque, Renaissance, seventeenth century)
cavalier poets (seventeenth century)
comedy of manners (seventeenth century, Restoration period)
Enlightenment (seventeenth century, eighteenth century)
neoclassicism (seventeenth century, eighteenth century)
pre-romanticism (eighteenth century)
picaresque novel (eighteenth century)
sentimentalism/sentimental novel (eighteenth century)
epistolary novel (eighteenth century)
comic novel (eighteenth century)
moral novel (eighteenth century)
romanticism (eighteenth century, nineteenth century)
gothic novel (eighteenth century, nineteenth century)
historical novel (nineteenth century)
post-romantic literature (nineteenth century)
neo-romantic literature (nineteenth century)
Transcendentalism (nineteenth century)
colonial literature (nineteenth century)
impressionism (nineteenth century)
expressionism (nineteenth century)
symbolism (nineteenth century)
aestheticism / "art for art's sake" doctrine (nineteenth century)
Pre-Raphaelite Brotherhood (nineteenth century)
realism (nineteenth-century, twentieth century)
naturalism (nineteenth century)
modernism (twentieth century)
futurism (twentieth century)
surrealism (twentieth century)
cubism (twentieth century)
dadaism (twentieth century)
imagism (twentiethcentury)
Harlem Renaissance (twentieth century)
the Lost Generation (twentieth century)
stream-of-consciousness novel (twentieth century)
Angry Young Men (twentieth century)
postmodernism (twentieth century)
campus novel (twentieth century)
magical realism (twentieth century)
historiographic metafiction (twentieth century)
postcolonial literature (twentieth century)
minimalism (twentieth century)
Beat poets (twentieth century)
confessional literature (twentieth century)
spoken word (twentieth century)

Concerning the differences in the history of British and general European literary phenomena, it has been often brought into discussion the so-called "complex of insularity" of the British cultural background, its strong regional and conservative features in relation to the rest of Europe. Throughout its history, British culture seems reluctant to accept the Continental influences, new developments in literature and other arts, new movements, trends and styles, whose origins have been in France and Italy, and to a lesser extent in Spain and Germany.

Hence the fact that English literature is a late phenomenon, from the very beginning and throughout its entire literary history. It may take a century or more to speak about English Renaissance and about the rise and consolidation of a literary tradition in English fiction, or decades for romanticism or symbolism, as if British literary background must finally yield to the acceptance of what in contemporary Europe has been already established as a dominant literary tradition, movement, or trend.

Still, many English authors on the side of the freedom of artistic expression remained for centuries unknown or wrongly evaluated, such as Donne and Hopkins, or, like Byron, Lawrence and Joyce, had to escape from the conservatism and reluctance of the fellow-citizens and produce their works in some other countries. It is claimed, however, that English literary "complex of insularity" ends with the synchronization in the first half of the twentieth century of the British with European modernism, due to the contribution of, among others, Joyce and Eliot, though in the second half of the last century English literature turns again to realistic and social concerns rather than literary experimentation, being traditional rather than innovative.

It might be that British literature, in general, has been traditional rather than innovative, but it passes nowadays, as many national literatures do, through a process of decentralization due to globalization, the country's former membership in European Union, new developments in sociology, anthropology, women's studies, cultural studies, and postcolonial and transnational studies. Perhaps the most significant factor of decentralization of British literature is the advancement of English as a world language, spoken worldwide by millions who have no other connection with Britain.

English literature might have been traditional rather than innovative, but it is an aberration to assume that it represents weak literary phenomena, lacking aesthetic strength and significance, and that it is investigated and taught merely because of some political, economic, colonial, postcolonial or linguistic causes.

British literature is rich and complex, studied in almost every country of the world and acclaimed by Anglo-American as well as international scholarship, as to remember just Emile Legouis and Louis Cazamian who, almost a century ago, in their celebrated *A Short History of English Literature* (1929), already saw English literature possessing "a greater capacity than other literature for combining a love of concrete statement with a tendency to dream, a sense of reality with lyrical rapture", and English writers characterized by "loving observation of Nature, by a talent for depicting strongly-marked character, and by a humour that is the amused and sympathetic noting of the contradictions of human nature and the odd aspects of life".

British literature is an important part of the world literary heritage, answering and assuming during its history most of the innovation and development in arts and literature, and having its own contribution to world literary practice and literary doctrine, attributable to such major British literary voices as Chaucer and Gower in the Middle Ages, Shakespeare, Marlowe, Spenser and Sidney in the Renaissance, Donne, Marvell, Milton and Dryden in the seventeenth century, Pope, Swift, Defoe, Richardson, Fielding and Sterne in the eighteenth century, Blake, Wordsworth, Coleridge, Byron, Shelley and Keats in romanticism, Dickens, George Eliot, Emily

Bronte, Charlotte Bronte, Tennyson, Robert Browning, Swinburne, Arnold, Ruskin, Pater, Wilde and Carlyle in Victorian Age, and, in the twentieth century, Joyce, Woolf, Lawrence, T. S. Eliot, Shaw, Hughes, Beckett, Pinter, Golding, Murdoch, Fowles, Barnes, Mitchell, Spark, Lodge, Larkin, Ackroyd, McEwan, and many other writers of all these periods, whose works are landmarks in the history of English as well as European and world literature and thought.

Finally, a few terminological explanations may properly conclude our answering of the three questions, which we have focused upon in this Introduction, as well as strengthen the acquired knowledge.

With regard to literary criticism, the interconnected terms "criticism", "critic", "criticise", "critical", and "critique" entered English language at the beginning of the modern period, largely around 1600. The etymology of all these words starts in ancient Greek, namely from Greek *krites* ("judge, a person offering reasoned judgement or analysis") and its derivation *kritikos* ("skilled in making judgement"), as well as *krinein* ("to decide, to separate") and *krinô* ("I judge", or "to separate and distinguish in order to be able to judge"), which is also the root for the word "crisis". From Greek they passed into Latin, then French and finally English.

The term "critic", for instance, having in 1580s the meaning of "the one who passes judgement" and from c.1600 on that of "censurer, the one who judges quality of books", entered at that time English from medieval French *critique*, which comes from Latin *criticus* ("judge, critic of literature") which derives originally from Greek. "Criticism", from "critic" and "-ism", meant around 1600 "the act of criticising" and from 1670s on "art of estimating literary works". "Criticise", formed by "critic" and "-ise/-ize", meant in 1640s "to pass, usually unfavourable, judgement", then "to discuss critically" from 1660s and "to censure" from 1704. "Critical", from "critic" and suffix "-ial", meant "censorious" in 1580s, received its meaning of "pertaining to criticism" in 1740s, but also had a medical meanings from c.1600 and the meanings "of the nature of crisis" (1640s") and "crucial" (1840s). "Critique", around 1700, meaning "the art of criticism", is from French *critique* or *critick* and Latin *critica* as the feminine of *criticus*, but it also derives ultimately from the Greek *krites*, *krinô*, and *kritikē* ("the art of discerning").

Concerning imaginative writing, it is interesting and also necessary to point out that in place of the terms familiar nowadays "author" and "literature", the words "poet" and "poetry" were used for centuries until late into modern period to label all creative literature and the writer, in general. The etymology begins in ancient Greece and Rome, with the Greek word *poiëin*, meaning "to make, to do, to compose". It gave the Greek *poesis* ("a thing made, composition, poetry"), *poema* ("thing made or created, work of poetry"), and *poetes* ("maker, poet, author"); the Latin *poesis* ("poetry"), *poema* ("poetry, verse"), and *poeta* ("poet, author"); Vulgar Latin *poesia*; Old French *poesie*, *poetrie*, and *poete*; Old and Middle English (c.1300) "poesy"; Modern English (c.1500) "poetry", "poem", and "poet".

Thus, the terms "poetry" and "poet" signified literature and author, in general, and referred to all genres, which was mainly due to the fact that the greater part of imaginative literature produced until the rise of the novel was actually written in verse form. Philip Sidney in *The Defence of Poesie* insists that "it is not rhyming and versing that maketh poesy. One may be a poet without versing, and a versifier without poetry". Literature was, therefore, named as "poetry", a text of literature of whatever genre as "poem", and the author as "poet". Drama was labelled "poetry", as in Dryden, for whom plays are "dramatic poesie" and Shakespeare and Jonson are "poets". Even novel was included in poetry, as in Fielding, who calls his novel *Joseph Andrews* a "comic epic poem written in prose". Gradually, in the course of literary history, the words "poetry" and "poet" were limited to the meaning of literature written in verse form.

The term "literature" originates from the Latin *littera*, meaning letter of alphabet, and its form *litterarum*, referring to books, manuscripts, letters, acts, memories, and literary and scientific works. Terry Eagleton points to the fact that throughout the periods of literary development in England, and especially in the eighteenth century, "the concept of literature was not confined as it sometimes is today to "creative" or "imaginative" writing", that it "meant the whole body of valued writing in society: philosophy, history, essays and letters as well as poems", "conformed to certain standards of "polite letters"", and that it was only in the romantic period that the modern definition of "literature" began to develop, "the privilege accorded by the Romantics to the "creative imagination"" leading to "a narrowing of the category of literature to so-called "creative" or "imaginative" work" and literature became "virtually synonymous with the "imaginative"" (Eagleton 15-17).

Today, the term "literature" denotes the entire imaginative writing and all the works which belong to all literary genres and forms, including narrative, lyrical, dramatic, or fictional prose, poetry, drama, or, to be more specific, novel, short story, poem, play, epic, tragedy, ode, satire, dramatic monologue, etc. Also, the term "literature" has another meaning: "if we describe something as "literature", as opposed to anything else, the term carries with it qualitative connotations which imply that the work in question has superior qualities; that it is well above the ordinary run of written works" (Cuddon 505-506).

This is the reason why anyone concerned with the history of literature and that of literary criticism should pay attention to the ways in which certain terms derive etymologically from others and the ways in which they change their meanings, as one should bear in mind that the criticism of "poetry" and "poets" produced before the nineteenth century actually means criticism of imaginative literature, in general.

To conclude this rather long but necessary part of our book, the argument to be considered in the field of literary studies dealing with the history of English literature is that the literary texts produced by different writers in different periods of British history and civilization are not merely a category which needs to be included in an overall literary system of English or international cultural heritage for the sake of rendering its completeness and aesthetic validity.

It is rather that they are different in kind, unique and representative of a type of literary discourse which should be studied as a system in itself, and which, if properly comprehended, may perform the function of breaking down the existing views and theories about English literature, in general, or a particular literary manifestation in Britain, reorganizing them and suggesting new ones.

In our series of books, we attempt to argue that, following the principles announced by Yuri Tynyanov, the investigation of literary history is possible in relation to the view of **literature as a system, interrelated with other systems and conditioned by them** and by assuming that the movement of literature through history represents **substitution of systems**.

A more detailed and comprehensive presentation of Tynyanov's principles and opinions on historical investigation of the literary phenomenon may provide a vector methodology to those concerned with the diachronic movement of literature, as we shall see in the Preliminaries to this book.

PRELIMINARIES

LEARNING LITERARY HERITAGE THROUGH CRITICAL TRADITION OR BACK TO TYNYANOV

> The point is that most people don't want what you and your colleagues think of as history – the sort you get in books – because they don't know how to deal with it. Personally, I've every sympathy. With them, that is. I've tried to read a few history books myself, and while I may not be clever enough to enrol in your classes, it seems to me that the main problem with them is this: they all assume you've read most of the other history books already. It's a closed system. There's nowhere to start. (A character in *England, England* by Julian Barnes, London: Jonathan Cape, 1998, pp. 70-71)

Keywords: Tynyanov, Shklovsky, Eliot, Bakhtin, system, literary system, system of elements, substitution of systems, centre versus margin, innovation versus tradition, internal change, function, order, depersonalization, *ostranenie* (defamiliarization), literariness, intertextuality, dialogism, chronotope

It is a remarkable coincidence that the *fin de siècle* of all centuries before and during modernity represents an important breakthrough in the literary advancement: around 1370, *Sir Gawain and the Green Knight* is said to have emerged on the literary scene; around 1387, *The Canterbury Tales* came to claim the rise of Englishness in the literary art; 1470 saw the publication of *Morte d'Arthur*; the end of the sixteenth century saw Elizabethan drama and Shakespeare; the end of the seventeenth century proclaimed the age of reason and, particularly in English literature, neoclassicism; the eighteenth century ended in romanticism and the dominance of poetry (in English literature, with Blake, Wordsworth, and Coleridge), and, also in English literature, the novel is founded; the nineteenth century ended with the innovation of symbolism and aestheticism as origins and precursors of modernism; and the last decades of the twentieth century, as postmodern, also revealed the flourishing of literary innovation and experimentation under the auspices of postmodernism, which mainly manifest themselves in imaginative prose.

The movement of English literature (or any other national literature, or the world literature, in general) through history is the main concern of the history of literature (literary history), a distinct discipline of literary evaluation which is nowadays alive and applied – and still developed and attempted to be conferred with scientific and methodological apparatus – despite the postmodern laments over the death of history, originality, meaning, reality, and authorship, along with the mourning of the end of reflexiveness, reflexivity, reflection, and the impossibility of language to truthfully represent whatever an artist would endeavour to reflect.

In its diachronic perspective focused on literary periods, movements, trends, authors, and texts, the historical investigation of literature is interrelated with literary theory (offering terminology and general principles of research) and literary criticism (providing the way of approach to particular texts), which, in turn, are indispensable from literary history (history of literature), as we have seen in the Introduction to this book.

In the discussion of the rise and consolidation of an English literary tradition, one should focus on the elements of the literary system in order to conduct a general, surveyistic as well as coherent approach to the complexity of the literary phenomenon considered diachronically from its Anglo-Saxon beginnings to the present day.

Rewriting Jakobson's structure of communication, Guy Cook identifies author, reader, text, performer, society, texts and language to be the main elements of the literary communicative situation, or the elements of the literary system. Among these elements is language; the formal, particularly structuralist and post-structuralist, interpretative arrangements of Shklovsky (*O teorii prozy*, 1929) and Lotman ("Lektsii po strukturalinoi poetike", 1994) – concerning art as language and system of signs, and the written language of the novel, poem and other literary works as their instrument and material – argue that language influences diachronically the essence of every cultural system, including literature and fiction. In turn, written language is indispensable from the instability and dynamics of various historical and cultural circumstances.

In order to be closer to the objective theory of art, from a formalist perspective, the aestheticization of written language, as a central aspect or element in the literary act of communication, prompts literariness and becomes possible by means of a set of literary devices, figures of speech, verbal nuances, and so on. Shklovsky, over a century ago, already showed that these devices would eventually make things unique and complicate the form of a work of art in order to increase the difficulty and time of perception since this process in art is an end in itself and must be prolonged.

This principle working in art and literature, called *ostranenie* ("defamiliarization"), has become the fundamental credo of modernism and is still successfully applied nowadays in literary practice, such as in the works of magical realism.

Adding Bakhtin to Cook, Shklovsky, and Lotman, other canonical principles, underpinning the development of literature and representing elements of its consolidated pattern, include chronotope, *raznorechie* (heteroglossia), polyphony, carnivalesque, and, especially, dialogism.

Adding Tynyanov to Bakhtin, Cook, Shklovsky, and Lotman, literature is to be viewed as a system of elements with centre and margin, with dominant and peripheral elements which fight to move into centre, to resist what denies them.

These elements do not disappear; they always are; they just exist; they are "Lord's", as Shklovsky says about his "images", just as T. S. Eliot speaks about impressions and experiences which do not change but are continuously recombined and rearranged.

> Based on Tynyanov, a "rule" of literary development would declare periods, movements, trends, genres, subgenres, even texts, and so on, to be literary systems placed in a diachronic relationship of substituting, following or succeeding each other by continuing and rejecting each other, as well as by being influenced by contemporary socio-cultural stimuli and developments in philosophy and science.

In the light of Tynyanov's ideas on literary work and literature conceived as systems, speaking solely about literary practice, its development in the context of literary history is based on the "fight" between the aspect of "innovation" and that of "tradition". These two aspects are represented diachronically by different periods, movements, trends, types of text, and so on, which either continue or reject and either follow or replace one another.

> These aspects, therefore, constitute the central (tradition) and marginal (innovation) elements within a literary system, which are engaged in a battle for dominance and to be central, to achieve defamiliarization, by which allowing development, change, and advancement of literature through history.

> The movement through history of a national literature can be better explained by drawing on theories of genre and literary development, of which one of the most congenial theorization, still valid and viable nowadays, belongs to Yuri Tynyanov, whose main reasoning would be that **literature is a system of central and peripheral elements** – in other words, tradition (centre) versus innovation (margin) in the fight over supremacy, which means for tradition to stay in the centre, whereas for innovation, it implies to proclaim demarginalization, to move into centre, and by this, to claim the right to build up a new system – **and the development or historical advancement of literature is the substitution of systems**, in other words, the substitution of various periods, movements, trends, genres, subgenres, styles, textual typologies, and so on.

Amid the huge amount of critical attention given to English literature, in general, and amid the multiplicity of theoretical perspectives to be applied to its analysis, Tynyanov's theories are appropriate and applicable also because they characterize national types of literature with their own characteristic features and peculiarities of historical development.

Drawing on the assumption that a literary work, like literature in general, is a system of interrelated and interdependent elements, the Russian formalist scholar discusses the genre in his essay entitled "Literaturnyi fakt" ("Literary Fact") and the development (history) of literature in "O literaturnoi evolutii" ("On Literary Evolution"), both written in 1927. Both works postulate the formalist theory of system and that of internal change in literary history.

In "Literary Fact", in matters of its principles, rise, development, sources, death and rebirth, these aspects of the genre, along with the migration and transformation of the genre, co-exist with and depend on the larger literary process, namely, the emergence of new literary trends, movements, forms, as well as views and conceptions in literary history.

The genre represents, in this respect, Tynyanov argues, not "a fall from the system", "not a planned evolution", not a "development", but "a jump or leap" and a shift, "a substitution of systems", and is therefore innovative and "unrecognizable" ("Literaturnyi fakt" 255-256). Like a literary work or movement, or literature in general, a genre is a system, but not a static, motionless system; it is a structure that may fluctuate, emerge from other systems, and weaken to become vestiges of subsequent systems.

A new genre replaces an old one, or becomes its successor, and the decline and rebirth of a genre are to be understood, as Tynyanov shows, in relation to the concentric model of literature, which is organized by the principles of "centre" and "margin": moving within this structure, a genre degenerates or dies out when it departs from the centre towards the periphery, but revives its literary potential when it approaches the centre, or "in its place from the trifles of literature, from the backyards and bottoms of literature, a new phenomenon emerges in the centre" (Tynyanov, "Literaturnyi fakt" 257-258).

Tynyanov emphasizes the diachronically inconstant feature of the literary periods, movements, and genres, which are viewed as literary systems, their dynamic, not static, essence, which is based on the perpetual clash between tradition and innovation, the permanent conflict over hierarchy, which involves various elements in their position within the system as centre and margin, in other words, as central or peripheral, dominant or marginal elements. An element or a form originally not considered literary is placed into a literary system, or it diverges from another element or form, and thereby it may give birth to a new trend or genre as a new system. Once established, a literary genre or trend never goes out of existence since its elements may emerge in either dominant or marginal positions in various other systems, namely newly emerging periods, movements, trends, genres, subgenres, and so on.

The medieval ballad, for instance, receives a new expression in romanticism by Coleridge. Also, in this period, the historical element becomes dominant in the system of what is established as the historical novel by Scott. In Wieland and especially Goethe, the element of ordeal from medieval romances re-emerges as an important element in the Bildungsroman literary system to determine the inner change of the character and prompt his or her identity formation.

Focusing primarily on literary genres, Tynyanov develops the formalist theory of internal change in literary development. After providing a concentric model of literature, he postulates the principle of the conflict between centre and margin, theorizes the obliteration and rebirth of genres, and insists on the migration and transformation of genres, according to which, moving within the literary system, a genre is forgotten or silenced if it moves away from the centre, and is renewed when it comes closer to the centre.

A particular genre becomes dominant in a certain period and develops its system of elements: it attracts writers, who become more imitative than creative, expands temporally and territorially, and, in this way, a literary tradition or convention is established. Confronted by innovation and originality, the genre may lose its dominant position and be replaced by a new one which becomes dominant.

The way in which Tynyanov discusses the genre is true for literary periods, movements, trends, species, and works, i.e., all literary phenomena which constitute, in the formalist view, literary systems with distinct characteristics.

We also follow in our study the **theory of internal change**, and start from the premise of literature to be a system of elements which denote either centre or margin prompting a battleground for innovation and tradition.

In order to explain this practically with direct reference to a literary tradition established as literary system, a good example would be the subgenre of the novel known as the Bildungsroman. Just like with various genres, in Tynyanov's opinion, the thematic and, to a lesser extent, structural elements of various literary systems – literary systems are represented diachronically from ancient times to the end of the eighteenth century by different periods, movements, trends, genres, subgenres and text categories – perform individual breakthroughs and survive, or are modified, receive new positions, and interrelate anew around the central element of identity formation as established by Goethe in his canonical novel of formation *Wilhelm Meisters Lehrjahre*. In doing so, these elements, primarily thematic, are placed into and become elements of the new Bildungsroman literary system; among them, pseudo-biographical material, childhood experience, education, ordeal, chronotope of road, epiphany, and others become central and peripheral elements of the literary system of the Bildungsroman, whose dominant and central element is formation.

The Bildungsroman, being currently perpetuated by various writers around the world, reveals that changes still occur within its literary system. These changes have occurred and occur for both internal and external reasons, such as the newly emerging trends (magical realism, for instance), the audience, the publisher, or various social, cultural and political developments.

Unlike the romance, or the picaresque novel, or the gothic narrative, the Bildungsroman stays to the present day one of the few "strong" genres, or rather subgenre of the novelistic genre, as to be more correct terminologically in accordance to the categorisation by literary theory and criticism. The Bildungsroman proves, historically, literary vitality and multifaceted creative consistency, since, in its depiction of the life of a particular individual, this fictional subgenre relies on and confirms the view that literature has always been and will always be, to a lesser or greater extent, a reflection of the personal experience of the author.

The formalist theory of internal change covers the domain of genres, and also those of literary periods, movements, trends, types of texts, including the Bildungsroman, and so on; nowadays it is also applied in feminist, minority and cultural studies and in postcolonial theory. In postulating intertextuality – new texts emerge as imitating, completing, competing, negating, or parodying other texts – the formalist theory of internal change alludes to Bakhtin's dialogism, Shklovsky's *ostranenie*, and Eliot's new combinations of elements.

"A new art emotion" is what T. S. Eliot declares, in "Tradition and the Individual Talent" (1919), to be novelty in literature, its significance and the real artistic and poetic achievement. Tradition is for him an "order", which is a term identical to that used by Tynyanov; for Eliot, likewise, order is not static or ideal but is continuously modified by new works which attempt to acquire their place in literary history, making order simultaneous, bringing it into the present of literary activity when intertextuality is at work.

The poet is not an individual separated from history, and the significance of his poetry stands in its relation to the past: "No poet, no artist of any art, has his complete meaning alone. His significance, his appreciation is the appreciation of his relation to the dead poets and artists" (Eliot 44).

The ideal order established by tradition becomes a simultaneous order when the past and present are united and expressed concomitantly: the simultaneous order is a kind of archive. Accordingly, the individual talent does not need to invent something or attempt to produce originality, since everything has been already written, but to recombine, rearrange the elements of order, keeping in mind – and here Eliot is not far removed from "dialogism" in Bakhtin and "intertextuality" in Kristeva – that "the past should be altered by the present as much as the present is directed by the past" (Eliot 45).

Another important aspect in the act of artistic creation is, for Eliot, the "process of depersonalization" based on the continuous surrender to tradition and "self-sacrifice": the poet does not express a personality, but "a particular medium"; poetry, in Eliot's famous anti-Wordsworthian declaration, "is not a turning loose of emotion, but an escape from emotion; it is not the expression of personality, but an escape from personality" (Eliot 52-53).

Actually, the process leading to novelty or "new art emotion", as articulated by Eliot, is not far removed from a formalist perspectives: it begins with (1) learning, acquiring the knowledge of canonical works as standards of greatness (as later Harold Bloom would insist), in other words, evolving an awareness of the past tradition, order and the world, the human condition; it continues with (2) self-sacrifice or surrender to past tradition; which leads to (3) poet losing personality and acquiring "depersonalization" or impersonality; so that (4) the poet becomes a medium for the expression of existing elements, "impressions and experiences"; (5) the poet thereby produces new, original combinations of impressions, experiences, images, feelings, phrases, etc.; which results in (6) the ideal order becoming simultaneous; which means, finally, that (7) a "new art emotion" emerges to take its place in the order or, in Tynyanov's terms, in the literary system.

The modernist author T. S. Eliot is viewed, as a critic, in relation to Anglo-American "New Criticism", whereas Yuri Tynyanov represents Russian "Formalism"; they are united in their pursuit of a formal approach to literature, hence certain similarities of their critical thinking.

Examples of a common pursuit and similar concepts and perspectives of literary investigation are to be found in the work of the formal and formalist Viktor Shklovsky, namely in his "Art as Technique" (1917), in which self-sacrifice and depersonalization become ostranenie ("defamiliarization") and the key concepts are again "rearrangement", "recombination" of elements and images so as to pursue the technique of art which is "to make objects "unfamiliar", to make forms difficult, to increase the difficulty and length of perception because the process of perception is an aesthetic end in itself and must be prolonged" (Shklovsky 778). "Art is thinking in images", and poetry is a special way of thinking, namely, thinking by means of images, where thinking in images allows for "economy of mental effort" (Shklovsky 775).

"Images", in Shklovsky (or "elements", in Tynyanov, and "impressions and experiences", in Eliot), change little diachronically, or, actually they are the same; they pass or are taken unchanged from poet to poet: "from century to century, from nation to nation, from poet to poet, they flow on without changing" (Shklovsky 776); they belong to no one but the Lord, and they are identical in the works of various poets.

Like Tynyanov and Eliot, Shklovsky draws attention to the fact that a certain poet would never invent or produce new images. Like Tynyanov, for whom elements are linked to co-exist in the system in correlation and interrelationship, and, like Eliot, for whom impressions and experiences are combined in new and original ways to produce a new art emotion, Shklovsky contends that the poets should remember images rather than create them – since images are given to poets – in order to rearrange and combine them in new and original ways.

As in Tynyanov and Eliot, elements, images, experiences, feelings, themes, concerns, motifs, ideas, etc. are static; what is continually changing is their relation, or combination, or arrangement. The motivation for such arrangements and combinations focuses on impression, in that poetic imagery "is a means of creating the strongest possible impression" (Shklovsky 776). Shklovsky's "impression", like that of Henry James and especially Walter Pater, concerns the process of artistic perception; as in Pater, personal impression is a means of fighting stereotype or unconscious existence, or, as Shklovsky calls it, fighting "habitualization", the process of "algebrization", "the over-automatization of an object" (Shklovsky 778).

Hence, the requirement for successful and accomplished artistic endeavour is "ostranenie" or "defamiliarization", by which the sensation of life is recovered, things are felt, the stone is made "stony", and the purpose of art is achieved, namely, "to impart the sensation of things as they are perceived and not as they are known", since "Art is a way of experiencing the artfulness of an object; the object is not important" (Shklovsky 778). One should remember here that the romantic critical theory already pointed at this feature of literature – Wordsworth and Shelley stipulating the ability of poetry to achieve unusual, unfamiliar expression – as later the nineteenth-century avant-garde did.

Shklovsky's view of the arrangement of images in various new ways – just like Tynyanov's view of elements and Eliot's of impressions which are arranged and combined in new, original ways – represents one way to understand the historical movement of literature through periods, movements, and trends.

Poets and their works are classified or grouped according to the arrangement of images, the "development of the resources of language", and "the new techniques that poets discover and share" (Shklovsky 776), where this "grouping" would allow the foundation of new trends and movements.

To us, such ideas represent a congenial way to understand the movement of literature as a system diachronically, including the rise, consolidation, fall, further development, and change of various periods, movements and trends.

In matters of literary genre, Viktor Shklovsky talks about "the canonization of minor genres", such as the romance, the picaresque novel, or the gothic narrative. The Bildungsroman is also such a historically emergent literary fact, first in German pre-romanticism with Goethe, to become aesthetically strengthened by the realists and modified and diversified by the modernist and postmodern writers.

To revert to Tynyanov, a literary system, as a particular period, movement, trend, literary species, category, type, genre, or subgenre, demonstrates in the system of literature, in general, that "the literary fact is multi-structured and in this respect literature is a continuously evolving order" ("Literaturnyi fakt" 270) consisting of a myriad of diverse forms within which occur a myriad of "merging episodes of the constructional principle with the material" ("Literaturnyi fakt" 269).

Tynyanov further applies his conception of literature as a system to the discussion of literary development, or, in his words, "literary evolution", whose principles are, also in his terms, "fight" and "substitution". In his study "O literaturnoi evolutii", Tynyanov compares the domain of the history of literature to a colonial state driven by an "individualistic psychologism" and "a schematically causal approach to the literary order" (270). The divergence between them leads to a methodological discrepancy in the field of the historical investigation of literature. The former type replaces the problem of literature with the question of the author's psychology and the issue of literary evolution with that of the genesis of literary phenomena. The latter leads to the disagreement between the literary order and the standpoint from which the observation of this literary order takes place.

This place of observation constitutes social orders, and the construction of a closed literary order and the approach to evolution inside it (that is, to literary variability) would frequently come up against neighbouring cultural, domestic and, in the broad sense, social orders, and as such are doomed to incompleteness. Moreover, the theory of value in literary science has brought about the danger of studying major but isolated works and has changed the history of literature into what Tynyanov calls "the history of generals", meaning "great works" or masterpieces of literature (the literary canon), to the detriment of the study of mass literature.

The very term "history of literature" is a problem as well, continues Tynyanov, as it seems to be extremely broad and pretentious, suggesting the study of the history of *belles lettres*, the history of verbal art, and the history of writing, in general. Meanwhile, the historical investigation of literature has forked into the investigation of the genesis of literary phenomena and the investigation of the "evolution" of the literary order, or literary mutability.

The problem plaguing the historical approach to literature is the lack of theoretical methodology and the lack of an awareness of the character of research. The solution for making the history of literature a science, conferring on it the necessary methodological rigour, must be its striving for "reliability" and veracity ("O literaturnoi evolutii" 271). The study of literary development must avoid the theory of "naïve evaluation" and the subjective response; it is also necessary to reconsider the notion of "tradition", which is the abstractization of one or more literary elements in a system.

The central concept in literary evolution, which is responsible for literary change and development, is the **"substitution of systems"** ("O literaturnoi evolutii" 272). In order to analyse this essential issue in the context of studies on literary history, Tynyanov starts from the fundamental assumption that a literary work is a system, as is literature itself. In his opinion, the foundation of a science of literature and the investigation of the historical progress of literature are possible only in the view of literature as a system interrelated with other systems and conditioned by them.

All the elements of a literary work are the elements of a system, in the sense of a literary system which is a system of functions of literary order which are in continual interrelationship with other orders. All the elements of the system of a literary work are interrelated, interdependent and interacting. Some elements of a work in prose, such as rhythm, are also elements of the system of a work in poetry, and their study shows that the role of such elements is different in different systems.

The interrelationship of each element with every other in a literary work as a system, and, therefore, with the whole, is what Tynyanov calls the "constructional function of the given element" ("O literaturnoi evolutii" 272). This function is a complex entity: it shows that a distinct element is, on the one hand, interrelated in the order with similar elements of other works-systems and even of other orders, and, on the other hand, interrelated with other elements within the same system. Tynyanov names the former "auto-function" and the latter "syn-function". Both operate simultaneously but are of different relevance. The lexis of a given literary work, for instance, is related at once to the literary lexis and the general verbal lexis, and to other elements of this work.

Tynyanov points to the mistake of extracting certain elements from a system and, without their constructional function, of correlating them outside the system with a similar order of other systems. It is also impossible to study synchronically a literary work as a system outside its relation to the general system of literature; otherwise, such a study is another abstractization. The isolated study of the literary works is applied, successfully enough, to the evaluation of contemporary works, since the interrelationship of a contemporary work to contemporary literature is involuntarily taken as an established fact.

However, Tynyanov argues, even in contemporary literature, isolated study is impossible because the very existence of a text as literary depends on its differential quality, which is on its interrelationship with either literary or extra-literary order. In other words, its existence depends on its function: what in one period would be a matter of casual social communication, in another would be a literary fact, or vice versa, depending on the whole of the literary system in which the given text appears.

Therefore, "studying the work in isolation, we cannot be sure that we speak in correct terms about its construction" ("O literaturnoi evolutii" 273). The auto-function (the interrelationship of an element to the order of similar elements in other systems and other orders) is a condition for the syn-function (the constructional function of the element).

To summarize, according to Tynyanov, the constructional function is the correlation of each element of the literary work with other elements of the system, and thus with the whole system. It is a mistake to separate the elements from the system and to correlate them outside the system, which is to neglect their constructional function. The existence of a literary fact depends on its differential quality, meaning its function.

Next, Tynyanov offers examples of poetry and prose, and focuses on the novel and its adjustment genres of story and novella to insist again that "the evaluation of literary phenomena does not occur outside their interrelationship" ("O literaturnoi evolutii" 276) and that, unfortunately, the evolutionary relation between the function and the formal element has not been studied. There are examples in literature of how the evolution of literary form determines the change of function; examples of how a form with indefinite function calls and builds up a new one; and examples of how function searches for its form.

The variability of functions of a formal element of the system, the appearance of a new function of the formal element, and its association with the function are important issues of literary evolution. Again, the whole research depends on the consideration of literature as an order, a system, where "the system of literary order is first of all the system of functions of literary order in continuous interrelationship with other orders" ("O literaturnoi evolutii" 277). Each literary work is correlated with a particular literary system depending on its deviation, its difference, as compared to the literary system with which it is confronted. Moreover, since a literary system is a system of the functions of the literary order which is in continual interrelationship with other orders, such as social and cultural, orders or systems change in their composition, but the differentiation of human activities remains.

Due to the specificity of its material, the growth of literature, like that of other cultural orders, coincides neither in rate nor in character with those systems or orders, such as social, with which it is interrelated. The evolution of the constructional function occurs rapidly; that of the literary function occurs over epochs, and the one concerning the functions of the whole literary system in relation to the neighbouring systems occurs over centuries.

> To follow Tynyanov's line of argumentation, to understand the development of literature as the "substitution of systems" is to perceive it as the change in the interrelationship of the elements of a system, which is the change of functions and formal elements.

A system does not represent an equal interrelationship of all elements, promoting instead the differential interaction of its elements, where through a group of dominant elements producing the deformation of other elements, a new literary work emerges in literature and acquires its literary function by means of these dominant elements.

Drawing especially on these theoretical assumptions by Tynyanov, as well as on those by Shklovsky and Bakhtin, the books of our project focusing on English literature aim to demonstrate the diachronicity of the literary phenomenon as an order or system of elements. We argue that English literature is a literary system which has passed through development and change of its thematic and formal elements and functions in order to establish itself as a continuous movement of periods, trends, genres, subgenres, authors, texts, and so on, each a literary tradition or system with preceding systems as cornerstones.

The substitutions of literary systems leading to new ones vary from epoch to epoch; they may occur rapidly or slowly; they do not necessarily require the complete renewal or replacement of the formal elements of the systems, but rather "a new function of these formal elements" (Tynyanov, "O literaturnoi evolutii" 281). A potential collation of certain literary phenomena must consider functions in addition to forms.

Tynyanov concludes his study by summarizing his ideas: the study of literary evolution is possible only by viewing literature as an order, a system which is interrelated with other orders, systems, and is conditioned by them. The study must move from the constructional function (the interrelationship of each element with other elements of the system, and thus with the whole system of the literary work) to the literary function (the interrelationship of a literary work with the literary order), and from the literary function to the verbal function (the interrelationship of a literary work with the social conventions), while clarifying the issue of developmental interaction of functions and forms. Also, the investigation of literature in its development "must go from the literary order to the nearest correlated systems, not some distant ones, although these could be important" ("O literaturnoi evolutii" 281), such as social conventions, cultural doctrines, historical background, the author's psychology, daily life and personal experience, and the tastes and interests of the reading audience.

Concerning the two components – social or historical, on the one hand, and biographical or psychological, on the other – that is, the author's times and life, from a formalist perspective, literature is above all interrelated with social conventions, and as such the correlation takes place first of all through its verbal aspect. In other words, the interrelation between literature and society is realized through language, and in relation to the social background the prime function of literature is its verbal function. Using the term "orientation" to denote the author's creative intention, Tynyanov and the formalists suggest that the intention is changed by the structural function (the interrelationship of elements within a work) into a catalyst, that "creative freedom" yields to "creative necessity", and that the literary function (the interrelationship of a work with the literary order) completes the process.

Simply stated, the "orientation" of a literary work proves to be its "verbal function", its interrelationship with social conventions. It would be futile to study the verbal function of literature in relation to some distant conditions, such as economic, as it is useless to study the author's psychology, environment, daily life, and class directly in order to establish the origins of the literary phenomena. Clearly, Tynyanov and the formalists believe, the problem here is not one of individual psychological conditions, but of objective, evolving functions of the literary order in relation to the adjacent social order.

Likewise, in discussing practical criticism, David Daiches states that the approach to the literary work should be different from going to biography or psychology to discover the author's intention, for "it is less personal intention than artistic tradition that is the real question" (265), where literary tradition is the object of study of the history of literature. Earlier, W. K. Wimsatt together with Monroe C. Beardsley condemned both "affective fallacy", which leads to a confusion between ends and means in judging the literary work in terms of its results in the mind of the audience, and "intentional fallacy", which is an error of evaluating a literary work by trying to assess what the author's intention was and whether it has or not been fulfilled.

In the historical studies of British literature, or any national literature, or the history of world literature, on the whole, it is clear that literary history, which provides a chronological vision on literature, is confronted with repeated methodological crises, as this discipline is unable to fully synchronise itself with the innovations which constantly take place in modern literary theory and criticism. As Tynyanov has already warned on this matter in his formalist attempts to renovate the history of literature through the theories of literature as a system, literary evolution, and the genre, the historical investigation of literature might still have no clear theoretical awareness of how to study a literary work or what the nature of its significance is. Rene Wellek and Austin Warren, in their celebrated *Theory of Literature*, also claim that the history of a national literature is hard to envisage and remains a distant ideal; strongly bound to their Russian formalist origins, they assume the theory of the literary system and claim that literary history must be the study of systems of "literary norms, standards, and conventions" and must be "the tracing of the changing from one system of norms to another" (264-268).

Wellek and Warren believe that the separation of criticism from the diachronic dimension of the literary history and its subsequent consolidation as a distinct domain were caused by the distinction between the consideration of literature as a simultaneous order and the view on literature as diachronic order, a line of works arranged chronologically and regarded as constituent parts of the historical process. Our study attempts to balance the levels on the assumption that neither the research of the text as a synchronic phenomenon nor the historicization of literary experience are to be neglected. To achieve an adequate comprehension of the literary works of different writers and periods, it is necessary to overcome the gap between literary criticism and literary history by fusing the synchronic and diachronic dimensions in literary analysis, and by strengthening the relationship between text and context.

To revert to Tynyanov, the two main types of the historical investigation of literature – the investigation of the genesis of literary phenomena and the investigation of the growth of a literary order or system – are both problematic, as problematic is to re-examine the problem of "influence", one of the most complex issues of literary history, in relation to the existence of specific literary conditions. Also, coming back to the concept of "tradition" in literature, it is to be remembered that what may be called "traditionalism" is, as to give an example from Tynyanov, the fact that each literary movement in a given period seeks its supporting point in the preceding systems, as each new genre, or form, or type of literary text does.

In the process of literary development, tradition continues tradition and rejects innovation, just as innovation continues innovation and rejects tradition, making literary systems – which we view as literary periods, movements, trends, genres, subgenres, texts, and so on – follow, replace, substitute each other. This process implies the struggle between tradition and innovation in terms of a binary opposition involving centre and margin, or central and peripheral elements, where the differential interaction of the elements of a system, the existence of some "dominant" elements which produce as such the "deformation" or marginalization of other elements, mean actually, in Tynyanov's opinion, literary evolution as substitution of systems.

Yuri Tynyanov's views on the literary work and literature conceived as systems and on the development of literature as substitution of systems are applicable in other domains of the humanities, such as linguistics (since language itself is a system), translation studies, and cultural studies, and in different literary disciplines, such as comparative literature, where, in particular, the issue of "reception" – the study of the process of reception of a literature (as a system) in another literature or another cultural background (also conceived as systems) – receives a strong theoretical and practical basis. Although highly important for the elucidation of the status and role of literary history as a scientific discipline, Tynyanov's theory of the literary system, due to its normative principles and methodological rigour, may not always be appropriate to the study of literature. This is especially the case when we face some national peculiarities of literary history, or when the individual creative imagination is both ready to assume an established tradition, model or pattern of writing and to pursue unexpected innovation, literary experimentation, and modernization of the literary discourse.

However, like many other concepts and principles of the formalists, and from the Russians' ranks also those of M. M. Bakhtin, Tynyanov's idea of literature as a system of dominant and peripheral elements turns out to be an important issue for postmodern theoretical and ideological debate regarding the "centre and margin" dichotomy. Bakhtin himself focuses on the concepts of "self and other"; he also coins the terms and discusses chronotope, polyphony, *raznorechie*, carnivalesque, dialogism, unfinalizability, *roman vospitaniya* ("the novel of education" or Bildungsroman), where these and other principles and ideas on literature are the most congenial to our approach to the rise and development of a national literature, English, and world literature, in general.

To return to the idea of system and the "centre and margin" dualism, this binary opposition is nowadays discussed in cultural, postcolonial, social, feminist, and literary studies. The postmodern attitude towards dominant elements, and, in particular discourses, is twofold: (1) to come within dominant discourses and try to modify them from within, and (2) to accept and proclaim marginalization and try to make fringe move into centre.

The relationship of centre and margin, or dominant and peripheral elements, can be applied to literature both diachronically and synchronically. From a diachronic perspective, we would link two explanations in the discussion of the development of literature, in general, one late modern by Tynyanov, based on his theory of system, and another postmodern, based on the concepts of margin and centre. In its shift from centre or a dominant position to margin or periphery, literature becomes ex-centric (outside the centre), and "ex-centric" means "eccentric", in the sense of being unconventional, original, new. Thus, innovation emerges by rejecting tradition as centre within tradition, and moves towards the margin to become a peripheral phenomenon; if strong enough, innovation may eventually become a centre and establish itself as tradition, as it happened with baroque, romanticism, symbolism, modernism, and, more recently, with magical realism.

Innovation and tradition in literature are reified by various following each other periods, movements, and trends as literary orders or systems; their rise is based doubly on rejection of some prior literary systems and continuation of other previous literary systems, and is influenced by contemporary developments in other more or less distant systems, such as cultural, linguistic, scientific, sociologic, and so on.

Although postmodernism rejects the notion of system, we should still pay attention to Tynyanov pointing to literature as a system containing dominant and peripheral elements when we speak about centre and margin from a postmodern standpoint to explain the development of literature by recourse to such concepts as innovation and tradition. We ought especially to recall Tynyanov's theorization of literature as a system, the evolution of literature as substitution of systems, and the elements of the literary system as interrelating and interacting both (1) among themselves and (2) with the elements of other literary and non-literary (social, cultural, political, ideological, artistic, etc.) systems.

From a synchronic perspective and within national boundaries, a literary system may be described in terms of three criteria of development with regard to the interrelationship of its elements: (1) concerning individual authors, for example Alexander Pope as centre and Thomas Gray as margin, or Shakespeare as centre and Ben Jonson as margin; (2) the substitution of periods and movements, for instance neoclassicism as centre and romanticism as margin at the end of the eighteenth century, where subsequently romanticism becomes itself a centre and replaces neoclassicism; and (3) the shift of periods and movements, for example realism as centre and modernism as margin changes to modernism as centre and realism as margin in the first half of the twentieth century.

The centre and margin dichotomy in feminism and in social studies is actualized as male/man as centre and female/woman as margin, heterosexual versus sexual minorities, dominant nationality or race versus national or racial minorities, and so on. In postcolonial studies: white versus non-white, colonizer/West/Europe as centre and the colonized/Non-West as margin. The opposition emerges also within each of the two elements taken separately. In Europe as centre, for example, Western Europe is centre and Eastern Europe is margin, which can be seen in literature as well: in anthologies of literature you would barely find Alexe Rudeanu in the company of Ian McEwan. The margin may move into the centre, along with the emerging issue of identity, when an author is translated but especially when he or she assumes the language of the centre, its values, mentality and attitudes, but, above all, enhances the centre, just as Eliade, Ionesco, Kundera, Kis, Safak, and others have done. Another example would be Latin America as margin which, in its relation to the West as centre, nevertheless produced a type of reversal of the binary opposition: after producing outstanding literature (Marquez and Coelho, among others), the erstwhile margin becomes centre when it is imitated by the already existing centre, as is the case, in English literature, of Angela Carter and her novels of magical realism.

The basic term "system" in Tynyanov and formalism receives a new life through Linda Hutcheon's "constant" and "system" as well as Bran Nicol's "dominant" in their explanation and evaluation of the postmodernist literature. Hutcheon, in *A Poetics of Postmodernism* (1988), speaks about a constant, meaning a central, dominant element, in postmodern fiction, namely that "the assertion of identity through difference and specificity is a constant in postmodern thought" (59). Furthermore, Hutcheon views modernism and postmodernism as two incompatible ideological "systems", where postmodern fiction rejects from the system of modernism such elements or features as the modernist ideology of artistic autonomy, individual expression, and the deliberate separation of art from mass culture and everyday life.

Nicol, likewise, considers "postmodern" as adjective to refer to "a particular period in literary and perhaps cultural history" and, at the same time, to a system or "set of aesthetic styles and principles", whereas, postmodernism, as an aesthetic phenomenon and the reflexive or reflecting mentality and artistic practice of postmodernity, refers to a system or "set of ideas developed from philosophy and theory and related to aesthetic production" (2). Furthermore, Bran Nicol introduces the notion "dominant" in his consideration of three main features or elements, which are mostly important, or dominants, in the postmodern novel (xvi), itself conceived as a literary system. They are identified by Nicol in his book as (1) a self-reflexive acknowledgement of a text's own status as constructed, aesthetic artefact; (2) an implicit (or sometimes explicit) critique of realist approaches both to narrative and to representing a fictional "world"; and (3) a tendency to draw the reader's attention to his or her own process of interpretation as s/he reads the text (6).

In conceiving the postmodern fiction as a system with certain dominant or central elements, Nicol relies on Jakobson's formalist concept of "dominant" which determines and rules the other components or elements of the system or structure, stays in the centre of the system and guarantees its integrity, and changes over literary history.

It is certain and there is no further need to argue that Jakobson with his theory of communication relies entirely on the formalist conception of the system containing various elements possessing specific functions and, to the present, his theory has remained highly influential in both linguistics and literary studies. It is also worth mentioning here another approach which, drawing on the assumption that a particular literary work is a literary system within the larger system of a genre within the general system of literature and interrelated with other socio-cultural systems, is based on Itamar Even-Zohar's theory of polysystem. Even-Zohar views literature as a polysystem, a system of systems, a complex and heterogeneous structure, coherent yet dynamic, in that its elements are in a constant agonistic relation among themselves. Applicable along with formalism to the study of literary history and genre, this view of literature as a kind of system widens the approach to literature, whose system is regarded in relation to other systems and domains such as culture and cultural studies, translation, anthropology, and so on.

Jakobson and French structuralism, on the whole, later Hutcheon and Nicol, to say nothing about Itamar Even-Zohar, to a certain extent Julia Kristeva, and even Homi Bhabha – as well as our humble contribution, we would like to believe – maintain Yuri Tynyanov's line of thinking and concepts alive, which have developed and emerged nowadays more like a kind of "neo-formalism".

Within this neo-formalist framework of reasoning, in order to strengthen the understanding by the students of the mechanisms working to make possible the movement of literature through history, it is to comprehend again that speaking solely about literary practice in the light of Tynyanov's ideas, its development in the context of literary history is based on the "clash" between "innovation" and "tradition". They stand to each other as centre and margin, the dominant element versus marginal element in the system of literature, each striving against marginalization and for the supremacy of its aesthetic validity, longevity and potency. They are represented diachronically by different periods, movements, and trends which follow and replace one another. Just like the literary genres, they are systems whose elements are correlated as depending again on their central and peripheral nature. Literature on the whole is a system with an on-going battle between central and marginal elements, where mutations happening on the level of any element generate and determine mutations on the general level of the system.

> If we conceive of the **literary work and literature, on the whole, as systems**, the interrelationship between "tradition" and "innovation" in the historical advancement of literature acts upon a literary system, which, by placing a group of its elements in the "dominant" position, makes the marginalization and deformation of other elements possible. A new work, or writing style, or subgenre, or genre, or trend, or movement emerges in literature and takes on its own literary function through this "dominant": this is the factor which stipulates the **substitution of systems** and determines the change and development of literary phenomena in the course of succeeding periods.

This is true as much of genres as of periods and movements. For instance, the literary system of the medieval romance changes in the Renaissance into the system termed by the noun *roman* ("novel") when elements of extended narration, setting, character representation and others become "dominant", whereas others, like verse form and the supernatural element, are extinguished.

On the contrary, when other elements, such as love intrigue, subjective and psychological experience, the fantastic and the irrational involved in action, are placed in the "dominant" position, the literary system of the romance is substituted in the second half of the eighteenth century by the system of a particular type of poetry called by the adjective "romantic". Another example: the element of "the revival of ancient classical tradition" in the literary system of the Renaissance becomes "dominant" in relation to the social and cultural orders (systems) of the seventeenth and eighteenth centuries, making possible the substitution of the system of the Renaissance literature by that of Enlightenment and neoclassicism.

This is also true about any particular literary tradition, or type of literary text. The "dominance" of such elements as adventure, ordeal, trial, the road chronotope, moral issues of personal conduct, love experience, autobiography, change of condition with respect to the social background, representing the system of the picaresque novel, to which the "dominant" element of *Bildung* or character formation (emergence or becoming, as in Bakhtin), implying inner change, is added in Goethe's *Wilhelm Meisters Lehrjahre*, makes possible the rise of the fictional system of the Bildungsroman in the nineteenth century. This type of novel, now a literary tradition, seeks its support in the previous systems, especially in the ancient and picaresque narratives and the romantic tradition, but places, in turn, a group of its elements in the "dominant" position, which makes possible the deformation of other elements, and as a result the related fictional types of *Entwicklungsroman, Erziehungsroman,* and *Künstlerroman* emerge in world literature.

A literary system can, therefore, be a literary period, such as the Renaissance, whose main elements are humanism, individualism, observation, rationalism, deduction, revival of the ancient classical tradition, etc.; it can be a literary movement, such as romanticism, whose central elements are imagination, subjective experience, dualism of existence, escapism, rebelliousness, and so on. A literary system can be also a genre, such as the novel, or a subgenre, for instance, the Bildungsroman.

Concerning this novelistic tradition, as to further exemplify our line of reasoning, we regard the literary discourse of the Bildungsroman as a well-structured literary pattern and likewise as an ordered system of elements whose aesthetic values stand within the larger system of the novel. The novel, as a self-standing system, belongs, along with other literary genres and types of text, to the system of literature. Literature, in turn, is a system framed within the general system of culture and should be approached in relation to other cultural systems. Such an analysis takes into consideration the national peculiarities of a literary system (here English), its relation to world literature, as well as the interrelationship between national culture and the world cultural phenomenon in general.

The peculiarity of the Bildungsroman as a literary work centred on the process of character formation – as both self-formation and guided formation – implies certain interpretative considerations. A critic should examine such elements of its system as (1) the author, particularly in his or her relation to the character, and the degree of their identification and separation, as well as the character as an autodiegetic narrator, since the Bildungsroman is an autobiographical type of fiction; (2) the reader, since the Bildungsroman is intended to be representative of the human condition; but, especially, (3) the content, or the thematic level, and (4) the form, or the narrative level, with their distinct but interrelated arrangements within the text of the whole process of an individual's development and formation.

In matters of (3) the content, or the thematic perspectives, particular concerns represent the milieu or society, the family background, parental figures, education, professional career, sentimental experience, ordeal, the philosophy of living, epiphany, moral didacticism, and others. In matters of (4) the form, meaning the structural perspectives, the focus is on the type of narration, point of view, narrator, narratee, mode, voice, and especially chronotope and its typology, and language as a means of both textualization of the process of growth and maturation and expression of the authorial point of view on this process. These elements are at the same time the main thematic and narrative aspects of the Bildungsroman literary system.

The elements to be focused upon in the study of such a particular type of text as the Bildungsroman may recall the elements of Roman Jacobson's structure of communication in general (sender, receiver, message, context, contact, and code) and those of literary communication as stated by Guy Cook: author, reader, text, performer, society, texts, and language. Such elements emerge from the condition of the Bildungsroman as a literary phenomenon which represents a specific type of fictional discourse framed within a specific type of communicative situation, a literary discourse intended to be communicated to the reader; in other words, the text of the novel of formation is involved in a literary communicative situation, it is the central element of a particular type of literary communication involving its author and reader and being organized as a literary system.

The Bildungsroman is to be considered a particular novelistic subgenre structured as a literary system in the line of such established literary and non-literary traditions as picaresque fiction and biography. Romanticism is a literary system in the line of such movements and trends in literature as metaphysical poetry, neoclassicism, aestheticism, or realism. The Renaissance is a literary system similar to such periods in the history of literature as medieval period, Victorian Age, the period of modernism, or the postmodern one.

They are phases and aspects of the diachronic movement of English literature and, as such, they are matters of concern of literary history, theory, and criticism. However, one should avoid making his or her study of English literature a compilation of unverified critical and theoretical categories simply due to their wide dissemination. In our case as well, instead of heavily borrowing ideas and providing quotations from historical, critical and theoretical studies in an attempt to relate and apply them to the analysis of English literature, it is necessary to consider the essence of different opinions and ideas, to adapt them according to the vector of research, and, especially, to follow the interpretative perspectives emerging from the direct, textual, contextual and comparative approach to English literature.

> We suggest to our students that a particular subgenre, such as the Bildungsroman, as well as the novel or fiction, generally, together with a poetic or dramatic text, or poetry and drama, or a particular literary period, movement, and trend, along with literature, in general, can be studied as systems of elements which would become concerns and objects of study of various trends and schools of the large domain of literary theory and criticism.

Literature, on the whole, and the particular elements of the literary system represent the main concern of the history of literature as well, especially in the light of Paul Ricoeur's hermeneutic perspectives of the textual arrangement and text analysis with regard to the human experience considered diachronically: (1) the implication of language as discourse, (2) the implication of discourse as a structured literary work, (3) the relation between verbal and written forms in the discourse and the structured literary work, (4) the structured literary work/discourse as the projection of another world, (5) the structured literary work as the projection of the authorial life which is transfigured through the discourse, and (6) the structured literary work as the self-comprehension of the reader (94).

In our books, the "world" of the literary system of English literature receives evaluative attention from three perspectives, which are the long-established domains of literary theory, literary criticism, and the history of literature. An accurate approach to English literary phenomenon would require the symbiosis of the three directions of research; unfortunately, much of the modern literary theory and criticism addresses the literary work as a synchronic phenomenon, removing the text from its temporal and spatial context.

The study of literature may avoid references to some distant systems, such as science and economy, but it should not ignore the importance of the private, social and/or historical factors, and especially cultural, philosophical and theoretical ones, since it is within these contexts that the literary significance of the work can be better clarified.

We agree with those who, like Brian Vickers, attempt to balance the impact of the internal and external factors acting upon the historical movement of literature in that a particular period, movement, trend, or genre is punctuated by social events, such as changes of governments or industrialisation, but it also necessarily obeys its own internal logic and is subjected to the organization and interrelationship among the elements of its system.

In his presentation of the seventeenth century, Vickers states that "[p]olitical events do impinge on literature, nowhere more dramatically than in the closing of the theatres in 1642, but the introduction, development, and ultimate decline of literary modes or genres follow their own laws, depending on the innate vitality of a form of the inventiveness of the writers using it" (160).

The emphasis on cultural, theoretical, philosophical, scientific, and historical dimensions and the consideration of various social and biographical influences on literary work must not, of course, exclude the synchronic dimension, methodological principles and the scientific rigour of literary theory and criticism to which literary history has access. Especially in the case of the diachronic advancement of English imaginative writing – which has a long developmental history – without understanding literature in its movement through history, the dualism of tradition and innovation, the origins of the literary work, the author's artistic sensibility and especially his or her theoretical and philosophical views, and the social and cultural circumstances and context of the act of literary creation, the critic would scarcely offer competent judgement on the value of the text, its author, period, movement, trend, or genre.

Despite the apocalyptic death verdict announced by so many concerning the future of literary history, the fact that any literary work is not historically determined, or that no literary text is an expression of an epoch, or that its production has no connection with the individual experience of the author, would never be proved. It is counterintuitive to think that a literary work can be properly understood by some criteria lacking temporal significance.

Therefore, it is crucial to shoulder the effort of joining the synchronic and diachronic research, and to examine the literary work as projected on a diachronic scale, in relation to both its past and its contemporary perspective. In this case, the history of literature should endeavour to find ways to innovate its discourse by getting support from other disciplines of the humanities, such as cultural anthropology, social history, sociology, linguistics, and cultural studies, but especially from the most recent and world-wide acknowledged theoretical and critical modalities advanced by literary theory and literary criticism.

Possessing scientific consistency, the history of literature is expected to form together with literary theory and criticism a distinct unified discourse of aesthetic evaluation of the literary phenomena. If continuously and adequately modernized, this discourse would be efficient enough to sustain the proper study of national and international literary heritage, and even eliminate the general illiteracy caused by the deformed vision of the literary truths from the past.

The books of imaginative writing might then remain an important stimulus for the aesthetic and intellectual needs of the human race, despite the complexity of new cultural alternatives and the changing rhythm of human existence at the beginning of a new millennium.

Likewise, the books of literary history or history of literature might remain important guides into the cultural heritage, which needs to survive and stay known, despite the claims, which are still heard nowadays, in the aftermath the postmodernity, that history and historicism are dead or writing history is an equivalent to writing stories which encompass, like fiction, events and characters specific to the narrative. A character, in Julian Barnes's *England, England*, states that concerning the reception by readers of the historical books, it occurs in view of history as a system which is closed and the reader is expected to have already read other books of history. The statement is given at the start of these Preliminaries.

To justify our own series of books on the movement through history of English literature, and contrary to what is stated in Barnes's novel, we do not expect readers to have read books about English literature since we aim our work to be their starting point in learning or strengthening the knowledge about a remarkable share of the international cultural depository, a part of which – focused on particular periods, or movements, or trends, certainly on genres and unavoidably on various authors and their works – our readers will discover in the following.

GENRE THEORY FOR POETRY

> **Keywords:** literary genre, poetry, verse, narrative poetry, lyric poetry, poet, poem, typology, thematic level, structural level, theme, idea, motif, meaning, imagery, rhythm, figurative language, stylistic devices

The modern critical thinking got accustomed to make divisions and categorizations in its approach to literature. Literary theory and literary criticism, and especially literary history divide the literary phenomenon into periods, movements, and trends following the temporal principle and grouping authors of imaginative writing through identifying their shared artistic credo and common literary doctrine as well as similar thematic concerns and, to a lesser extent, structural similarities of method and means of artistic expression.

The literary science also categorises literature into types called "literary genres" with a special focus on literary practice, having text in the centre of attention and chiefly with regard to its formal typology.

The separation of literature into genres is indeed done chiefly according to the form of the literary work, the most general naming of genres in this respect being prose, poetry, and drama or fiction, poetry, and drama, where "fiction" is used to designate imaginative prose, the product of the art of literature, which is to be differentiated from other types of written prose, such as scientific or journalistic ones.

Each genre is a distinct system of elements which are termed and categorised – apart from form – also according to its producer (writer or author), subgenres or species, work of literature or text and textual typology, the organization of language as a literary discourse, as well as the act or action performed by each genre.

The author of prose or fiction is open to rich labelling: he or she is often called prose writer or fiction writer; in case he or she writes only short fiction, such a writer can be also called short fiction writer or short-story writer; the producer of novels is commonly termed novelist; the author of fiction or author of imaginative prose are other terms often used along others alike. The persona speaking in a text of fiction representing the author's voice and delivering his or her point of view is called narrator. In the case of poetry, the writer is named poet, while his or her textual self is either called lyric I (in lyric poetry) or narrator (in narrative poetry). The author of drama is dramatist or playwright.

Each genre is made of literary works whose generic name is text. The text of prose or fiction is simply called prose text or text of fiction, but it displays a distinct typology which includes novel, short story, novella, and so on. In poetry, the text is called poem, whose typology is large, perhaps the largest of all genres: a poetic text can be simply lyric poem or narrative poem, but more often it bears various names such as epic, romance, sonnet, elegy, ode, hymn, dramatic monologue, and others.

The text of drama is called play and its typology is likewise complex: tragedy, comedy, tragicomedy, history play, interlude, masque, etc. Unlike in fiction and poetry, the text of drama can be also performed, the relationship between text and performance being actually the most discussed topic of critical theory focused on drama.

Every literary work or text of each genre has its specific form, where the form of prose or fiction is called prose, the form of poetry is verse, and dialogue is used to give form to a dramatic text.

Each genre is involved in a particular act of communication between the producer and receiver of literature performing in the course of delivering the message a particular action or activity: prose or fiction narrates; poetry expresses and narrates; and drama shows.

Literary Genres	prose / fiction	poetry	drama
Author	novelist, fiction writer, author of short fiction, and so on	poet	playwright, dramatist
Text	novel, short-story, novella, and so on	poem	play
Form	prose	verse	dialogue
Action	narrate	express, narrate	show
Speaking persona	narrator	lyric I, narrator	character

The problem with the division of literature into genres – or, in other words, with grouping the literary works into genres – according to the form of the text is, first, that novels and other types of fiction narrate just as some works in verse, such as epic, metrical romance, or various narrative poems do; second, the speaker in lyric poetry is called "lyric I", whereas in narrative poetry, likewise written in verse, the speaker is "narrator", is a structural device in the text which is also responsible for the telling of the story in the works of fiction written in prose.

If one considers action rather than form of each genre to be more appropriate for the categorization, then a more correct consideration of the literary genres would state **narrative genre, lyric genre, and dramatic genre**.

In this case, the narrative genre would include texts written in both verse and prose and belonging to both narrative poetry and fiction or imaginative prose, namely novel, short story, novella, epic, romance, or a narrative poem such as *The Canterbury Tales*, meaning all literary works which narrate stories through the voice of a narrator and contain narrative or story as the central element of their system regardless of the form (prose or verse) of the literary work. The lyric genre would then include only lyric poetry meaning literary texts written in verse form and expressing feelings and states of mind through the voice of a lyric I, among which ode, sonnet, hymn, elegy, dramatic monologue, and other textual types of lyrical expression. The dramatic genre or drama remains the most fixed and normative type in matters of form, action, and typology, and is formed of plays such as tragedy, comedy, morality, mystery, interlude, and so on. Also, the specificity of drama and what makes it stand apart from the other two genres is its stepping beyond its status as literary production in literary field into the larger artistic and cultural sphere acquiring there the status of theatrical performance, and the relationship of text and performance has become one of the most discussed issues in drama and theatre studies.

Literary Genres	Narrative genre	Lyric genre	Dramatic genre
Type of literature	fiction (imaginative prose) and narrative poetry	lyric poetry	drama
Author	novelist, fiction writer, author of short fiction, poet, and so on	poet	playwright, dramatist
Text	novel, short-story, novella and other types of fiction plus narrative poem	poem	play
Subgenre / species	picaresque novel, gothic tale, realist novel, Bildungsroman, stream of consciousness novel, epic, romance, and so on	ode, elegy, hymn, sonnet, dramatic monologue, and so on	tragedy, comedy, morality, tragicomedy, interlude, history play, masque, and so on
Form	prose, verse	verse	dialogue, performance
Action	narrate	express	show
Speaking persona	narrator	lyric I	character

Despite an apparent complexity and confusion, in the strictest sense of terminology a competent scholar would tend to be more precise in all classifications and terminological acceptations. For instance, narrative is genre; novel is subgenre (also referred to as species or type); and picaresque novel, gothic tale, realist fiction, psychological novel, Bildungsroman, stream of consciousness novel, postcolonial novel, historiographic metafiction, or novel of magical realism are sub-subgenres (also referred to as subspecies, or subtypes, or subcategories).

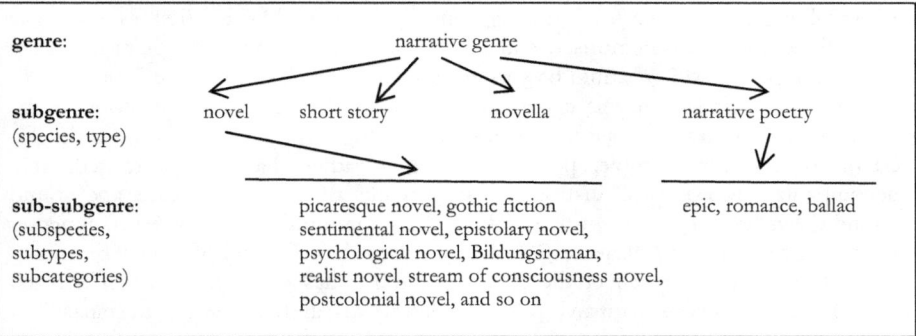

Even more accurate classifications may be attempted, beginning again from the general to particular. For example,

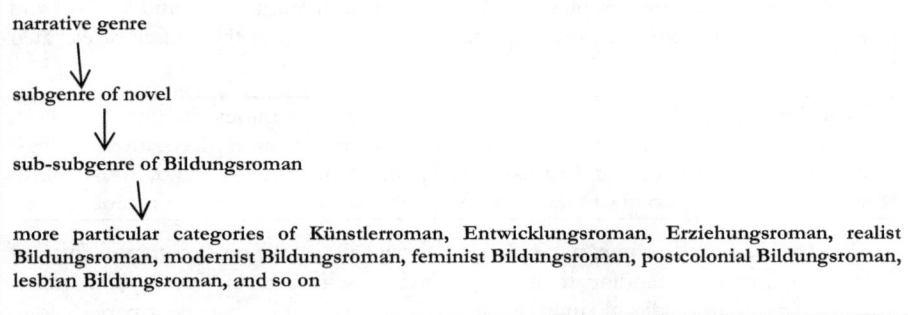

Genre terminology, however, blurs nowadays and many terms have become terms of abuse used randomly: lyric genre would be the more correct label but one can find statements such as poetic genre or that sonnet is a genre specific to Renaissance; likewise, one can say that tragedy is among the most important dramatic genres; also, Bildungsroman is called a novelistic genre or a type of novel, and so on.

Genre classifications also blur, especially in contemporary period when no writer would follow and no critic would impose strict parameters of writing. Authors of imaginative writing, in particular, in their attempt to experiment and innovate the literary discourse, striving for originality, would often mix genres and break the established rules. This common practice has emerged diachronically since long ago, where Shakespeare, for example, introduces tragicomedy (critically defended by Dryden during Restoration in his treatise *An Essay of Dramatic Poetry*); Sterne, Carlyle, Joyce, and Lodge subvert many novelistic conventions; T. S. Eliot remodels dramatic monologue, in *The Love Song of J. Alfred Prufrock*, and, in *The Waste Land*, achieves a pastiche and collage of genres and subgenres.

...

Poetry is one of the oldest literary forms to achieve symbolical representation of experience in the framework of an imaginative and creative activity itself part of a larger cultural framework encompassing other aesthetic practices such as painting or dance.

The origins of poetry are to be found in the beginnings of writing or perhaps even of speaking, and certainly of singing, since poems established first as an orally transmitted tradition, memorised and passed on as songs by word of mouth long before the poems/songs would be written down as texts. The history of poetry relies on the view that language is a material, just like colours, sounds, or stone, to be worked with and transformed into pieces of art. Originally, as it is the case of Anglo-Saxon poetry, for example, poems were sung rather than simply recited, and, accompanied by a musical instrument, such works of art fusing words and sound would deliver message and music combined in a communicative experience aimed at providing meaning and pleasure. The music or songlike features of poetry remain to the present helpful to deliver the meaning and emphasize the idea, which is often done by repeating consonants, vowels, syllables, words, and even lines and stanzas.

Those familiar with William Wordsworth's poem *Tintern Abbey* might remember the lines "All thinking things, all objects of all thought, / And rolls through all things", in which the use of alliteration regarding the sound "th" alluding to "thought" and "thinking" emphasizes the idea that in maturity the mind is "lord and power", responsible for the process of thinking and nature is the source of elevated thoughts.

> The history of the art of poetry is therefore a continuous attempt to create, surprise, impress, defamiliarize in order to attain ornamentation, decoration, effect – similar to music by sound and to painting by image or imagery – and, above all, to conceive and assert a point of view, a message, a discourse containing a meaning.

Poetry has soon become, particularly in ancient times, the most common form of linguistic expression standing to name creativity itself since in Greek *poētēs* means "creator" giving in medieval language *poetria*. In ancient and subsequent periods long into the middle of modernity, "poetry" with its variants and synonyms "poesie" and "poesy" would be used to designate imaginative writing (i.e. literature) on the whole as well as its various genres, and "poem" to speak about a particular literary work. It should not then sound strange when Dryden, during Restoration period, refers to drama as "dramatic poesie" and Fielding, during the eighteenth century, calls his novel *Joseph Andrews* a sort of "comic epic poem written in prose". "Poem", in turn, also comes from Greek *poiēma* meaning "something created, made", just like "poesie" from *poiēsis* which comes from *poiēin* ("to make").

Ancient times also established the discipline of "poetics" which is actually the theoretical system or framework providing rules and principles of poetic composition. The classic example is Aristotle's *Poetics*, which looks at the nature of literature, the philosopher assuming the task

> to treat of Poetry in itself and of its various kinds, noting the essential quality of each; to inquire into the structure of the plot as requisite to a good poem; into the number and nature of the parts of which a poem is composed; and similarly into whatever else falls within the same inquiry.

It is then more true to assume, as Northrop Frye does, that by "poetics", Aristotle meant a "theory of criticism whose principles apply to the whole of literature and account for every valid type of critical procedure" and in doing so, the classical philosopher approaches

> poetry as a biologist would approach a system of organisms, picking out its genera and species, formulating the broad laws of literary experience, and in short writing as though he believed that there is a totally intelligible structure of knowledge attainable about poetry which is not poetry itself, or the experience of it, but poetics. (Frye 14)

Nowadays, the term "poetics" is used to designate the science or discipline of any creative activity which produces aesthetic products – we can hear of a "poetics of fiction", for example – and the term has become synonymous to "aesthetic principles" governing the nature of any literary form.

Undergoing a long process of change, from its original community essence, as part of ceremonial practice involving music and sometimes dance, poetry has become an extremely individualistic form of verbal art, a mimetic activity focused on inner world, a means of expressing private and intimate feelings and thoughts. In English literature, the romantic poet William Wordsworth is credited with having begun the modern poetry of the self, where the poet's subjective experience becomes the subject-matter of a poetic text. Actually, with the romantic advancement of the expressive theory of authorship, lyric poetry definitely separated from the collective spirit as well as narrative element to establish itself as a form of art which by means of language achieves rhythmic expression of intensely personal, which is emotional and psychological, perception of and response to the world and the self, and the relation of these two.

Apart from the standpoint of form, called "verse form", advancing rhythm or metre as the first characteristic of poetry, this highly imaginative genre – either lyric or narrative – has great thematic significance in its contributing to our experience of life and knowledge and prompting a variety of essentials for human existence, such as an idea, an attitude, a vision, a feeling, and above all, a meaning. Poetry can be also didactic, often claimed to provide cathartic moral didacticism; it may enlarge the "circumference of knowledge"; it may give historical insight; but its main purpose is to please.

Hence the view about the superiority of poetry over other genres; poetry as fusing visual arts with the art of music; and even of poetry being superior to or encompassing or replacing various other domains, such as history and philosophy, as well as being indispensable from scientific endeavour, as for Mathew Arnold, who also calls poetry "criticism of life". For Theodore Watts-Dunton, poetry is an "artistic expression of the human mind"; earlier, Percy Bysshe Shelley declared poetry to provide "moral improvement of man"; Robert Frost combines the idea of giving of pleasure with usefulness: poetry "begins in delight and ends in wisdom".

Edgar Allan Poe, however, speaks solely about "poem per se", which is a "poem and nothing more", a "poem written solely for the poem's sake", just as late nineteenth-century avant-garde art and literature, including English aestheticism of Walter Pater, Oscar Wilde, and the Pre-Raphaelites poets, would declare and assert the doctrine of "art pour l'art" or "art for art's sake" and the concept of "aesthetic hedonism".

Poetry, like literature and art in general, can be therefore viewed as an independent aesthetic phenomenon, self-contained and autonomous, with intrinsic values, having a significance of its own, an existence in itself, and its production and reception, including critical, need no extra-literary implications.

Poetry can appeal to our various senses of sight and sound, various emotions may be sparked off, memories and thoughts may be called forth, even learning may be strengthened, but the immediate and ultimate purpose or effect of poetry is aesthetic pleasure, as it was once and forever asserted by Samuel Taylor Coleridge during the romantic period:

> A poem is that species of composition, which is opposed to works of science, by proposing for its immediate object pleasure, not truth; and from all other species – (having this object in common with it) – it is discriminated by proposing to itself such delight from the whole, as is compatible with a distinct gratification from each component part.

Moving away from the diachronic towards the synchronic to stay closer to literary field and leaving aside historical movement of poetry and its socio-cultural or personal implications, the students of literature would learn that **"poetry"** is the generic name given to one of the three literary genres – poetry, prose, drama – when the division considers the form of the text. With regard to its purpose or modality of communication with the reader, it would be more appropriate to differentiate between lyric genre, which includes lyric poetry of feeling and thought, and narrative genre, which includes narrative poetry along imaginative prose.

Poetry is commonly classified into **lyric** type, when it expresses emotional and psychological states, and **narrative (epic)** type, when it tells a story involving characters and events. Poetry can be also classified as **dramatic** when it employs dramatic forms and techniques, such as monologue, dialogue, emotional conflict, tense situation, and so on.

The term "lyric" comes from the name of a musical instrument called "lyre"; poems are nowadays recited rather than sung, but the word is used to designate poems which rely on a particular, subjective experience (a feeling, a thought, a memory, an impression, and so on) which becomes the source of emotional appeal textualized to express feelings and thoughts.

The speaker in the lyric poetry is "lyric persona" or "lyric I" disclosing primarily feelings to render a personal vision, an individual subjective experience and the meaning seems hidden, themes and ideas are implied, the reader being invited to understand the lyrical movement, the organization of the verse, and to consider the sounding of the text and, above all, its imagery in order to step on a proper path of understanding.

Narrative poetry contains a "narrator" that renders a particular authorial point of view and recounts the action either as being involved in it as a character or not, just as in prose fiction, and, similarly to novels or short stories, narrative poems are constructed by elements such as narrative and narration (linear, chronological, or non-linear which can be concentric, for example, as in *The Rime of the Ancient Mariner* or *The Canterbury Tales*), narrator (autodiegetic, homodiegetic, and heterodiegetic), point of view (omniscient, detached, limited), chronotope, mode, tone, voice, and so on. Narrative poetry tells a story in verse form unfolding themes and ideas through plot, setting, and characters, and making meaning more accessible to the reader.

More than prose and drama, the poetic genre with its both lyric and narrative types – as well as dramatic – is open to artfulness, a special way of craftsmanship which would link words into lines which in turn are grouped in stanzas which represent actually the largest units in verse, where the poet, as a creative writer, aims at both formal effects and a suggestive, allusive, implied, effective expression of meaning.

Verse is the form of poetry, be it narrative or lyric, which implies particular use of vowels, consonants, syllables, words as well as construction and delimitation of lines in order to achieve metre, rhythm, rhyme, and other formal effects, each with its specific typology. Lines, for instance, can be "end-stopped lines" or "run-on lines" along more specific structures such as a three-line and seventeen-syllable organization of the type of poem called "haiku" or the five-line poem with a specific form called "limerick".

Poetry itself, particularly lyric and narrative, displays an impressive typology, where its various types or kinds of text, as subgenres or literary species of the poetic genre, emerged diachronically to live longer or shorter lives than others and some of them to survive nowadays.

Types of lyric poetry include, from a diachronic perspective, those categories which, first in ancient times, played communal roles and were limited to political and religious spheres of social life. Many of them, actually, were dedicated to divinity; as such, sometimes supplemented by dance, they would be songs sung most of the time by a chorus around the altar and almost always accompanied by a lyre or flute. Devoted to the worship of Dionysus is dithyramb; paean is dedicated to Apollo; the worship of various other gods are achieved through hymns; also, a poem sung in solemn procession to the altar or temple is prosodion.

As opposed to the hymn, which is dedicated to the gods, enkomion is in honour of men; a praise poem sung to a victor in an athletic contest is epinikion.

Poems at various other occasions include skolion (song sung at a banquet), hymenaios (nuptial song), threnos (funeral lament), partheneion (poem sung by a chorus of maidens). Standing apart are erotikon, which is love poetry, both sacred and profane, and hyporcheme, which is a unique combination of a song and a dance.

Many of these types disappeared from our literary practice and literary history; others survived but modified some of their thematic and structural elements; new kinds of poetry emerged on literary scene in later periods either to perish sooner or later or, on the contrary, to strengthen their creative presence on the literary scene.

Among these lyric poems, in which subjectivity plays the dominant role, more commonly known and historically more persistent are hymn, sonnet, song, ode, elegy, ballad, dramatic monologue, vers de societe, rondeau, and other types or subclassifications of the lyric poetry.

Hymns (Greek "song in praise of a god or hero") came to represent a lyric category originally expressing religious emotion, sung by chorus, and later to the present turning more secular and generally expressing exaltation and praise less of gods and more of famous people and important events, and when sung, it may denote a nation and be identified with a national anthem.

Ode (Greek "song") is a lyric poem which also expresses exaltation and praise but it deals with a single theme, focuses on a single person, object, or event, and is directed to a single purpose. It usually deals with public nature and accomplished individuals, but romanticism turned to exalt natural beings (*Ode to the West Wind* by Shelley) or objects of art (*Ode on a Grecian Urn* by Keats) while keeping the subgenre's stately gravity and solemn diction. The ode is the most complicated and elaborated in form of many other lyric types. Originally used in Greek dramatic poetry, it was sung by the chorus that, accompanied by music, would strictly follow its division into "strophe", antistrophe", and "epode" in order to render the rise and fall of emotion. In English poetry, the distinction is between three types of odes: the "Pindaric" or regular, the "Horatian" or homostrophic, and the "irregular".

Elegy (Greek "lament") is a poetic composition very similar to ode but it generally praises and acclaims those who died leaving behind a sense of greatness mixed with grief, which places mourning as a central element in its literary system. Along exaltation and praise accompanied by mourning and lament, the elegy contains also a meditation set forth by the death of a particular person or by a solemn event. Originally, in both Greek and Latin classical writing, the meditation in elegy would concern not only death but also destiny, love, war, and so on, or be merely informative, and what distinguished this lyric category was more its use of elegiac meter than its subject matter. Generalized observation and reflection concerning human condition are added to a sentimental type of mourning by Thomas Gray in *Elegy Written in a Country Churchyard*; earlier, Milton developed in *Lycidas* the so-called "pastoral elegy" as a particular subtype of elegy.

Sonnet (Italian *sonetto*, "a little sound" or "song") is a poem emerging on literary scene in Italy in the thirteenth century to express love and other feelings, present a short narrative, state a proposition, or raise an issue, which is followed by a resolution, comment, acceptance, evaluation, solution, or answer to the question. The two basis subcategories are the Italian or Petrarchan sonnet and the English or Shakespearean sonnet, both invariably of fourteen lines but different rhyme schemes. The English form is distinguished by four divisions: three quatrains (usually with rhyming alternate lines) and a rhymed concluding couplet, with its typical rhyme scheme *abab cdcd efef gg*. A rare sonnet type is the Spenserian sonnet which combines the Italian and the Shakespearean forms. From Thomas Wyatt through William Shakespeare and Milton to William Wordsworth, Dante Gabriel Rossetti, W.H. Auden, and Geoffrey Hill, the sonnet has always been a strong presence in English literature.

Dramatic monologue, although a rather old form (some speeches in Dante's *Comedy*, for example), is considered a Victorian poetic creation, particularly by Robert Browning, who brought it to a very high aesthetic level to be used occasionally by Alfred Tennyson and, in the twentieth century, by T.S. Eliot. In this lyric poem, a speaker, different from the author (who assumes a different identity such as of a character from myth, history, or literature), utters the entire text in a dramatic situation or moment of existence which sparks off the range of feelings. The use of implication reveals the circumstances surrounding the speech and may offer an insight into the personality of the speaker. The poems of this lyric category, more in an implied than explicit manner, point to a problem, its nature and causes, and eventually suggest solutions.

Along these classifications of lyric poetry standing more for a kind of "high art" and representing aesthetically esteemed categories, there other types of lyric poetry which are more popular with the larger public, representing a more accessible form of entertainment and gratifier of the human aesthetic needs, such as **doggerel** (crude verse), for example, or **nursery rhymes**.

There are also lyric texts in verse form which do not fit into any classifications or varieties and are regarded as just **lyric poems**, such as *The Chimney Sweeper* by William Blake or *The Second Coming* by William Butler Yeats.

Types of epic or narrative poetry include epics, metrical romances, and ballads. **Epic**, with its origins in antiquity, can be succinctly defined as "a long narrative poem in elevated style presenting characters of high position in adventures forming an organic whole through their relation to a central heroic figure and through their development of episodes important to the history of a nation or race" (Holman and Harmon 171). Epics can be anonymous (oral or folk) and literary, written by poets whose names claim authorship. Some of the best known epics are Homer's the *Iliad* and the *Odyssey*, the Indian *Ramayana*, the Spanish *Cid*, the German *Nibelungenlied*, and others; in English, certainly *Beowulf*, the great monument of Anglo-Saxon literature, and John Milton's *Paradise Lost* can be called an epic or Puritanism.

Metrical romance, or verse romance, or simply "romance", a literary product of medieval culture, shares with epic, besides its verse form, a central character, predominantly a male protagonist, as well as a narrative movement involving deeds of value or various formative adventures accompanied by a sense of moral didacticism.

But the heroic age reflected in the epic is changed in romances by a chivalric one and the outstanding hero of the epic is replaced in romances by more humanised and individualized knights, kings, or distressed ladies; in romances, action is motivated by love, religious faith, or simply the desire for adventure; romances exhibit mystery, fantasy, imaginative flight, and a certain degree of light-heartedness; romances are primarily romantic tales in verse – with a distinct narrator placed amid a rather loose narrative structure – about actions and adventures, such as quest or rescue or journey or search, all coming next to the supreme experience of love. Originally twelfth-century Old French creations, their English versions are mostly known as "Arthurian romances" with such classics as the fourteenth-century anonymous verse romance *Sir Gawain and the Green Knight* and the fifteenth-century *Le Morte Darthur* by Thomas Malory, the latter showing that romances can be also written in prose form.

There are narrative texts in verse form which are also not of a particular kind; they are simply called narrative poems, such as *The Canterbury Tales* by Geoffrey Chaucer.

The type of poetic text termed "**ballad**" – which is classified either as lyric or narrative (epic) – is actually beyond a concrete subclassification within the poetic genre since it appears to be more of a mixture of the two varieties of poetry blending lyrical expression in mood and message with various narrative qualities of form and structural matter. The main types of ballads are "folk ballads" and "art ballads". Whatever its type, the ballad requires a brief and concise narrative unity, a short narrative movement containing typically one character involved in usually one event – which is the narrative element of the ballad – but this event or experience of the protagonist is dramatic as well as symbolical for human nature and becomes representative for our condition, in general, with intense emotional and spiritual implications – and this is the lyric element in the ballad.

The famous art ballad *The Rime of the Ancient Mariner*, for example, appealing to the notion of "lyrical ballad", mixes lyric and narrative subgenres in that its author Samuel Taylor Coleridge chooses the ballad type of a lyric-narrative thematic framework to focus on a single character involved in one event, both the protagonist and his experience having universal and symbolical appeal and being representative for human existence in general: here, crime and punishment, the act of murdering of the albatross and its consequences.

Apart from the common categorization of poetry into the two great type-divisions – lyric and narrative or epic – with their further classifications and divisions, there is a third type known as "dramatic poetry" or "poetic drama". The lyric drama of the romantics, for example, represented in the best possible way by Shelley (*Prometheus Unbound*) and Byron (*Manfred* and *Cain*), shows how the art of poetic composition may return to its original status of combining in one literary discourse individual, subjective experience of personal emotion with matters of collective interest and become a vehicle for tragedy, drama, history, myth, the symbolical and generally representative for human condition. Some plays like Shakespeare's *The Tempest* can be called poetic drama; and poems designated as dramatic monologues by Tennyson and Browning can be named dramatic poems, though more commonly they are included in the realm of lyric poetry. Also, based on mood and purpose, poetry can be classified as pastoral and didactic.

The creation of poetic imagination, the result of the literary composition of the genre of poetry in verse form – covering all types or sub-categories of either lyric or narrative poetry – is called "poem". A cultural product, a literary artefact, a work of art, oral but mostly written, a poem is the text of poetry and like every literary text, it consists of a thematic level (or content, what the text is about) and a structural level (or form, how the text is written).

The thematic level has as its main elements theme(s), idea(s), and meaning(s), where the thematic movement of the text and especially its figurative language forming the structural level would help us to better understand the theme and its related ideas, which leads and means to discern a particular meaning. In its simplest acceptation, this process could be taken to represent the practice of literary interpretation:

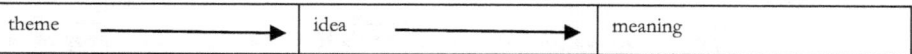

The theme in a poem, as in literature in general, whether it is directly stated or implied, represents the authorial concern expressed in the work, his or her subject-matter or topical interest which would constitute the essence of the work to be artistically rendered and receive personal perspective and vision. A thought or a concept, personal or universal – love, time, nature, separation, art, etc. – change its transcendental, intrinsic, and abstract standing to be concretised and individualised. A careful reading by paying attention to details in order to understand the content, the movement in the text and the focus through rational discernment on the sound and form of the text, and especially on some words and lines which appear as key-elements in the structure of the text, particularly those that build up images, would assist the receiver of the poetic work to understand what this work is about, what are its themes and what are its ideas which are related to the theme. A text may have one theme, or a number of themes, or a main theme among other, minor themes, but the themes are always to be accompanied by ideas which refer to the themes explaining or illuminating them.

The idea in a poem is ultimately the author's opinion about the theme (concern or subject-matter) chosen to be discussed and aesthetically rendered in the art of poetry. The theme or the concern in a poem is meaningless without any expressed ideas or viewpoints on this theme; a poetic or another type of text says nothings if it only speaks about something without sharing an attitude, an explanation, a vision on a particular matter of concern chosen to be the theme of a literary work.

The apprehension of the theme together with the range of ideas results in understanding of the meaning, which may have several levels and which is the writer's way of sending a message to the world and communicate with the reader in order to reveal his or her attitude on existence, a private vision, an individual conception, a point of view rooted in a personal philosophy of life. As Coleridge declared during romanticism, the meaning together with the artificial arrangement of the text by rhyme, metre, and other constituent elements into a whole would necessarily result into a sense of pleasure.

Closer to us, Bakhtin argues that writing comes with points of view and intentions of its author preserved in the multi-layered nature of language which means heteroglossia or polyglot social contexts; these contexts are to be fused together and lose their worlds of reference in order for poems to achieve autonomy and artistic unity. There are poets, of course, who would reject such an autonomy, particularly postmodernists who conceive poems as a space in which notions and concepts are floated before the reader, who avoid canon and the established excellence of poetic rhetoric, and who reject the inward and self-referencing tradition.

Apart from the theme(s) and idea(s), on the thematic level, there are also motifs used by the poets to reveal the course of lyrical expression and help the reader to see the theme and understand the ideas: for example, the first stanza from John Donne's *A Valediction: Forbidding Mourning* introduces the motif of the separation of the soul from the body, which would direct the reader towards the main thematic perspective in the poem, which is the departure of the speaker leading to a temporary separation of the lovers.

But more important are various figures of speech, also referred to as tropes or stylistic devices, from the structural level, which, by creating imagery and, to a lesser degree, by producing musical effects, lead the reader into the thematic context of the text pointing to its range of themes, ideas, motifs, and eventually meaning.

On the structural level, there are two perspectives of the language use in poetry, revealing the creation simultaneously of both melodic (musical) effects (based on rhythm) and pictorial effects (based on imagery). For this, the poetic art necessitates a figurative use of language. This occurs when the poet uses various methods or techniques, or modes of handling the vowels, consonants, syllables, words, and so on, of a language, which are called figures of speech or stylistic devices, in order to achieve artistry, produce an aesthetic discourse, create poetry with its literary essence which is accompanied by musical and pictorial dimensions sparked off by figurative language which point out and clarify the thematic features of the text.

Figurative language is the language of poetry. It consists of figures of speech (stylistic devices) which are actually words or phrases used deliberately by writers against their proper, direct, and accurate linguistic standing to consequently receive an altered, indirect meaning which would be different from its actual, literal one. Used mostly in poetry, figurative language is also the material of literature in general, where, possessing different and deviant meanings, it prompts the beautiful, the special, the aesthetic, the defamiliarised, placing literary discourse within the realm of art.

The comprehension of the figurative language supports the approach to the thematic level; in other words, to understand figurative language is a possibility for the understanding of the thematic level when we lack non-textual information (such as the knowledge about the author, his or her period, the movement or trend he or she belongs to, or the characteristics of his or her literary activity or views on literature, and so on).

The two perspectives of the use of figurative language in poetry prompt stylistic devices to be classified into two groups. The first perspective is on pure structural or formal level and, concerned with how the poetic text is written and how it sounds, it encompasses melodic effects similar to those from the art of music and deals primarily with the rhythm in poetry. Its **Group 1** includes figures of speech which are viewed in relation to poetry's musical (melodic) effect and sound or sounding.

In other words, the **first perspective** of the structural framing of the poem handles language regarding textual organization and focuses on verse form, metrical organization, line, stanza, word and phase structure, which concerns the levels of phonology, morphology, and syntax.

The keywords for the understanding of this perspective are **repetition**, **recurrence**, **inversion**, and **change** of certain language units such as vowels, consonants, syllables, words, lines, stanzas, and so on. The main structural elements as figures of speech or stylistic devices aligned to this first perspective include the following:

Line	a single unit of words in a poem, sometimes called "verse"; can be regular or irregular; in English verse, the most popular are four- and five-beat lines
Stanza	a single unit of a number of lines in a poem having a definite measure and rhyming system which is repeated throughout the poem; can be regular or irregular; usually consists of four lines; major types: "heroic couplet" (lines of 2 iambic pentametres with rhyming pattern *aa*), "Spenserian stanza" (9 lines of 8 iambic pentametres and 1 iambic hexametre with rhyming scheme *ababbcbcc*), "ottava rima" (8 iambic pentametres rhyming *abababcc*), "ballad stanza" (alternation of iambic tetrametres with iambic dimetres *abcb*), "sonnet" (14 iambic pentametres with 3 quatrains with cross rhymes and a couplet at the end rhyming *ababcdcdefefgg*)
Rhyme	repetition or recurrence of identical or similar sounds particularly at the end of the line, called terminal sound combinations of words; it is commonly known as rhyme or end rhyme; it can also be internal rhyme, full rhyme, perfect rhyme, incomplete rhyme, impure rhyme, eye-rhyme (depends on spelling not sound, e.g. meat-great), consonant rhyme, vowel rhyme; types or models of rhyme: couplets (*aa*), triple rhyme (*aaa*), cross rhyme (*abab*), framing or ring rhyme (*abba*); unrhymed verse is called "blank verse"
Rhythm	it can be simply defined as more or less regular alternations of similar units; it represents an inescapable element of poetry arising from the exercise of breathing and the attempt to achieve shape and regularity in individualising the use of a language to achieve effects similar to those of music; the systematic regularity in rhythm is metre which is realised through a repetition or recurrence of beats or sets of stressed and unstressed syllables as a pattern of utterance in the line; related concepts are syllable, foot, metre, metrical pattern, metrical scheme, metrical form; no regular metre is called "free verse"
Refrain	repetition of line(s) or stanza(s)
Onomatopoeia	words or phrases are used to imitate or suggest sounds to which they refer; various combinations of speech-sounds are associated with whatever produces the natural sound; these speech sounds may be produced by people, animals, birds, natural phenomena, and so on; "direct onomatopoeia": use of words which imitate the sound of what it describes, e.g. "Slathery / Slithery / Hisser / Don't miss her!" (*Cat!*); "indirect onomatopoeia": words or phrases producing sounds which relate to or disclose the meaning, e.g. long vowels in "the slender stream / Along the cliff to fall and pause and fall did seem" (*The Lotus-Eaters*) alluding to the movement of water
Alliteration	an important phonetic stylistic device which aims at imparting a musical effect which is achieved through the repetition of similar, usually consonant, sounds usually at the beginning of successive words; for example, "I caught this morning morning's minion, kingdom of daylight's dauphin, dapple-dawn-drawn Falcon, in his riding …" (*The Windhover*)
Consonance	the repetition of consonant sounds at the end of the neighbouring words; e.g. earth – birth
Assonance	the repetition of vowel sounds within the stressed syllables of neighbouring words

Parallelism	the repetition of similar or identical words or phrases in neighbouring lines
Anaphora	the repetition of a word or phrase at the beginning of succeeding each other lines in a poem
Climax	a succession of words describing a character or event from the least important to the most important feature (e.g. stanzas 5 and 6 from *Elegy Written in a Country Churchyard*)
Anticlimax	a succession of words describing a character or event from the most important to the least important or even ridiculous feature
Enumeration	a succession or listing of words or phrases, usually synonymous adjectives, describing a character or event
Inversion	change of word order
Chiasmus	changed or inverted word order so that one half of a sentence balances the other one
Allusion	a reference or connection, explicit or by implication, made to people, events, myths, and so on; aligned to parody, it opens the perspective of intertextuality
Ambiguity	poetry itself is based on ambiguity through its figurative language; there are instances in text when words and phrases are deliberately used to suggest more than one meaning; e.g. "Whose woods these are I think I know" (*Stopping by Woods on a Snowy Evening*)
Emphasis	a kind of grammatical deviation employed in order to draw attention to an idea or statement; for example, "I am become a name" (*Ulysses*)

In relation to "rhythm" in poetry, a particular consideration is required for the understanding of the two other concepts, indispensable from the structural level, or better saying, responsible for the actual organization of the poetic discourse in the form of a literary text, which are foot and metre.

Foot	unit or set or beat of stressed and unstressed syllables; in other words, foot is the unit of metre whose repetition creates line or verse and produces the rhythm in poetry; types of foot (also called **metrical patterns**): "iambic metre" (one unstressed syllable followed by one stressed syllable, or rising duple), "trochaic metre" (stressed unstressed, or falling duple), "dactylic metre" (stressed unstressed unstressed, or falling triple), "amphibrachic metre" (unstressed stressed unstressed), and "anapaestic metre" (unstressed unstressed stressed, or rising triple)
Metre	a systemic regularity in rhythm, a sequence of feet representing the rhythmic pattern of the line or verse; in other words, a regular pattern of stressed and unstressed syllables within a line; types according to the number of feet repeated in a line: monometer (1 foot), demeter (2 feet), trimeter (3), tetrameter (4), pentameter (5), hexameter (6), septameter (7), octameter (8)

Verse is rarely completely regular, but we may rely on its being conventionally classified into iambic metre, dactylic metre, anapaestic metre, and dactylic metre, such a terminology deriving from classical prosody. Additionally, metre can be also considered with regard to whether the syllables or the stresses are being counted, and whether these counts are fixed or variable; the classification so prompted includes accentual verse (fixed counts of stress but variable syllables as in popular verse, nursery rhymes, and ballads), syllabic verse (fixed counts of syllables regardless of stresses), **accentual-syllabic verse** (conventional metre with both stress and syllables fixed, developed by Chaucer to become the conventional type of English poetry from Renaissance to the present), and free verse (no restrictions on either stress or syllables).

Letters and sounds form syllables which form feet which create metre, and all these constitute repeated patterns which actually produce **rhythm** in poetry and represent the metrical organization of a particular poetic text, its mode of versification responsible for effects similar to those from the art of music.

The name of the pattern emerges from the type of foot, depending on syllables, and that of metre, depending on the number of feet: the first line from a famous poem by Yeats, for example, namely "When you are old and gray and full of sleep" is designated as iambic pentameter since it consists of 5 feet (pentameter) each representing a pair of syllables of which first is unstressed followed by a second stressed one, such a verse pattern of beats being called "iamb".

When you are old and gray and full of sleep
‿ ✓ | ‿ ✓ | ‿ ✓ | ‿ ✓ | ‿ ✓ |

This first perspective of the usage of language in writing poetry, which prompts the sound or musicality of poetry and is strictly related to matters of versification, is indispensable from another, second perspective of language use in poetry, which prompts imagery or poetic image with artistic effects similar to those from the art painting. A poet is therefore a writer as well as a musician and now also a painter producing an image which is like a picture created by words. Images in a poetic text are combined in what is called "imagery", which is expected to appeal mainly to the visual, to be related to sight and create in the mind of the reader a kind of painting of what is described or alluded to in the poem. Images may also appeal to other senses, such as taste or smell, and they necessarily also refer to emotional and psychological states, in the case of the lyric poetry, or to action and narrative movement, in the case of narrative poetry.

This second perspective of the language use in poetry also belongs to the structural level but mediates between the structural level and the thematic level; it is stronger linked to the thematic dimension of the poetic text and its comprehension supports better the approach to the thematic level because – by its creation of imagery responsible for pictorial effects – it helps to identify and understand the theme(s) leading to the understanding of the idea(s) and finally to the realization of the meaning of the text, which is a process called text analysis or interpretation.

The second perspective of the structural organization of a poem manages language regarding contextual meaning and verbal discourse and deals primarily with imagery in poetry, or the creation of effects similar to those from the art of paining. Its **Group 2** includes figures of speech which are viewed in relation to pictorial effect, imagery, theme, idea, and eventually meaning, which concerns the levels of semantics and pragmatics. The keyword here is comparison. The main stylistic devices affiliated to this second perspective include the following:

Metaphor	the most powerful means of creating poetic images based on comparison; it achieves similarity or resemblance of certain features of usually two corresponding concepts framing the relation between the dictionary/literal and contextual/implied logical meanings; in other words, hidden/indirect/implied comparison or affinity of usually unrelated concepts by asserting that one is another without using "like" or "as"; for instance "All the world's a stage" (*As You Like It*) discloses a relation between the dictionary and contextual logical meanings based on the **affinity** or similarity of certain properties or features of the two corresponding concepts, which are "world" and "stage"
Simile	like metaphor, it is based on comparison of seemingly different concepts, but it is a direct/explicit comparison in which the **similarity** or association is stated openly by using "like" or "as"; e.g. "I wandered lonely as a cloud" reveals how one object is characterised by being brought into contact with another object belonging to an

		entirely different class of things
Metonymy		a kind of metaphor based on a different type of relation between the dictionary and contextual meanings, but the features of the corresponding concepts are **associated** rather than presented as similar or resembling each other; in other words, one concept is called by the name of another concept with which it is associated: for example, "this clay will sink its spark immortal" (*Childe Harold's Pilgrimage*)
Symbol		a concrete being or event standing for a concept or idea or everything else abstract; a common example would be "rose" symbolising love, passion, beauty, or a young girl
Allegory		a kind of extended metaphor or symbol with large implications, involving a symbolical representation of beings or events as concepts or ideas; for instance, the experience of crime and subsequent punishment of the character in *The Rime of the Ancient Mariner*
Hyperbole		a deliberate exaggeration of a feature or peculiarity; e.g. "And this maiden she lived with no other thought / Than to love and be loved by me" (*Annabel Lee*) is used to intensify one of the features of an object, event, phenomenon, state, or person in question to such a degree as it might show even its utter inadequacy or absurdity
Personification		a kind of metaphor in which concepts, abstract ideas, objects, plants and animals possess human qualities and act as human beings; for instance, "daffodils ... Fluttering and dancing in the breeze" (*I Wandered Lonely as a Cloud*)
Oxymoron		a combination of contradictory words, expressions, concepts and meanings, which are semantically incompatible; here, the meanings of the two words clash, being opposite in sense; e.g. "dark light", "cold fire", "hateful love", "true lie", "magical realism"
Paradox		a self-contradictory or illogical statement which is apparently false and in which contradiction or absurdity reveals deeper meanings and truths; for example, "I must be cruel only to be kind" (*Hamlet* by William Shakespeare) or "War is peace. Freedom is slavery. Ignorance is strength" (*1984* by George Orwell)
Periphrasis		a long-length statement whose meaning could have been conveyed more briefly; for instance, the line "The curfew tolls the knell of parting day" can be expressed by a single word "evening", which shows that a person, object, and phenomenon can be re-named by phrases which bring out some particular feature of this person, object, and phenomenon
Pleonasm		an expression in which the meaning contained elsewhere is repeated in what precedes or follows it, which makes the statement be rendered redundantly; for example, "a false lie"
Tautology		a kind of pleonasm representing a statement in which an idea is unnecessarily repeated by using different words, as in "my uncle is male"
Pun		or paronomasia; a common stylistic device based on the play of words with a similar sound but different meanings for comic effect; for example, "The Importance of Being Earnest"
Zeugma		or syllepsis; the use of a word to refer to two or more words although it is often logically connected to only one of them; e.g. "Kill the boys and the luggage!"
Irony		comic effect is provided through a bitter allusion based on the discrepancy or opposition between dictionary/literal and contextual/implied meanings; in other words, words convey meanings which are contradictory to their dictionary/literal meaning; for instance, "my tongue / Could scarcely cry 'weep! 'weep! 'weep! 'weep!' / So your chimneys I sweep, and in soot I sleep" (*The Chimney Sweeper*); irony is often classified into types: situational irony, cosmic irony, dramatic irony, and Socratic irony
Sarcasm		another category of the comic genre which provides bitter and more aggressive comic effect through malice and remarks expressing mockery and contempt; e.g. "The grave's a fine and private place / But none, I think, do there embrace" (*To His Coy Mistress*)
Satire		more often text itself as a whole than a particular word or phrase is considered to

	be this figure of speech; it provides comic effect concerning people, ideas, institutions, or social events and circumstances with the task to criticise and disclose the problems, vices, follies, and faults through the use of irony, sarcasm and, above all, exaggeration; a revelatory example would be *Gulliver's Travels* which, employing exaggeration of exaggeration, first aims at contemporary travel-books as to focus consequently on politics, social issues, philosophy, science, and eventually human condition in general
Parody	phrases, or parts of a text, or even a whole literary work, for example *Pamela*, can be considered parody when the writer deliberately imitates the thematic context (rather than form) of another writer's work, or style, or viewpoint, and so on, to achieve, often through intentional use of exaggeration, a comic, particularly humorous, effect
Understatement	deliberate presentation of a situation as being less important, serious or valuable than it really is
Rhetorical Question	a special syntactical stylistic device representing a question with no answer expected and therefore used for effect, persuasion or confirmation of an idea; for example, "O Wind, / If Winter comes, can Spring be far behind?" (*Ode to the West Wind*), which in its essence is a reshaping of the grammatical meaning of the interrogative utterance, and stands not as a question but a statement expressed in the form of an interrogative sentence
Epithet	a kind of label, name, byname or nickname used to express a quality or characteristic of a person or thing; this stylistic device is a subtle and delicate means of displaying the writer's emotional attitude to his or her communication; for instance, "Your Highness" for a noble person, "Hollywood" for the American film industry, or, as in *Ulysses* by James Joyce, "a great sweet mother" for sea
Euphemism	the substitution of a word or phrase having unpleasant or offensive meaning by a milder indirect term; e.g. "pass away" for becoming extinct
Allusion	an indirect reference to a historical, mythological, literary, biblical fact or to an aspect or event of everyday life, which is made in the course of writing or speaking
Repetition	certain words or phrases originating in emotive language are repeated less to reveal that the speaker is under the stress of strong emotion than to aim at logical emphasis which is necessary to fix the attention of the reader on the key-word or key-phrase of the utterance
Enumeration	a stylistic device by means of which homogenous parts of an utterance are made heterogeneous from the semantic point of view

These figures of speech are responsible for the creation of imagery, another next to rhythm essential and indispensable element in the literary system of poetry. Imagery is defined as the content of thought where attention is directed to sensory qualities, which means mental images, figures of speech, and embodiments of non-discursive truth. Sight, sound, smell, taste, touch, muscular tension and bodily awareness are the seven mental images identified by psychologists, which poets use to different extent in order to achieve a particular purpose in the creation and assertion of the meaning.

Modernists and postmodernists, in particular, take images as inseparable parts of language and consequently of a meaning, and focus on the images themselves; by this, these poets leave behind the earlier use of imagery either to depict morality in art or to clarify, order, enforce, decorate, and persuade. The meaning was pre-existing and imagery would just disclose it by its images representing fixed devices providing mental representations of sensory experience and recreating aesthetically various aspects of personal life, nature, society, and so on.

Imagery can still be used to externalise thought, to give continuity by fixed and recurring leitmotifs, and to create mood and atmosphere, but images also operate from subject to analogue, become concepts or feelings; they may become typically for individual poems or writers and express personal meanings, or they may express the deepest essences of a community.

The most important figures of speech – both for the aesthetic release of the text and its comprehension by the reader – are **metaphors**, which constitute elements or concepts which are being compared up to eventually lose their identity, where one is or becomes another. The first line of Matthew Arnold's poem *To Marguerite* – "Yes! In the sea of life enisled" – shows that life is a sea and people are islands, which expresses a sense of loneliness and separation that would come to dominate the whole mood of the poem providing also its main theme and ideas.

Symbols are also in the frontline of those stylistic devices which assist the reader in his or her endeavours to come close to the thematic range of a poetic text: the "pleasure dome" in Coleridge's *Kubla Khan*, with its "sunny" appearance but "caves of ice", is a symbol of something or someone that represents form without essence; "chimney" in Blake's *Chimney Sweeper* stands as a symbol of dirt, misery, harshness of life, suffering, and even death with regard to the condition of the children, and, concerning mature life, it stands for an experienced, sinful existence of the adults whom the child redeems by his purity and innocence.

In matters of handling the comparison, simile is usually viewed as the closest to metaphor, but unlike metaphors, similes represent elements and concepts which maintain their identity, one is like another.

Metaphor is based on **affinity**, as in "sea of life" or "All the world's a stage"; simile on **similarity**: "I wandered lonely as a cloud"; next to them is metonymy, which relies on **association**, as in "Hollywood" standing for the American cinematographic industry.

Since literature is imaginative, artistic, referential, aesthetic representation of existence, it can be simply defined as metaphor. Every literary work is therefore a metaphor as well as its constituent parts. The first line of *Elegy Written in a Country Churchyard* by Thomas Gray, for example, is a metaphor, or it actually contains at least three metaphors: first, "curfew" used for a bell ringing in the evening; secondly, "parting day" gives the impression of departure of a person; thirdly, "tolls the knell" is metaphorical with respect to both curfew and day.

Indeed, the whole literature is, in a way, a metaphor, for life, world, experience, a person's subjectivity, his or her self are something else or become the aesthetically rendered substance of another life, world, experience, a person's subjectivity, his or her self. For some, metaphor is associated with metaphysical poetry, romanticism, modernism and postmodernism, that is, what is innovative and experimental, whereas simile with realism; for others, metaphoric is synonymous to modernist, whereas metonymic is antimodernist.

In considering the relation between figurative and literal senses, when reading poetry we come to view metaphor to be "so central to our notion of poetic creation that it is often treated as a phenomenon in its own right, without reference to other kinds of transferred meaning" (G. N. Leech 150).

> Metaphor exceeds the limits of poetic art, coming to signify a mode of expression, a point of view on life rendered as transcendental value aimed to become atemporal yet bound to rhetorical exigencies.

Symbol, likewise, transcends the spheres of poetry and literature, as well as art, and reveals, according to Mircea Eliade in *Images et Symboles* (1952), certain aspects of reality – the most profound ones – which defy other means of becoming known; a symbol answers a necessity and performs a function: to disclose the most secret modalities of being (15).

To conclude, the main figures of speech, also called stylistic devices, which constitute the distinct, figurative language of poetry, can be conceived as following two perspectives of textual organization and in this respect can be classified into two parts or groups: (1) figures of speech related to verse form, or structure, and responsible for the sound of poetry; and (2) stylistic devices related to the contextual meaning, in general, which produce imagery. In both cases, the aim and function of the figurative language as used in poetry are to emphasize and create an effect which would lead to the apprehension of the meaning and other elements on the thematic level.

Within the genre of poetry, figurative language must not be confused with complex poetic utterance, ornamented use of language, or stylized diction, as some students do.

First, concerning language use in poetry, we ought to remember that it is to be **figurative language** in order to be considered language of poetry, which means that it relies on figures of speech, various metaphors and symbols, words and phrases with indirect meaning establishing the dichotomy between dictionary meaning and contextual meaning, the outcome being imagery, or poetic image, and musical (melodic) effects, as well as a message, idea, meaning, and so on. In interpreting poetry, it appears obvious that the figurative meaning becomes necessary because the literal meaning is absurd.

Second, this figurative language can be used in two ways: either as applying a **complex, ornamented, sophisticated language** or in a **plain, direct manner, the poet using concrete language with specific words instead of an abstract language with allusive or general words**. In either case, the user of language is a poet and the resulted work is a poem.

To sum up, the language used in poetry should be figurative language, but the poet may choose to be more traditional and make the language of his or her poetry more complex and ornamented – as if to adhere to what were earlier in modernity "poetic diction" and "decorum" – or to construct his or her poetic discourse by means of more plain, concrete, and direct utterances, as in modernist and postmodernist conceptions on literary practice.

The poet may even avoid the traditional, common shape or form of the text and choose to write "concrete poetry" in which letters, words, lines, and even punctuation create strong visual effects making the shape of a poem look like its subject-matter. Mary Ellen Solt, for example, arranges words to form a picture; others may even replace pen and paper with wood, steel, or concrete.

An example of the former way of writing could be again the first line from *Elegy Written in a Country Churchyard* – "The curfew tolls the knell of parting day" – which Thomas Gray uses to deliver the idea that evening has fallen.

An example of the latter could be the text of *This Is Just To Say* by William Carlos Williams:

I have eaten
the plums
that were in
the icebox

and which
you were probably
saving
for breakfast

Forgive me
they were delicious
so sweet
and so cold

To give a final example: in order to express the idea that evening has fallen, for instance, we can say (1) "The curfew tolls the knell of parting day", which blends figurative language with ornamented language resulting in poetry; (2) "the day has died", which is a combination of figurative language and plain language also alluding to a poetic statement; or (3) "the day is over" or another plain utterance which commonly is not viewed as poetry. Certainly, all this is relative and there are no certain rules since one may talk using figurative language without his or her discourse being necessarily a poem.

The language used in poetry, Aristotle stipulated long ago, is to be a mixture of ordinary and unfamiliar words: ordinary words to clarify and unfamiliar words to make language shine, sound beautifully, and avoid what is prosaic and trivial.

Language is used in poetry as well as literature, in general, to convey aesthetic statements; it is a means of communication and represents the material used to build up discourses containing messages in various other domains of human activities.

Language is the object of study of the science called linguistics, a generic and large field of expertise in social and human studies. Among those independent disciplines arising from within the larger field of linguistics as the science of language is stylistics, which concerns the subsystems of the literary language (language styles) and those language expressive means whose usage determines particular aims or effects of utterance. Every language style can be better revealed by its particular use of expressive means and devices, where certain interaction of these means and devices allows us to distinguish one style from another.

Despite its etymologically being related to the term "style", the subject of stylistics has so far not been definitely outlined and clarified. It will not be an exaggeration to say that among the various branches of General Linguistics the most obscure in content is stylistics. This is due to a number of reasons. First of all, there is a confusion between the terms "style" and "stylistics". The former concept is so broad that it is hardly possible to regard it as a term. We speak of style in architecture, literature, behaviour, dress and in other fields of human activity. Even in linguistics the word "style" is used so widely that it needs interpretation. The majority of linguists who deal with the subject of style agree that the term applies to the following fields of investigation: (1) the aesthetic function of language; (2) expressive means in language; (3) synonymous ways of rendering one and the same idea; (4) emotional colouring in language; (5) a system of special devices called "stylistic devices"; (6) the splitting of the literary language into separate subsystems called styles; (7) the interrelation between language and thought; and (8) the individual manner of an author in making use of language.

The term "style" is also applied to the teaching of how to write clearly, simply and emphatically. The purely utilitarian approach to the problem of style stems from the practical necessity to achieve correctness in writing and avoid ambiguity. These heterogeneous applications of the word style in linguistics have given rise to different points of view as to what is the domain of stylistics.

There is a widely held view that style is the correspondence between thought and its expression. The notion is based on the assumption that of the two functions of language – a means of communication and a means of expression of ideas, of shaping one's thoughts (the first function is called "communicative" and the second "expressive") – the latter finds its materialization in strings of sentences specially arranged to convey the ideas and also to get the desired response.

Many great minds have made valuable observations on the interrelations between thought and expression. The main trend in most of these observations may be summarised as follows: the linguistic form of the expressed idea always reflects the peculiarities of the thought. And vice versa, the character of the thought will always in a greater or lesser degree manifest itself in the language forms chosen for the expression of the idea.

That thought and expression are inseparable from each other is a well-established fact. But to regard this as the true essence of style is misleading, in as much as what is mainly a psychological problem has turned into a linguistic one.

However, although the inseparability of thought and expression is mainly the domain of logic and psychology, it must not be completely excluded from the observation of a stylist. The character of the interrelation between the thought and its expression may sometimes explain the author's preference for one language form over another.

The linguistic problem of thought and expression, mistakenly referred to as one of the problems of style, has given rise to another interpretation of the word "style". The term is applied to the system of idiosyncrasies peculiar to one or another writer, and especially to writers who are recognized as possessing an ingenious turn of mind. This generally accepted notion has further contributed to the general confusion as to how it should be understood and applied. It is only lately that the addition of the attributive "individual" has somehow clarified the notion, though it has not put a stop to further ambiguity.

The term "individual style" is applied to that sphere of linguistic and literary science which deals with the peculiarities of a writer's individual manner of using language means to achieve the effect he or she desires. Deliberate choice must be distinguished from a habitual idiosyncrasy in the use of language units; every individual has his or her own manner of using them. Manner is not individual style in as much as the word "style" presupposes a deliberate choice. In order to distinguish something that is natural from something that is a result of long and perhaps painful experience, two separate terms must be used, otherwise the confusion might grow.

When someone declares that "style is the man himself", this person has in mind those qualities of speech which are inherent and which reveal an individual being's breeding, education, social status, and so on, where all qualities of both types are interwoven with individual style.

Stylistics yet differentiates and draws a definite line of demarcation between that which is inherent, comes natural as an idiosyncrasy of utterance and that which is acquired, the result of the writer's choice.

Then, "individual style" is to be used for an individual choice of language means of expression, particularly in writing, whereas inherent, natural idiosyncrasies of speech can be better termed "individual manner".

Also, "individual style" is often identified with "style" in general, and "style" discussed in literary field is sometimes taken to be synonymous with "genre" and sometimes with "literature" in general, where in this case, "genre" would be synonymous with "substyle".

Seemingly, the most individual style in its essence is **literature** – a cultural phenomenon, one of the arts, the verbal art, also referred to as imaginative writing or creative writing – which in stylistic terms can be called the "**belles-lettres style**".

Undeniably, the science of stylistics, in its going beyond the strict formal-structural analysis of language, focuses, among other things, on literature and literary genres, including poetry, and on those figures of speech (stylistic devices) which constitute the main elements of poetry and literature, in general, as well as of other language using domains and styles of human activity and interaction, identifying, classifying, characterising, and exemplifying these stylistic devices and means of expression.

Concerning their **categorization**, for example, stylistics prompts three groups, namely **phonetic expressive means and stylistic devices, lexical (or lexico-phraseological) expressive means and stylistic devices, and syntactical expressive means and stylistic devices**. Stylistics also deals with the **classification of the vocabulary** of a particular language (for instance, archaic words, slang, professionalisms, dialectical words, and so on). Not the least, stylistics considers the **functional styles** of a particular language, namely **literature (or the belles-lettres style)**, **publicistic style**, **newspaper style**, **scientific prose style**, and the **style of official documents**.

In the light of stylistics, language used in literature (imaginative writing) constitutes the substance of the theoretical and practical scrutiny performed in relation to the so-called "**belles-lettres style**", which is a generic term for three substyles: (1) **the language of poetry**, or verse; (2) **emotive prose**, or the language of fiction; and (3) the **language of the drama**.

In these **substyles** – roughly corresponding to what are more commonly known to us as literary **genres** – the most general properties of the belles-lettres style are materialized and, at the same time, each of these substyles also enjoys some individuality. Each of these substyles "has certain common features, typical of the general belles-lettres style, which make up the foundation of the style, by which the particular is made recognizable and can therefore be singled out" (Galperin 255).

The common features of the three substyles of literature include first of all the common function which stylistics terms "aesthetico-cognitive" and which is not far removed from the common conception about the twofold purpose of imaginative writing which is to please and to instruct. As Coleridge already argued, the pleasure is caused not only by admiration of the chosen language means and their peculiar arrangement but also by the fact that the reader is led to form his own conclusions as to the purport of the author. One would say that nothing gives more pleasure and satisfaction than realizing that "one has the ability to penetrate into the hidden tissue of events, phenomena and human activity, and to perceive the relation between various seemingly unconnected facts brought together by the creative mind of the writer" (Galperin 255).

Language used in literature or belles-lettres style, in general, and the language of poetry or verse, in particular, have long been viewed as a code of rules which can either be observed or broken. This opinion of linguistic deviation has its limitations: the reader can be surprised by the difficulty of deciding whether a given metaphor is the invention of a writer or an established part of language. Language is used not only in literary composition, but in everyday gossip, in scientific reports, in commercial or political persuasion, and in a multitude of other situations involving inter-human communication. Also, there is no firm dividing between poetic and ordinary language, so it would be artificial to enforce a clear division between poetic language and other literary kinds, as Coleridge, for instance, does. The relation between the language of poetry and ordinary language discloses at least 3 aspects: (1) poetic language may violate or deviate from the generally observed rules of language many innumerable ways, some obvious, other subtle; (2) most of what is considered characteristic of literary language – for instance, the use of various figures of speech – has its roots in everyday use of language; (3) the poet enjoys a unique freedom among other users of language to range over all its communicative resources, without respect to any historical or social context to which they belong – this means that a poet can draw on the language of the past tradition or can borrow aspects of other, even non-linear uses of language.

Still, figurative language, once more, is the language of poetry and it requires special modes of expression, particular choices of words, a rhetorical rather than grammatical substance of the literary discourse, which necessitates, among other things, distinct rhyme, rhythm, metre, and metrical units. And the expression of a meaning too, a meaning which would express a particular poetic style, or a school of poetry, or a literary trend or movement, or period – each claiming its aesthetic views and principles as indisputable truths – as well as the whole conception of a particular literary voice belonging or not to certain periods, movements, and trends. Leaving aside the more formal considerations of the poetic or figurative language, rhythm, metre, imagery, and so on, we may talk about writing poetry which would be appropriate to context as well.

To remember medieval poetry in English literature, for instance, it prompts allegory, dream-poetry, and moral didacticism. Metaphysical poetry pursues wit, conceit, persuasion, argument. Neoclassical poetry relies on reason, rule, order, measure, poetic diction, decorum. Romantic verse promotes imaginative flight, individual expression, dualism of existence, escapism, reverence for nature and countryside, rebelliousness. Nineteenth-century avant-garde attempts to innovate the poetic discourse and advances the objective theory on art. In twentieth century, originality and experimentation flourish by modernism and postmodernism further championing innovation and free verse while co-existing with several revivals of more traditional, strict verse as encouraged by the Georgians, the Movement poets, the Neo-Romantics, and the New Formalists.

English verse in its advancement through history developed a distinct literary voice, established a kind of national tradition, but it would also periodically attempt to break with the past and convention, proclaim freedom from traditional metre, and pursue free verse as well as freedom to use sound and visual effects, to diversify and play with the meaning in order to continuously defamiliarize and reshape our normal expectations in language.

In doing so, poets may rely on tradition or embrace innovation but almost exclusively assert the view that aesthetic and cognitive aspects of the literary discourse interpenetrate, and that literary convention, historical content, language, rhythm, imagery, theme, versification, prosody, ethics and so on may be brought into one poetic system.

The main representatives of English and American poetry are Geoffrey Chaucer, Philip Sidney, William Shakespeare, John Donne, John Milton, Alexander Pope, William Blake, Samuel Taylor Coleridge, Walt Whitman, Edgar Allan Poe, Alfred Tennyson, Robert Browning, Mathew Arnold, Emily Dickinson, Robert Frost, T.S. Eliot, Philip Larkin, Seamus Heaney, and a great number of others. Exploring the formal resources and those of poetic imagery, these and other writers would create poetry in an attempt to deviate from the ordinary use of language or, in more experimental endeavours, even violate as far as possible the contemporary expectation of what poetry should sound like, mingling the surprisingly colloquial with the surprisingly unusual to make a poem explode.

On the thematic level, it is impossible to specify particular concerns and viewpoints of these and other poets to be more important than others, but on the structural level, "iambic pentameter" is the most common type of metre in English literature having formed the metrical entity called "heroic couplet", which is a couplet of rhyming iambic pentameters. The heroic couplet dates as back as medieval period with Chaucer using it in the fourteenth century. A more extensive use of the heroic couplet as iambic pentameter with pairs of rhyming lines *aabb* occurred with John Dryden and Alexander Pope who perfected the form.

The heroic couplet became the dominant and omnipresent type of English verse in seventeenth and eighteenth centuries in both drama and poetry whose flourishing and peculiar features on the seventeenth-century English literary scene, along with the genre of fiction, we shall see in the following.

1.

THE INTELLECTUAL BACKGROUND

> ***Keywords:*** monarchy, Puritanism, Restoration, Francis Bacon, French classicism, Thomas Hobbes, rationalism, Rene Descartes, empiricism, John Locke, ancient versus moderns, neoclassicism, John Dryden

The seventeenth-century British historical and social scene, in particular between the death of Elizabeth and the accession of James I in 1603 and the inauguration of the Hanoverian Dynasty by George I in 1714, saw more profound transformations on all levels than any other centuries. It was the period of uncertainty concerning the future of the country and the whole purpose of life since it was a period of Revolution and Restoration, of increasing divergence in religion and politics, and the main changes addressed actually the political and religious life of the century. The world of the seventeenth century, Andrew Sanders argues, "had been turned upside down; crowns and mitres had been knocked off heads only to be restored in a world that looked more cynically and questioningly at all forms of authority. Many of the private convictions which had been revolutionary in the 1640s seemed reactionary in the 1680s" (272).

1.1 The Period and Its Historical, Social and Cultural Implications

Concerning the general historical and cultural background of the seventeenth century, one of the most spectacular political changes regarded the undoubted power of the kings and queens of England, whose unlimited prerogatives had no longer constituted matters of private interest but were under the control of the Parliamentary majority.

If James I accessed to the throne by heredity, George I succeeded by an act of Parliament; the Tudors could choose ministers, decide matters of foreign policy, and control economy by arbitrary actions on customs, industrial and financial institutions, as it seemed best to them, but at the end of the seventeenth century and in the early eighteenth century these actions were under the control of the executive.

James I united the kingdoms of England and Scotland, but only a century later, by the 1707 "Act of Union" between England and Scotland, the Parliament achieved a more solid union of the two crowns. The Parliament managed many other important regulations in most spheres of social life, which made possible, among others, the establishment of the Bank of England, and, at the end of the seventeenth century, Great Britain became a leading world power holding a large empire in Asia, Africa, and America.

Important changes were also produced in the religious outlook and religious institution concerning its social status, which manifested themselves in the gradual diminishing of the power of State Church, the Puritan triumph by the middle of the seventeenth century and the toleration of Protestantism by 1714. Applied to those who, starting with the second half of the sixteenth century, aimed at purifying the Church of England, the term "Puritan" came to name a movement that was highly influential in the seventeenth century in both England and the New England colonies in America.

The beginnings of Puritanism go back to the middle of the sixteenth century, and the Elizabethan period and the first half of the seventeenth century saw its development as a movement while acquiring political control over Parliament even though James I promised to "harry the Puritans out of the land", the Catholic Church desired its autocratic power restored, and Charles I fought popular rights and suppressed Parliament proclaiming, in December 1641, the Church of England to be "the most pure and agreeable to the Sacred Word of God of any religion now practised in the Christian World".

A consequence of the conflict between the King and Parliament, between the followers of Charles I, who were called "Cavaliers", and the members of the Puritan or Parliamentary party, who were called "Roundheads", was the Civil War that lasted from 1642 to 1646. Led by Oliver Cromwell, who came to power during the war, the Puritans abolished the monarchy by executing Charles I in 1649 (by whose side also ended his life Archbishop Laud, the King's chief instrument of his ecclesiastical policy) and established the Puritan "Commonwealth", also called the "Interregnum" period, or the period of "Commonwealth Interregnum", or "Protectorate", which lasted until the restoration of monarchy in 1660 and during which the country was ruled by Oliver Cromwell, who proclaimed himself "Lord Protector" of England.

Cromwell died in 1658, leaving power to his son Richard who, unlike his father, was an incompetent ruler. The political and social crisis of the country was solved by the return of Charles II to London and his restoration to the throne of England in 1660. The political death of Puritanism in 1660 and the subsequent persecution of the Puritans made thousands of them leave England for the Colonies.

Puritanism in England was an aftermath of Calvinism, an outgrowth of the Reformation, and later allied itself with the radical movement of Presbyterianism, objecting to certain forms of the Church of England, demanding certain reforms of the Church (as, for instance, by its 1603 "Millenary Petition"), and, in general, openly hating the Established Church of England (as, for instance, Thomas Cartwright, the first important exponent of Puritanism, did). An extreme form of Reformation, Puritanism exaggerated some of Protestant traits, aiming at a global restructuring of the religious institution, rejecting the religious ritual, opposing any kind of worship, and advising instead the reading of the Bible and preaching fundamentals of the faith.

The Protestant doctrine in Western Europe, in general, and, in particular, in England Puritanism and Presbyterianism extended themselves outside religious circle of ideas, reaching general social, economic, and cultural levels. What is now designated by the term "Puritan" as conservative and thwarting the development of the individual, art, and democracy, was in the seventeenth century a paradigm of simplicity and democratic principles.

Many of the Puritans were people of culture and education, some of them patrons of art, and it was the persecution of Charles I that made them turn callous religious and social reformers, wishing to establish a theocracy and involving themselves in all spheres of social life, and desiring to control politics and economy as well as literature and arts in relation to which they emphasised the ecclesiastical and the virtuous over the light-hearted, lyric, sensual, and chivalric.

The Protestant theology reached the literary level and came to be reflected in literary works, becoming the source of a distinct tradition of religious poetry in the seventeenth century, as in the works of John Milton and in the poems of the metaphysical writers George Herbert and John Donne. In the latter's "Holy Sonnet 14", for example, one can see the expression of the Protestant view that salvation cannot be achieved but can only come from God.

On a more general, social level, the Protestant concept of "actively serving God" developed in relation to the doctrine of individual consciousness, the right of the individual to religious and political independence, while individualism played an important part in the rise of capitalism by encouraging industrial and educational development as well as frugality, which determined an individual sense of purpose and faithful and honest work as a means of ensuring prosperity. The religious factors on the seventeenth-century English social scene are thus connected to and manipulative of the economic and cultural as well as political ones, in particular with regard to the institution of monarchy and its relationship with Parliament.

Although the King was restored to power in 1660, the institution of monarchy lost its decision making prerogatives and since then the major political and social actions in the country have been under the control of the Parliament.

Except the Interregnum period, the institution of monarchy in Britain has yet always been a relatively strong but continuous presence: following the rule of the House of Tudors from 1485 to 1603 (Henry VII to Elizabeth I), between 1603 and 1714 the country was ruled by the Stuarts (James I to Anne), followed by the reign of the House of Hanover from 1714 to 1901 (George I to Victoria), and in the twentieth century, the reign of Edward VII (1901-1910), George V (1910-1936), George VI (1936-1952), and since 1952 to the present the reign of Elizabeth II.

Considering the seventeenth century, the period is historically divided into four parts. The first was the "Jacobean Age" that saw the reign of James I between 1603 and 1625, and, in the field of thought and literature, the production of some of Shakespeare's major plays and sonnets as well as his death in 1616, Ben Jonson's *Volpone* (1606), Francis Bacon's *The Advancement of Learning* (1605), *The New Method* (1620) and *Essays* (1612, 1625), King James's translation of the *Bible* (1611), George Chapman's translation of *Iliad* (1598-1611) and *Odyssey* (1614-1615), and John Donne's sermons.

Second was the "Caroline Age" of the reign of Charles I between 1625 and 1649, which saw some of John Milton's major works (such as *On Shakespeare* in 1630, *L'Allegro* and *Il Penseroso* in 1633, and *Lycidas* in 1638), John Donne's and George Herbert's metaphysical poems, but also the closing of the theatres in 1642, the Civil War, and the execution of Charles I in 1649.

The third was the turbulent period of "Commonwealth Interregnum" that lasted from 1649 to 1660, the country being ruled by the Puritans led by Oliver Cromwell, the "Lord Protector" of England; it was a poor literary period except Milton's *Defence of the English People* (1651), Thomas Hobbes' *Leviathan* (1651), John Bunyan's *Pilgrim's Progress* (1658), Abraham Cowley's *Poems, Davideis, Pindaric Odes* (1656), and some translations of French romances and novels.

The last part of the seventeenth century was the "Restoration Period" between 1660 and 1700, which saw the restoration of the Stuarts to the throne of England in 1660, including the reign of Charles II, the son of the executed Charles I, between 1660 and 1685, followed by the reign of James II (1685-1688) and the reign of William and Marry (1689-1702). The first years of Charles II's reign were marked by the Plague that swept London in 1665 and killed as many as 70 000 people. A year later, a great fire destroyed half of the city's houses, yet the profits from the global trade carried by British merchants helped rebuild the city under the supervision of the architect Christopher Wren.

Charles II manifested himself as a patron of arts, inviting foreign painters and composers to live and work in London, re-opening the theatres, advancing the study of natural sciences by the Royal Society, and, in general, advocating artificial, stylized fashions and manners of a highly sophisticated society which came to be reflected in the Restoration comedy of manners as practiced by William Congreve, John Dryden, and others.

Charles II, John Dryden argued, "awakened the dull and heavy spirits of the English from their natural reservedness" and set free "their stiff forms of conversation, and made them easy and pliant to each other in discourse". Although a Catholic, Charles II kept his religious convictions for himself, unlike his brother James II who manifested himself as a devout Catholic appointing Catholics to high offices and dismissing the Parliament. When his son was born in 1688, meaning that another Catholic would be the next King, the Parliament reacted and several leaders invited Mary, James II's Protestant daughter, to rule England together with her husband, William of Holland, a Protestant himself.

In what was called the "Glorious Revolution", since there was no fight for the throne, James II, perhaps recalling the tragic fate of his father Charles I, escaped to France, and William and Mary came to the throne. By the 1689 "Bill of Rights" passed by the Parliament, England attained a limited constitutional monarchy, and witnessed the rise of the modern democratic principles, among which the right of the Parliament to approve all taxes and promulgate laws that no King or Queen could suspend, and henceforth England embarked on a process of progress, strengthening of stability, and increase of prosperity.

In literature and critical thought, the "Restoration Age" is dominated by John Dryden, but the period includes also Milton's *Paradise Lost* (1667), John Locke's *Essay Concerning the Human Understanding* (1690), the foundation of the Royal Society in 1662, the re-opening of the theatres, the rebirth of arts and literature, in general, along with the revival and institutionalization of the classical principles which make Restoration, the last part of the seventeenth century, to be the first of the three parts of the "Neoclassical Period" in British literature.

As part of neoclassicism, "Restoration", or the "Age of Dryden", representing the rise of neoclassicism, was followed by the "Augustan Age" (1700-1750s), or the "Age of Pope", representing the climax of the neoclassical period, and by the "Age of Johnson" (1750s-1780s) which reflected the decline of the neoclassical period and, in literature, the rise of a new poetic sensibility, that of pre-romanticism.

1.2 The Philosophical Advancement of Modernity

Many postmodern philosophers and theoreticians led by Jean-François Lyotard and Jacques Derrida, among others, would claim as well as modernity – roughly between Renaissance and the 1950s – to be foundationalist, essentialist, and realist, and to advance totality, order, stability, metanarratives, and a system of thought based on binary oppositions, which they attempted to reject and replace by difference, incredulity, alternative interpretation, playfulness, deconstructive reading, and so on.

Descartes, Locke, Hume, Hegel, Kant, Comte, Husserl are among the main founders and promoters of the modern thought with its essentialist, foundationalist, and realist approach to knowledge, science, existence, theology, reality, history, individual, and so on. First in line should be placed Francis Bacon, perhaps the most influential writer at the beginnings of modernity, with a total of seventy books, among which most literary works are his *Essays* (1597, 1612, and 1625) and most influential are *The Advancement of Learning* (1605) and *Novum Organum* (1620).

1.2.1 Francis Bacon and the "New Method"

It was the first half of the seventeenth century that saw the fundamental works of Francis Bacon (1561-1626), Viscount St Albans, one of the most eminent European intellectuals of the seventeenth century and one of the most important English scholars of all times.

Rejecting contemporary to him scholastic application of Aristotle's ideas, which he saw as unfruitful and useless, and apart from his devotion to and involvement in politics and public affairs, Bacon dedicated all his life to scholarly studies and scholarly scientific writing. His series of *Essays*, which from 1597 to 1625 increased in number to fifty-eight works, represent brief and comparatively informal studies on various subjects, from the arrangement of a house to the issues of moral good, written in a concise and clear style, similar to that of the Latin author Tacitus, and thus different from the artificial and ornamental manner of expression of the Elizabethan and Jacobean prose.

The major influence comes from the ancients as well as from Renaissance and contemporary thinkers, in particular the great French philosopher Michel de Montaigne (1533-1592), an earlier contemporary of Bacon. Montaigne and Bacon are the first to use the term "essay" in modern sense to designate their works. Before that, the essay "began to take form in the epistolary writings of Cicero and Seneca, Plutarch's *Moralia*, the compilations of *sententiae*, *exempla*, and *lectiones* of late antiquity and their humanist counterparts" (Gray 271).

Bacon's most important writings were not in the field of pure literature but in the domains of thought, science, morals, and politics. Philosophy with its various trends and especially the various scientific domains and disciplines must not be isolated but should cross-fertilize each other. His main contribution was the formulation of the methods of modern science, in particular natural science, concerning the advancement of knowledge on the basis of unlimited fresh observation, experiment, and inductive reasoning.

These are the three main pillars of Bacon's scientific method developed in *Novum Organum* ("The New Method"), written in Latin and published in 1620. Here Bacon provides an interesting classification of the "idols", or phantoms, which mislead the human mind in the pursuit of knowledge – the "idols of the tribe" inherent in human nature, the "idols of the cave" representing the errors of the individual, the "idols of the market-place" resulting from the mistaken reliance on words, and the "idols of the theatre", or schools, resulting from false ways of thinking – offering instead a clear demonstration of the applicability and importance of the inductive method of observation and reasoning.

Also, in all his work, Bacon relies on *vita activa*, a Renaissance concept advancing a way of living dedicated to serve society and implying the necessity of true intellectual reforms, as well as "moral knowledge" (on humans), "civil knowledge" (on government, justice, negotiation, and so on), the analysis of cause and effect in philosophical and social terms, and promotion of fundamental ethical principles such as *philanthropia* (goodness of nature).

In *The Advancement of Learning* (with its actual title *Of the Proficience and Advancement of Learning, Divine and Human*), in particular, Bacon expresses the strongest in his period belief in the importance of knowledge which should be continuously pursued and renovated despite all restrictions, including the suspicions of the Church about the study of Creation. In this book, which is considered the first philosophical work in English, Bacon develops the famous metaphor about "letters" (meaning written texts) that "pass through the vast seas of time" to perpetuate knowledge. Then again, science can no longer be derived only from books, such as by Aristotle and other ancients, but from direct observation and pertinent experiment.

This is actually the "new method" of scientific research in *Novum Oraganum*, which largely rejects deduction from fixed premises being instead inductive, working from individual observations to general laws. Owing to his attempts at conceiving and asserting new principles and methods which would refresh and advance scientific development, Bacon is truly one of the main founders of modern philosophy and science, a highly influential personality for the centuries to come as well as in his own times and country, where, in 1660, when the Royal Society of London was founded, Francis Bacon was honoured as its inspiration.

1.2.2 The Advancement of Classicism: French Contribution

Following the period of Baroque, the seventeenth century further extended the direction of classicism in European practice and theory of art. Classicism as the most important cultural aspect of the century owes its critical relevance to the major French thinkers of the period. Among them, Francois de Malherbe and Michel de Montaigne seeking to achieve the purification of native language for clear communication, and Chapelain, Corneille, d'Aubignac, Bouhours, Rapin, and Boileau, the last three, especially, as the real founders of the classical, in English studies also referred to as "neoclassical", theory.

The word "classical" dates from the eighteenth century with reference, first, to important ancient authors (Sophocles, Cicero, Terence, and others), who serve as models, as well as to some seventeenth-century writers (Boileau, Racine, Corneille, Moliere, and others) who imitate the ancient models, follow their rules of composition, and whose style is "correct" and elegant, and for this themselves coming to be labelled "classics".

The term "classicism" was initially used in the first decades of the nineteenth century (presumably by Stendhal in 1823) pejoratively, as it was the age of romanticism, to denounce a type of literature which seemed obsolete and useless, and then positively (as by Goethe in 1829) and finally laudatory with the meaning of "eternity" and "perfection". Likewise, the adjective "classical" refers to ancient Greek and Roman and later to seventeenth and eighteenth century European art and literature (corresponding to the term "neoclassical" used for English literature), and, likewise, it is synonymous to "perfect" and "eternal".

Regarding the literary practice in the seventeenth century, Europe was mainly dominated by French authors, namely by Racine, Corneille, Moliere, La Fontaine, Boileau, and others who reacted against the cultural extravaganza of the Baroque and institutionalized classicism.

Concerning the literary genres, towering over the entire period is drama, in determent of other existing genres (lyrical poetry, narrative poetry, novel, novella, short story, fable, and so on). Within drama, in determent of other dramatic forms (comedy, tragic-comedy, historical play, dramatic pastoral, and others), the dominant type of text was tragedy. The public would ask for fidelity to actuality in its textual and scenic representation, and the classical tragedy, conceived as *mimesis*, "behaves towards external reality with certain faithfulness which other genres are not able to achieve" and "from Sophocles and Euripides to Racine and Goethe, Claudel and Ibsen, O'Neill and Durrenmatt, the tragedy, drama, and tragic farce take place in some clearly defined time and place, which point to the history and ethnography of a civilization, and to a geography of a place that can be recognized" (Munteanu 139).

The predominance of the classical tragedy in the seventeenth century emerged also from the demands of the public concerning rules, order, measure, and common sense, and as supported and encouraged by Cardinal Richelieu.

Another reason for the supremacy of tragedy was the important theoretical input – about unities, rules, good taste, reason, and other aspects related to tragedy – which was provided, first, in 1639, by La Mesnardiere (in *Poetique*) and Jean Francois Sarasin (in *Discours sur la tragedie*), and later by Racine and Corneille, among others. The word "tragedy" was already familiar to French people at the end of the sixteenth century, but its meaning referred to an epic narration of cruel and murderous events. Only later the term came to name a particular dramatic form.

Also, as inherited from the ancients, namely from Aristotle's *Poetics*, tragedy was labelled "tragic poem", not "tragedy" like nowadays, meaning that in the seventeenth century, and "unlike today, drama and poetry were not totally distinct genres" (Clement 15). Coming from Greek "goat song", it is agreed among the scholars that the term "tragedy" originally "denoted a form of ritual sacrifice accompanied by a choral song in honour of Dionysus, the god of the fields and the vineyards. Out of this ritual developed Greek dramatic tragedy" (Cuddon 983).

The most discussed topic in relation to drama was its form rather than thematic level, including action, situation, convention, character, conflict, language, dialogue, and other aspects of the structural level. Concerning character, for instance, the ancient heroes were revived but also new myths were created, such as those of Don Juan and Faust. French classicism conceived of character by "revealing a dominant, a feature which is fundamentally human and around which all the other features are structured. It could be avarice, pride, honour, snobbism, or folly" (Ceuca 45-46).

Regarding the verbal discourse in drama, the French classicism "follows concision and eloquence, but also the soundness of the verse"; later, "in Romanticism, there will be imagism, metaphor, comparison, epithets. Realism brings language close to a common usage and imposes prose instead of verse" (Ceuca 44).

Among the major representatives of the seventeenth-century classicism, Pierre Corneille (1606-1684) and Jean Racine (1639-1699) were primarily tragedians. Moliere (Jean-Baptiste Poquelin, 1622-1673) was the greatest master of comedy, but who initially wanted to become a tragic author and actor. It is said that Moliere turned to comedy "only after the failure of his single tragedy (*Dom Garcia de Navarra*), and would admit comedy as a "major" genre only after ascribing to it the rules of tragedy" (Clement 9). Jean de La Fontaine (1621-1695) was a major fabulist and poet.

Nicolas Boileau-Despreaux (1636-1711), commonly called Boileau, and Rene Rapin (1621-1687) dominated the age as poets and critics. Apart from Boileau and Rapin, the literary theory and criticism of the seventeenth century owes its significance also to Racine and Corneille. The former expressed his ideas, revealing obedience to classical rules and being mainly concerned with the history and nature of tragedy, in a series of prefaces. The latter develops his *ars poetica* in three "Discourses" written for the 1660 publication of his complete works, in which the main concern is again tragedy, discussed in all its aesthetic, historical, and moral dimensions.

Corneille starts from ancient theories, but reformulates the notions related to the three "unities", formulates new concepts (such as "suspension" and "preparation"), redefines "exposition", prefers complex action, and favours characters that display energy, personality, and free choice. In particular in *Of the Three Unities of Action, Time, and Place* (1660), Corneille established the neoclassical theory of drama which was followed by Dryden. Many of his principles are valid nowadays, especially in the traditional drama.

Racine also gives importance to the free decision of the hero but accepts the omnipresence of destiny and, like Corneille, shows the failure of man to dominate events. For Racine, there is a superior, cruel force that controls the events and the only resolution is death. Unlike Corneille, Racine favours the simplicity of action and emphasises the thematic efficiency of psychological and emotional states, as in the Preface to *Britannicus*: the action must be "simple, with as less as possible material (...) to be sustained only by the feelings and passions of the characters".

The tutelage for the critical theory of the period was provided by the French Academy, founded by Richelieu in 1634. The guiding principles of the critical theory were borrowed from Antiquity, namely from the works of Aristotle and Horace, whose influence was decisive and whose texts were frequently translated and commented starting with the middle of sixteenth century. The ancient theoretical texts were revived; or rather, there was a continuation of the revival of ancient classical tradition which started in the Renaissance. The ideas from the texts were assumed but also debated on and even modified or rejected.

On the whole, starting from these ancient texts, the seventeenth-century theoreticians developed a new "classical" doctrine which was expressed in different treaties, prefaces, and essays. The doctrine itself might be considered a wholly new literary genre, but this idea is thwarted by the wide range of theoretical concerns with rules, models, reason, rigour, clarity, common sense, moral and didactic values, *catharsis*, *mimesis*, verisimilitude, character, subject-matter, tragic and comic elements, structure of the dramatic text, and the unities of time, place, and action.

In this age of old and new rules, the only unquestionable voice was that of Aristotle, whose *Poetics* would often be evoked to validate or reject whatever matter related to the form and content of the literary text. On a more general philosophical level, the seventeenth century was governed by the works of Bacon, Galileo, Hobbes, Descartes, Pascal, Spinoza, Leibniz, and others who made it an age of reason, marking the rise of physical sciences and of empirical, experimental methods, and thus proclaiming the reign of mind and rationalism. The new scientific spirit of the seventeenth century declares its independence from the religious norms first through the work of Galileo Galilei (1564-1642).

A similar endeavour was made earlier by Nicolaus Copernicus (1473-1543) who opposed the medieval view of the universe by his new heliocentric theory. By his improvement and use of telescope and his astronomical studies, Galileo extended further the scientific revolution and determined new directions in philosophical thinking, which proclaimed the autonomy of the scientific reasoning and argument against the dominant views of the Holy Books:

> Galileo produced an *epistemological revolution*: he not only desacralised the sky, making of telescope an instrument of discovery which allows the scientist not to search for truth in old books, but especially conferred to the truth a new status, defining it rigorously as being the *exact essence of the mathematical calculation applicable to the entire nature*. (Graf 6)

Blaise Pascal (1623-1662), continuing Galileo's epistemology, also advocates the separation between the scientific truth and religious obedience, and opposes the "God of philosophers and scientists to the God of the Bible". For Pascal, as for others philosophers, the reason is the principal faculty of acquiring knowledge, possessing the capacity to judge the natural objects without any help from imagination or feeling. Every natural phenomenon, argues Pascal, can be explained by the power of reason, but he seems to reconcile rationalism with theology, since he accepts the miracle and considers it to be an event revealing the power of God to act upon nature to disturb the natural forces. The miracle provides exceptions in the work of reason and remains beyond human understanding.

Unlike Pascal, Baruch Spinoza (1632-1677) rejects the existence of miracles whatsoever. Another rationalist of the seventeenth century philosophy and a forerunner of the eighteenth century Enlightenment, Spinoza is the only thinker of the period who "takes the mechanicalism to its last consequences, formulating a radical criticism on metaphysics: nothing, not even the human being, surpasses nature" (Graf 13). Apart from the natural sciences, the opposition to religious views manifested in the seventeenth century also in the field of social and political philosophy, as in the works of Cyrano de Bergerac (1619-1655) and Bernard le Bouyer de Fontennelle (1657-1757), and, in Britain, the most popular thinker in this respect was Thomas Hobbes.

1.2.3 The Social and Political Philosophy: Thomas Hobbes and *Leviathan*

Thomas Hobbes (1588-1679), proving scepticism and materialism in his political philosophy, suggests a strong secular state in *Leviathan* (1651). In this work, Hobbes "tried to build a philosophy of mind, using solely the facts of memory and imagination. Reasoning is mere calculation, the manipulation of signs, and the reasoning is correct if the same signs are constantly attached to the same images" (Hampshire 35).

Leviathan was written in Paris during the English Civil War which broke out in 1642, and Hobbes's doctrine of legitimate government was developed in relation to political crisis resulting from the war. The book's aim was to prove the necessity of a strong central authority to avoid civil war and social conflict. In most general terms, in this work Hobbes sets forth his theory of the foundation of society and civil government, and the theory of social contract. According to Romul Munteanu, Hobbes wrote his *Leviathan* at the historical moment when the belief in human decency and wisdom decreased. Instead, the famous formula of *homo homini lupus est* came to express new views on interhuman relationship, and "man was presented as an egotistic being, controlled by desires to invade and conquer" (Munteanu 237).

"The passions that incline men to peace are fear of death, desire of such things as are necessary to commodious living and a hope by their industry to obtain them", claims Hobbes. On the one hand, the passions of man, his fear of death as well as some materialistic interests determine the human being to try to prevent or stop the war. On the other, they determine him to create a state (society) in which humans give up their natural rights and their natural condition which are anti-social and in which life is "solitary, poor, nasty, brutish, and short" and men are in civil conflict, in *bellum omnium contra omnes* ("the war of all against the all") resulting from human passions. Surrendering its selfish individualistic and animal nature, mankind tends to create a state which Hobbes regards as a "Leviathan" (an artificial man or monster) composed of humans that submit to the absolute authority of a ruler. Hobbes rejects the doctrine of "separation of powers" and puts forward that of the "social contract" which would assure a peaceful society formed by a population under the authority.

The authority, either monarchy or democracy, is actually the "Leviathan" whose power is derived from the population and which ensures peace and stability by its unlimited prerogatives. The power of the authority is absolute and subject to no law whatsoever; it controls actually all judicial, civil, military, and ecclesiastical laws. This yet might be a problem because, though the system is absolute and controversy is eliminated, political activity is also eliminated as well as freedom, and individual is a mere presence in society.

Leviathan is first of all a philosophical work on man and society, displaying a remarkable unity of concern and subject assisted by united form and style. Apart from the issues related to state and politics, Hobbes focuses on other aspects of human experience, such as science, reason, speech, sense, and imagination.

In "Chapter II. Of Imagination", Hobbes defines imagination as "decaying sense" which occurs in that moment of experience in which, "after the object is removed, or the eye is shut, we still retain an image of the thing seen, though more obscure than when we see it." For him, imagination and fancy are but one thing, just like imagination and memory, imagination and dreams, and imagination and understanding. He then discerns between "simple Imagination", when "one imagines a man, or horse, which he has seen before", and "compounded Imagination", when "from the sight of a man at one time, and of a horse at another, we conceive in our mind a Centaur". The former is related to things perceived by sense and represents the common human faculties of observation and awareness; the latter, however, means creativity, for it is nothing but "a fiction of the mind". Later Coleridge makes a similar distinction between the faculty of perception as "Primary Imagination" and the creative principle as "Secondary Imagination". Hobbes regards imagination as a sequence of mental images, or, as he calls it, "the Consequence or Train of Imaginations", meaning "Consequence, or Train of thoughts" by which he understands "the succession of one thought to another, which is called (to distinguish it from discourse in words) Mental Discourse". According to Hobbes, imagination "is found in men, and many other living creatures, as well sleeping as waking", but the difference between men and animals lies in the possession of language which enables the human being to give a form to the process of thinking, a form of both the train of mental images and the estimation of "the consequences of terms".

To revert to its political and philosophical message, *Leviathan* puts forward the idea of a State ("Leviathan") with a life which can be traced from its foundation under pressure of human needs to its dissolution through civil conflict which emerges from passion and ego-centrism characterising human nature. In the natural condition of mankind, which is in the state of nature, existence is anti-social, life is brutal and short, since each of the human beings has the right to defend himself or herself against the threat of violent death and, in order to overcome the fear of death, the only constant is war. In other words, the man is by nature a selfishly individualistic animal at constant war with all other men. The rights are born of necessity, and the self-defence against violent death is, in Hobbes's opinion, the highest human necessity, though it may lead to war.

According to Hobbes, the fear of violent death is the main reason which determines men to create a state (a society) by contracting to surrender their natural rights and to submit to the absolute authority of a sovereign. The peaceful society is to be formed by entering into a social contract, where society is a population above which are the authority (a sovereign) and the law which enforces the contracts. The authority, which might be represented by either monarchy (preferred by Hobbes) or aristocracy, or democracy, should be a "Leviathan" whose power is derived originally from the people. Hobbes advocates an absolute authority which should be able to ensure internal peace and organise a common defence against violent death in war; some abuses of power by the sovereign are to be accepted if they lead to peace. Hobbes's leviathan state is highly authoritative since the authority controls everything and the ruler has authority to assert power over matters such as faith and doctrine; if this is not done, it may give rise to conflict.

The book ends with a general "Review and Conclusion" in which the question is raised whether the population has the right not to remain loyal to the ruler who has lost the power to protect his subjects.

In essence, *Leviathan* aims at demonstrating the necessity of a strong central authority to avoid civil war and social conflict. Although the term "Hobbesian" is sometimes used in modern English to indicate the idea that "might makes right", Hobbes' political doctrine is actually based on the principle of "do no harm" to others and it refers mainly to the necessity of avoiding the selfish action, uncivilised competition, and ruthless struggle.

Largely, *Leviathan* expresses a royalist view of state which must have a hierarchy with a sovereign with absolute power and Church subordinated to him, where human beings subordinate themselves to the whole since individuals are selfish and act by self-interest against it, and, for civil society not to fall into anarchy, they must be restrained by state. Society is a living organism whose head is the ruler; Leviathan or commonwealth is an "artificial man" with sovereignty its soul, magistrates its joints, concord its healthy state, and so on, which makes Hobbes's work an allegory, a metaphor, an emblem-book in which philosophy and argument meet literature and imaginative flight.

1.2.4 Rationalists and Empiricists

Hobbes's ideas were highly influential throughout Europe during the age of Enlightenment, which owes actually much of its theoretical input to the ideas expressed in the seventeenth century in the writings of Hobbes as well as Newton, Pascal, Leibniz, Galileo, and especially of empiricists and rationalists, namely John Locke's and Rene Descartes's philosophical works.

Actually, rationalism and empiricism were the most important and, at the same time, countervailing philosophies of the seventeenth century, the former emphasising reason and innate ideas, whereas the latter highlighting experience and rejecting tradition and innate knowledge. The work entitled *Essay Concerning the Human Understanding* (1690) by John Locke (1632-1704), with its concern with the foundation of human knowledge and understanding, and the theory of the human mind/spirit as *tabula rasa* ("blank slate") filled later through the experience, represented one of the main sources of the empiricist school of thought in modern philosophy.

Empiricism departs radically from the rationalism of Descartes, but it influenced many British Enlightenment philosophers, such as David Hume and George Berkeley, and many writers and theoreticians of neoclassicism, such as Alexander Pope and Samuel Johnson. It also influenced the men of letters in later periods, such as William Wordsworth in whose poetry the development of the human/poet's mind is a major thematic perspective. It was not until the twentieth century that Locke's doctrine was rejected by Carl Jung and other philosophers who developed new theories of the abstract manifestations of the mind, pre-established forms of psychic behaviour, collective memory, and archetypes.

Thinkers commonly associated with empiricism are Bacon, Locke, Hobbes, Bayle, Berkeley, Hume, and others who developed a philosophy of science which emphasises the role of the experience, in particular the experience of the senses. According to this philosophy, the acquisition of the scientific knowledge and the formation of ideas are possible only through sensory perception, experiment, evidence, and the testing of all theories. These philosophers reject the role of simple observation, a priori reasoning, instinct, and intuition, and promote a scientific application which is methodologically empirical in its essence. Locke, Berkeley and Hume are three great empiricists excelling mainly in the field of epistemology, but, although contemporaries, they did not cooperate and remained different within one movement in philosophy. Similarly, at the beginning of the twentieth century, one would find Pierce, James and Dewey as the three distinct and contemporary voices of another movement in philosophy, which is pragmatism.

Empiricism, a philosophy representing originally Great Britain, opens with Francis Bacon, the guiding spirit of the scientific revolution, writing on all the sciences, philosophy, politics, law, ethics, and other topics, a total of more than seventy works. In *The Advancement of Learning*, dedicated to King James I, Bacon expresses his belief in the perpetual renovation of knowledge and argues that "science can no longer be derived from the books of Aristotle and Pliny but must result from first-hand observation and experiment. Instead of being isolated, scientific disciplines should cross-fertilize each other" (Vickers 163).

Bacon declares science to be the greatest force and the experience to be the only foundation of science. It implies the acquiring of knowledge through the inductive method, which is outlined in the *Novum Organum* and which means the development of general laws starting from the observation of particular facts. This new method of scientific thinking, argues Bacon, would be "free of the prejudices of the past and the received affections of the present (characterised as the "Idols" of the Tribe, the Cave, the Market Place, and the Theatre)" (Sanders 189).

Likewise, Sir Isaac Newton (1642-1727), in his *Philosophiae Naturalis Principia Mathematica* (1687), rejects whatever imaginative activity and promotes the scientific experimentation related to the method of induction. Induction is a way of reasoning which, as for Bacon, makes possible "the deduction of an observation out of particular cases of the general laws" (Graf 25).

Opposed by empiricism, but of equal value, was the influence of the philosophical work of René Descartes (1596-1650), also known as Renatus Cartesius (the Latinized form of his name). A highly influential French philosopher, scientist and mathematician, Descartes represents together with Baruch de Spinoza and Gottfried Leibniz the seventeenth century European rationalism. Descartes's most important philosophical writings are *Discourse on Method* (1637), *Meditations on First Philosophy* (also known as *Metaphysical Meditations*, 1641), and *Principles of Philosophy* (1644). In his philosophical work, in particular in *Meditations on First Philosophy*, Descartes aims at developing a fundamental set of principles that one can know as true without any doubt. The method employed is the so-called "methodological scepticism", by which he rejects any idea that can be doubted in order to acquire a firm foundation for genuine knowledge. The only unshakable knowledge is that man is a "thinking thing".

Thinking is the essence of the human being, as it is the only aspect about him that cannot be doubted and the only activity of which he is immediately conscious of. Descartes defines *cogitatio* ("thought") as "what happens in me such that I am immediately conscious of it, insofar as I am conscious of it". By what is known as the "wax argument", Descartes shows the limitations of the senses and proves that one should use his mind to properly grasp the nature of an object or phenomenon, concluding that "what I thought I had seen with my eyes, I actually grasped solely with the faculty of judgment, which is in my mind".

In his system of knowledge, Descartes rejects the sensory perception as unreliable and admits deduction and reason as the only reliable methods of attaining knowledge that takes the form of ideas, and the philosophical investigation is the contemplation of these ideas. The first item of undoubtable knowledge that Descartes argues for is *cogito*, or thinking thing, and the first principle Descartes arrives at is one of his most famous statements, which is *cogito ergo sum* ("I think, therefore I am"). Other famous statements by Descartes are *ex nihilo nihil fit* ("nothing comes out of nothing") and *dubium sapientiae initium* ("doubt is the origin of wisdom").

At the time when Descartes discovered rationalism, reason, cold calculation, mind, and the consciousness of *ego cogito*, there were voices that turned to heart and feeling, as Blaise Pascal did by discovering "the logic of the heart as over against the logic of calculating reason" (Heidegger 127). Indeed, Pascal, mainly acclaimed as mathematician, physicist, and philosopher, is also remembered for having opposed both rationalism and empiricism. By contrast to them, in order to determine the major truths in life, Pascal suggests a system in which, according to Heidegger,

> the inner and invisible domain of the heart is not only more inward than the interior that belongs to calculating representation, and therefore more invisible; it also extends further than does the realm of merely producible objects. Only in the invisible innermost of the heart is man inclined toward what there is for him love: the forefathers, the dead, the children, those who are to come. (Heidegger 127-128)

Due to his philosophical system based on the method of systematic doubt, Descartes is called the founder of the modern theory of knowledge, and as such he influenced much of his contemporary and of the later periods European philosophical thought, starting from Spinoza to Russell.

Although accepting the influence of some earlier Jewish philosophy, many scholars have considered the philosophical work of Baruch de Spinoza (1632-1677) to be the continuation or further development of Descartes. Indeed, the only work published during his lifetime, *Principles of Descartes's Philosophy* is an exposition of Descartes's philosophy in geometrical order. Spinoza has been acclaimed by some and condemned by others for his *Ethics*, a philosophical book published after his death, which, although rooted in many of Descartes's conclusions, is in many respects a rather original work presenting Spinoza's own thought. Rationalist, rigorous, deductive, and materialist, Spinoza develops his own metaphysical system, his own views of Cod, creation, nature, structure of the world, idea and body, mind and matter, cause and substance, and above all, his moral doctrine aimed at salvation of man and the nature of society.

Another seventeenth century philosopher who studied and assimilated Descartes's philosophy was Gottfried Wilhelm von Leibniz (1646-1716). In his work, one finds the same emphasis on reason and rationalism, the principle of order, the similarity between logic and mathematics, and the connection of his metaphysics with his logic, which is the great merit of his philosophical system. The distinction between two types of statements is at the centre of Leibniz's philosophy: first, those which are necessarily true and are established as true only by reference to the principle of non-contradiction, and, second, those called "contingent statements", which cannot be established as true by the principle of non-contradiction alone. Also, at the centre of Leibniz's system is the attempt to define such concepts as Identity, Subject, Necessity, Truth, Knowledge, Existence, and others. The discussion of these notions is organized in such a way as

> to allow a place for a benevolent God who has freely created a world which is entirely intelligible. The world that God has created must exhibit a few universal principles of order, which ought to guide us in framing hypotheses to explain phenomena; for we have in metaphysics an assurance that the actual world is the most rationally ordered of all possible worlds. (Hampshire 146)

In the same way, Alexander Pope, the most important representative of English neoclassicism in the eighteenth century, would declare in his *An Essay on Man* that the actual world is perfect in its rational organization and that humans fail to see its perfection due to their limited vision.

1.3 The Idea of Literature as a Critical Concern in the Seventeenth Century

The advancement of philosophy in the seventeenth century was matched by the further development of literary theory and criticism which largely came under the auspicious of a particular theory of art called "classicism" throughout the Continent and "neoclassicism" with reference to English literature and other arts.

English neoclassicism was mainly influenced by French ideas of the period, France being actually the country that institutionalized classicism in the second half of the seventeenth century and became the most important cultural influence in Europe.

Thus, apart from theoretical input from both empiricists and rationalists, both John Locke's and Rene Descartes's philosophical works, as well as that from Bacon, Hobbes, Spinoza, and Leibniz, of equal importance to the consolidation of the neoclassical doctrine in Britain were the leading French ideas from, among others, *L'Art Poétique* (1674) by Nicolas Boileau-Despréaux and *Réflexions sur la poétique d'Aristote et sur les ouvrages des poètes anciens et modernes* (1673) by Rene Rapin. Rapin's work was translated into English by Thomas Rymer (1641-1713), himself a man of letters who, in the Preface to the translation, exalts Aristotelian rules and defends the neoclassical position. Also, by reference to ancient models, Rymer performs a more textual examination of the works of Fletcher and Beaumont, in *The Tragedies of the Last Age* (1678), and later of Shakespeare.

It is his view that Shakespeare's *Othello* might be improved if the words are left out that made Rymer be rejected by fellow-writers and receive harsh replies, as from the contemporary satirical poet Samuel Butler (1613-1680). Another reply to Rymer, this time to his *Short View of Tragedy*, came from John Dennis (1657-1734) in *The Impartial*

Critic (1693). In the general context of the period's reverence for the classics, Dennis argues that a "strict adherence to Greek practices which were closely linked to the religious and cultural notions of the day would be an absurdity in modern drama" (Blamires 122).

Sir William Temple (1628-1699) in *Miscellanea, Of Poetry* (1690) and William Wotton (1666-1726) in *Reflections Upon Ancient and Modern Learning* (1694) also acclaim the achievements of the ancients but exhibit a certain degree of reserve regarding their strict imitation and the total dependence of modern literature on them. The blind admiration for the classics must be replaced by a true, more rational appreciation of their works. Also, Temple replies to the "rigid claims for the Aristotelian rules made by French critics such as Boileau and Rapin" and argues that the most "that can be claimed for rules is that they might prevent some men from becoming bad poets without helping anyone to become a good one. It is by the power of the poet to work on your feelings that can be judged" (Blamires 112).

Boileau influenced Alexander Pope, the most important representative of neoclassicism in English literature representing the Augustan Age of the first half of the eighteenth century, but the mastermind of literary criticism in the seventeenth century, particularly in its last decades called "Restoration period", is John Dryden, who can be truly called the founder or at least promoter of neoclassicism in English literature, although unlike both Boileau and Pope, Dryden would be more flexible with rules and prescriptions, nationalistically focus on English dramatic heritage and allow for experimentation and freedom of artistic expression.

1.3.1 The English "Battle of the Books" or "La Querelle des Anciens et des Modernes" in the European Context

According to Edgar Allan Poe, Boileau is a "French Horace", and indeed the classical views of Boileau and Rapin are anything but original. Their ideas are largely an extension of those of Horace and Renaissance critics, but Boileau and Rapin express an attitude of measure, common sense, reverence for rules, the concepts of "human nature" and "decorum", imitation of the ancient poets, and worship of reason better than anyone in the period, as Boileau states in his *Art of Poetry*:

> Whatever you write of pleasant or sublime,
> Always let sense accompany your rime;
> Falsely they seem each other to oppose, -
> Rime must be made with reason's laws to close;
> And when to conquer her you bend your force,
> The mind will triumph in the noble course; (...)
> Love reason then, and let whatever you write
> Borrow from her its beauty, force and light.

The *Art of Poetry* has remained one of the best known works of critical writing, especially where and when the classical spirit is concerned and promoted. All the main tenets of the neoclassical doctrine are to be found here, including the ideal of reason, strict rules of composition, decorum, urbanism, didacticism, and above all the imitation of the ancients, who portrayed human nature in the best possible way. In general, European culture has become centralised in France and with French contribution and France as its main source, in particular with the foundation of the French Academy in 1635 and the courses taught at the Academy, the classical ideas are dominant and classicism is now an institutionalised cultural doctrine throughout Europe.

Following the example of the French Academy, similar institutions were founded in Berlin (1696) and Vienna (1702), and around 1790, throughout Europe, there were more than one hundred academies of fine arts. But for the most of the period, the Paris Academy remained to be the institutional guide for the European artistic movement and critical thinking. However, the seventeenth and eighteenth centuries saw classicism being attacked by the "moderns", who challenged the view that writers should admire and imitate the great ancient Greek and Latin models because civilization had not produced anything better or more excellent to surpass the great classical tradition.

The main arguments of the moderns against the rule of the classics, as set forth and explained by Gilbert Highet, are (1) "the ancients were pagan; we are Christians. Therefore our poetry is inspired by nobler emotions and deals with nobler subjects. Therefore it is better poetry"; (2) "Human knowledge is constantly advancing. We live in a later age (…) therefore we are wiser. Therefore anything we write, or make, is better than the things written and made by the ancient Greeks and Romans"; (3) "Nature does not change (…) therefore the works of men are as good to-day as they were in classical times"; and (4) the works of the classics "were badly written and fundamentally illogical" (Highet 261-288).

The attacks on art and literature of the classical writers agitated the spirits of the literary world and initiated the conflict between the defenders of the classics (Dacier, Racine, Boileau), who created a deeper understanding of ancient literature and expanded the literary traditions of the Renaissance, and the "moderns" (Tassoni, de Saint-Sorlin, Perrault), who argued that modern literature possesses aesthetic values as high as those of the classical Greece and Rome.

The conflict is remembered as "the battle of the books" and "la querelle des anciens et des modernes". It is just one battle in the war between tradition and innovation, between authority and originality, between classicism and modernism. The war started in Antiquity, was reinforced in the Renaissance, peaked in France and then throughout Europe at the turn of the seventeenth century and is still going on. In English literature, this conflict was remarkably captured by the neoclassical man of letters Jonathan Swift (1667-1745) in his satire on the battle between the ancients and moderns known as *The Battle of the Books* (1704).

Concerning literary practice, the real benefit of the battle for both sides was "that it discouraged slavish respect for tradition, and made it more difficult for future writers to produce "Chinese copies" of classical masterpieces, in which exact imitation should be a virtue and original invention a sin" (Highet 288).

Concerning English critical thought of the period, the outcomes of the conflict in the seventeenth and eighteenth centuries were also beneficial for the development of literary criticism, whose standards improved, and ideas, though sharpened, became more refined. According to Marcie Frank, in the seventeenth century "criticism arises in response to the seventeenth century series of crises in aristocratic culture, and its historical orientation marks its contributions to the modern separation of literature as autonomous from political, legal and historical discourses." But there is no separation whatsoever between literature and criticism.

Like in the previous century, the seventeenth-century criticism remains inseparable from literature, especially from the drama of the period, as "together, both literary and critical discourses seek to distinguish themselves from the body of discourses that share a deep investment in the institution of genealogical inheritance as an authorizing and legitimating activity even as they also rely upon them" (Frank 13). However, after Sidney, there were, unfortunately, no important critical voices to assess the great literary achievements of the Elizabethan and Jacobean periods, and it was only with John Dryden that English literary criticism stood firmly again on its path.

Meanwhile, the history of criticism names John Milton with *Areopagitica* defending poetry and theatre, and the liberty of printing, in general, against Puritan attacks during Commonwealth period. Mention should be also made of an earlier critical endeavour, namely Ben Jonson's (1573-1637) emphasis on rules and decorum in the prologues written to his many plays and in the book *Timber, or Discoveries* (1640). Here Jonson speculates also on Shakespeare and his literary achievement, praising him but also entering polemics on behalf of the newly emerging neoclassical perspectives of measure and common sense: "He [Shakespeare] was (indeed) honest, and of an open, and free nature: had an excellent Phantasy; brave notions, and gentle expressions: wherein he flow'd with that facility, that sometime it was necessary he should be stopp'd".

The history of criticism also mentions a verse survey of English poets by Michael Drayton (1563-1631) entitled *Epistle to Henry Reynolds, Esquire, Of Poets and Poesie* (1627). Reynolds himself is the author of *Mythomystes, Wherein a Short Survey is taken of the nature and value of true Poesie, and depth of the Ancients above our Modern Poets* (1632). Other critics were the royalist refugees in Paris, among whom philosopher Thomas Hobbes and the writers Sir William Davenant (1605-1688) and Abraham Cowley (1618-1667). They came under French influence and contributed in their turn to the development of native critical theories. The most important seventeenth century English critic was John Dryden, of whose many literary and non-literary works the most famous one is the critical treatise *Of Dramatic Poesie, An Essay*, written in dialogue form and derived from Dryden's own practical experience as a playwright in many areas of drama.

1.3.2 Restoration, John Dryden and Prescribing Neoclassicism

In English literary history, the last period of the seventeenth century was the "Restoration Age" between 1660 and 1700, which followed the Puritan rule ("Commonwealth Interregnum") between 1649 and 1660. On the general social level, the "English Renaissance, which had begun as an opening up to new European learning and new European styles, ended as a restrictive puritanical assertion of national independence from European norms of government and aesthetics"; likewise, the "English Reformation, which had begun as an assertion of English nationhood under a monarch who saw himself as head, protector, and arbiter of a national Church, ended as a challenge to the idea of monarchy itself" (Sanders 185).

Following the abolition of monarchy and the subsequent Puritan period, the next period, which is called "Restoration", started from the restoration of the Stuarts (with Charles II) to the throne of England in 1660. This political event gave its name to a period that lasted for about forty years, during which there was a gradual restoration of arts and literature as well, a "second Renaissance" in British culture following the "Dark Ages" of Puritanism, as some critics prefer to call it. However, although "political events do impinge on literature, nowhere more dramatically than in the closing of the theatres in 1642, but the introduction, development, and ultimate decline of literary modes or genres follow their own laws, depending on the innate vitality of form of the inventiveness of the writers using it" (Vickers 160).

The main genre of the Restoration literature was drama, particularly "comedy of manners". Although Restoration drama aimed at reviving the great Renaissance tradition, it changed its both thematic and formal perspectives. Also, "the actors changed, with young women acting the female parts for the first time", "the plays and the audience changed. The audience was now rich, upper-class, young, cynical, and fashionable, at least until the end of the century, and the plays were written to match this audience" (Stephen 51).

Another type of play popular in Restoration was the "heroic drama" or "heroic tragedy", which was developed by Dryden as well as Sir George Etherege and Sir Robert Howard (1626-1698). The latter turns a critic in the prefaces to his plays initiating a controversy with Dryden especially over such a matter as blank verse or rhyme. Their interaction could be summarised in the following: Howard's 1665 preface to *Four New Plays* "replies to Dryden's defence of rhyming verse of drama in his dedicatory epistle to *The Rival Ladies* (1664). Dryden came back to the topic in his *Essay of Dramatic Poesy* (1668). Howard responded in his 1668 preface [to *The Great Favourite, or the Duke of Lerma*], and Dryden rounded off the exchange in his *Defence of an Essay of Dramatic Poesy* (1668)" (Blamires 84). Actually, the preface was the favourite form given by the Restoration writer-critics to their critical commentary on drama, among whom, apart from Howard, being Richard Flecknoe and Thomas Shadwell.

Restoration, the last part of the seventeenth century, is the first of the three parts of the neoclassical period in British literature which lasted until the 1780s. The eighteenth century in general is called the "Age of Enlightenment", and, in English culture, "Enlightenment" and "neoclassicism" cover almost the same period and are almost synonymous, the main difference being that the former is a philosophical movement, whereas the latter refers mainly to literary theory and practice. In rest, similar to the neoclassical movement, the Enlightenment

> celebrated reason, the scientific method, and human being's ability to perfect themselves and their society. It grew out of a number of seventeenth century intellectual attainment: the discoveries of Sir Isaac Newton, the rationalism of Descartes and Pierre Bayle, and the empiricism of Francis Bacon and John Locke. The major champions of its beliefs were the philosophers, who made a critical examination of previously accepted institutions and beliefs from the viewpoint of reason and with confidence in natural laws and universal order. (Holman and Harmon 169)

The beginnings of the Enlightenment and neoclassicism in British cultural background, which took place during the Restoration period as the result of some major Continental influences, were also the direct consequences of some major changes in the native literary taste which occurred in that period. Neoclassical doctrine itself should be regarded primarily as a new literary attitude that came to influence the rise of the English novel in the eighteenth century and to dominate the poetic production. Neoclassicism was actually expressed in poetry for over a hundred years during the late seventeenth century (represented by Dryden) and most of the eighteenth century (dominated by the work of Pope and Johnson).

John Dryden excelled as a poet, dramatist, and literary critic, and it was not in drama but in poetry and, especially, in literary criticism that Dryden established a pattern of writing and a number of theoretical principles which determined the character of neoclassical doctrine and literature in the next century. He created a new style in prose and poetry which influenced, among others, Alexander Pope, the most brilliant writer among the Augustans. One of the major proponents of the classical ideas into England during the Restoration period, John Dryden was the most prolific English writer of the second half of the seventeenth century, but he was chiefly acclaimed for being a prominent literary critic, as Samuel Johnson did in *Prefaces, Biographical and Critical, to the Works of the English Poets*:

> Dryden may be properly considered as the father of English criticism, as the writer who first taught us to determine upon principles the merit of composition. Of our former poets, the greatest dramatist wrote without rules, conducted through life and nature by a genius that rarely misled, and rarely deserted him. Of the rest; those who knew the laws of propriety had neglected to teach them. (…) Two *Arts of English Poetry* were written in the days of Elizabeth by Webb and Puttenham, from which something might be learned, and a few hints had been given by Jonson and Cowley; but Dryden's *An Essay of Dramatic Poesie,* was the first regular and valuable treatise on the art of writing.

This passage shows that Dryden was probably the first to write a treatise, which is *Of Dramatic Poesie, An Essay*, on the art of writing in a systematised way. Dryden's critical masterpiece, which was written to prescribe the ways authors should follow in writing after recovering themselves from Puritanism, also defends and compares English literature in relation to the general European one, and, in particular, to the recent French drama. The work proves the excellence of English literature in the general literary background of Europe. Imitating Plato in its form, Dryden's critical text is written as a fictitious dialogue, a formal debate on drama among four characters placed in a boat on the Thames and hearing the noise of a naval battle, probably an English victory over Dutch army in 1665, which offers a sense of patriotic pride to the context.

Also, in the course of critical debate, the character called Neander ("the new man") – the voice of Dryden himself and as such the defender of English drama – argues in favour of a national, English literary tradition: for instance, when asked by Eugenius, Neander states, at the beginning of his discussion on English playwrights Shakespeare, Beaumont, Fletcher, and Jonson, that in doing so "I shall draw a little envy upon my self", and, after arguing in favour of their value, he claims that "we have as many and profitable Rules for perfecting the Stage as any wherewith the French can furnish us".

Neander represents English literature and defends the native dramatic practice of the recent past, in particular English tragicomedy, as well as the rhymed heroic drama, which Dryden considers to be the greatest achievement of English drama. Apart from Neander, there are three other characters as speakers in the essay. Of course, such debates could not actually take place, but each speaker can be identified with a contemporary person, and certainly each has his own topical concern to discuss and defend in front of all the others.

Crites, whose name suggests a critical mind, and who was modelled after Dryden's collaborator and brother-in-law Sir Robert Howard, defends ancient dramatic tradition and clarifies the rules of the unities of time, place, and action. Eugenius, whose name means "well-born", refers to the famous Cavalier poet Lord Charles Sackville. He defends the moderns against the ancients on the grounds of scientific progress which makes poetry attain greater excellence. Lisideus, whose name is a Latinised anagram of "Sedley", is Sir Charles Sedley; he defends the recent French dramatic practice, which, due to Richelieu's protection of arts, has reached almost perfection by championing rules, measure, and order, and by using rhyme instead of blank verse. For Lisideius, and for Dryden himself, ancient theories are no less viable. For instance, Lisideius defines a play as "a just and lively image of human nature, representing its passions and humours, and the changes of fortune to which it is subject; for the delight and instruction of mankind". The first part of the definition clearly derives from Aristotle's *Poetics* and the last clause derives from Horace's *Ars Poetica*.

The perspective of binary oppositions – moderns against ancients (Eugenius versus Crites) and English against French (Neander versus Lisideius) – is congenial for embarking on a critical debate about drama in general, types of drama, and thematic and structural particularities of drama from four different perspectives.

However, Neander turns from a general discussion and defence of English drama to a critical, and, at certain moments, comparative appreciation of Renaissance playwrights, in particular Shakespeare and Jonson. Dryden first considers Fletcher and Beaumont, but briefly, his main attention being devoted to Shakespeare and Jonson. For Dryden, Shakespeare has "the largest and most comprehensive soul"; he is naturally gifted, the greatest of all writers, following in general but also breaking some of the Aristotelian and Horatian "rules", and thus combining in his works both the innovative spirit of the Renaissance and the revival of ancient classical models. When compared to Shakespeare, Jonson is "the most learned and judicious writer" which any theatre ever had, and, being "deeply conversant in the Ancients, both Greek and Latin", Jonson borrowed boldly from the ancient writers and faithfully followed the classical doctrine. Related to Jonson, these characteristics emerge clearly as some of the main principles of neoclassicism. Finally, when comparing the two playwrights, Dryden concludes that Jonson is "the more correct Poet, but Shakespeare the greater wit. Shakespeare was the Homer or father of our dramatic poets; Jonson was the Virgil, the pattern of elaborate writing; I admire him, but I love Shakespeare".

In the Restoration period, following the Puritan Commonwealth, Dryden defined drama as "a just and lively image of human nature" and assumed in his critical text the task to defend and revive English drama. In this respect, the task means to prescribe the future ways of literary development based on great predecessors, on the best dramatic tradition of Renaissance playwrights, namely Shakespeare and Jonson. Dryden is on the side of the moderns who have excelled the ancients in tragedy.

In *A Discourse Concerning the Original and Progress of Satire* (1693), Dryden claims that the moderns have excelled the ancients in satire as well. This work is considered inferior to his *Essay* for being his "longest piece of criticism" which, of all his works, "is the most heavily loaded with scholarship: all second-hand and acknowledged" (Sambrook 89).

As Restoration marked the beginnings of neoclassicism in English literature, Dryden's contribution to this was immense, and he is commonly approached as the first of English neoclassicists. Dryden was the most prolific author of the Restoration, truly a writer-critic who "embodies the spirit and ideas of the neoclassical period, the literary age that follows Sidney and the Renaissance" (Bressler 31).

Apart from being theoretical, Dryden's literary criticism reveals a relative fidelity to classics of a critic who may be considered to be "a pragmatic or liberal neoclassical critic", since he accepts the theoretical patronage of Aristotle and Horace, but allows for exceptions and agrees with those moderns who feel "free to improve upon it [the ancient model] when situation demands" (Dutton 36). Still, Dryden remains in spirit neoclassical, invoking in his defensive and prescriptive criticism the ancient classical "authorities" with their prescriptions and rules.

One may notice Dryden's adherence to classical inheritance in his admiration for Jonson and his thorough critical appreciation of Jonson, as compared to the more general and superficial one of Shakespeare, which shows that for Dryden Jonson is a kind of prototype found in the Renaissance of a complete neoclassical man, whose plays should be taken as models of dramatic writing. Dryden's *Of Dramatic Poesie, An Essay*, with its dramatic structure and critical focus on particular writers and literary works – the treatise also revealing the major aspects of the ancient Greek and Latin, and the modern English and French drama – appears to be less theoretical than practical in a period (Restoration) of consolidation of neoclassical principles that were to dominate English art and criticism for over a century preceding the rise of romanticism in the 1780s.

In this celebrated critical work, John Dryden combined dramatic expression and practical criticism, and pleaded for European recognition of his native literature and for the synchronization of British with the general European literature. He clearly prescribed to his fellow writers the classical and contemporary, in particular French, doctrines to be followed in thought and Elizabethan drama of Shakespeare and Jonson to be revived and the contemporary European models to be imitated in literature.

The next eighteenth century highly valued Dryden's contribution to critical writing, being considered by Dr Samuel Johnson to be the best English literary critic. Although in some degree neglected by romanticism and its aftermath, in the twentieth century, T. S. Eliot, another great writer-critic, praises Dryden and considers his work to be "the first serious literary criticism in English by an English poet"; likewise, David Daiches, another important critic, considers Dryden to be "the true father of English practical criticism".

Like in earlier periods, in the seventeenth century, including the Restoration period, and later throughout the eighteenth century, criticism was still far from focusing on particular authors and texts, that is, far from dealing with literature as we understand nowadays what the aims and concerns of literary criticism ought to be.

Instead, the criticism of these centuries, "based on classical models, dealt mainly with literature-related theoretical prescriptiveness" and the issue of genres (Urnov 5).

The privileged ones remained to be poets; dramatists were placed next to them, whereas the rising in the eighteenth century novelists were disconsidered. Dryden debated on drama. Addison wrote on tragedy, lyric and epic poetry, and on imagination and literature in general. Johnson wrote his *Lives of the Poets* in such a manner as if there were no contemporary novelists, even though Johnson himself played with fiction in *Rasselas* and showed a high estimate for this genre.

There was then the task assumed by the practitioners, the novelists themselves (Defoe, Richardson, and Fielding), to evaluate their own writings and promote them as a new and distinct genre of novel. Apart from these critical perspectives, there were also debates on ancients and moderns as a "battle of the books" (Reynolds, Temple, and Swift), on morality and literature (Mulgrave, Wolseley, Collier, and Congreve), on beauty in poetry (Hutcheson), and on the status and subjects of poetry (Thomson). Criticism assumed also other tasks, such as to advocate and institutionalize neoclassicism (Dryden, Pope, and Johnson), or the rejection of neoclassicism (Warton, Young, and Lowth), and even the concern with the status and role of the critic and criticism (Addison, Pope, and Hume).

The diversity of critical concerns paralleled the diversity of the form of the critical texts, ranging from verse and dialogue to essay and preface. Amid general theorisation and abstract debates on literary issues, there were some concerns with particular writers, such as Peacham, Dryden, Dennis, Johnson, and Fielding.

John Dryden, who introduced the term "criticism" as early as 1677, represents, after Sir Philip Sidney, the second important step forward in the history of English literary criticism with his *Of Dramatic Poesie, An Essay*. Among other things, Dryden succeeds to employ a variety of critical perspectives from ancient to contemporary French and unite them under the form of a natural, almost modern prose style. Above all, Dryden avoids the moral or theological assessment of literature and focuses on the literary practice of certain writers, in particular the comparative assessment of Shakespeare and Jonson, a recurrent theme in literary criticism, whom he prescribes as literary models.

In the eighteenth century, the theoretical principles of neoclassicism enjoyed their highest reputation as set forth by Alexander Pope in prefaces, *An Essay on Criticism*, and *An Essay on Man*. Alexander Pope was the dominant figure among neoclassical writers, his theoretical contribution and poetical practice exemplifying in the best way neoclassical optimism, self-confidence, and urbanism in an age pleased with its civilization. Pope also aptly expresses neoclassical emphasis on reason, order, common sense, rules in the creation of poetry, and imitation of the classics and the laws of nature, as we can see in *An Essay on Criticism* and *An Essay on Man*. The former reveals, actually, Pope's status as a neoclassical literary critic, but, being written by Pope in his earliest years of literary activity, this work does not provide an original contribution to literary theory, except the fact that it is addressed to critics and that it combines in one poetic discourse the theoretical ideas of neoclassical doctrine with the creation of a literary, poetic text based on such ideas.

This is also the principle of composition of a more original work which is the philosophical poem *An Essay on Man*. Like the previous one, this work displays Pope's alliance to neoclassical doctrine and the principles of "imitate the classics" and "follow the nature", as well as his wide knowledge and intellectual brightness combined with a dynamic literary expression.

During the neoclassical period, the most important and influential critical voices belong to Dryden and Pope, who, together with Johnson, are the true theoreticians and practitioners of neoclassicism, aiming at defining the present and future ways of English poetry by offering prescriptive definitions, which makes their criticism, apart from a reflection of the neoclassical mentality, to be also normative and prescriptive.

2.

THE LITERARY BACKGROUND

> ***Keywords*:** drama, Ben Jonson, Baroque, metaphysical poetry, conceit, wit, imagery, persuasion, argument, "feeling thought", Puritan period, Restoration period, drama, comedy of manners, heroic drama, picaresque narrative, *The Pilgrim Progress*

The writers of this revolutionary age became directly involved in the major contemporary historical and religious experiences and reflected in their writings the turbulent world they lived in, making politics and religion important aspects of their literary concern. Structurally and thematically, the writers treated their concern by developing new formulas and genres, such as metaphysical poetry or Restoration "heroic drama" and "comedy of manners", or rather taking older established forms, such as ode, sonnet, or pastoral poetry, and rewriting and revising the forms to express new and often controversial views on their world.

An example for the concern with political issues would be the imitation of the classical ode by Marvell to review contemporary political events (the rising of the Parliamentary party, the Civil War, and the execution of Charles I) that led to Oliver Cromwell's emergence as the country's leader in *An Horatian Ode: Upon Cromwell's Return from Ireland*.

An example for the religious concern would be the use of sonnet by Donne and Milton, which reveals the transformation of the purpose of the sonnet from a simple vehicle to express the lover's passion to a complex formula that could be used to worship God, render Protestant theology and religious fervour, in general, along personal anguish and pain of the poet, his own fears about time and life.

2.1 The British Seventeenth Century and Its Literary Practice

The literature of the seventeenth century in Britain, in particular between 1620s and 1690s, is generally considered in three main directions: the metaphysical poetry revealing the flourishing of the Baroque in British literature, the literature of the Puritan period, and the literature of the Restoration period.

Although the "Baroque Age" in the literature of Western Europe and Britain is considered to cover the period between 1580s and 1680s, which is between the decline of the Renaissance and the rise of the Enlightenment, and Puritanism developed in England from around the middle of the sixteenth century to its end in 1660, whereas the "Restoration Age" embraced the second half of the seventeenth century from 1660 to around 1700, the attempt at conceiving an exact outline of the literary history in Britain considers that metaphysical poetry flourished mainly in the first half of the seventeenth century, Puritanism reached its apogee in the middle of the century between 1649 and 1660, and Restoration as a literary period covers the second half of the century following the restoration of the Stuarts to English throne in 1660.

However, in the context of the entire seventeenth century it is difficult if not impossible to regard the three directions as clearly succeeding each other and to establish their precise dates, or rather it is inappropriate to do so, since, for instance, though Renaissance is considered to have ended with the death of Shakespeare in 1616, the great Renaissance writer Ben Jonson produced literary works reflecting classical models and therefore extending the Renaissance emphasis on ancient classical tradition until his death in 1637. His works co-existed with the metaphysical poetry of John Donne, which shows the co-existence in the period of traditional and innovative elements in literature. Similarly, the great metaphysical writer Andrew Marvell, whose spirit was largely Puritan, continued writing literary works until his death in 1678 though metaphysical poetry is considered to have ended as a regular trend by the middle of the century. Also, the Puritan poet John Milton's *Lycidas* came in 1637 in the metaphysical period and his greatest works came in the 1660s and 1670s in the Restoration period which exercised a strong reaction against Puritanism. In the case of these writers as well as of many others, the mere chronology could be disregarded.

In most general terms, the Baroque period succeeded the classical style of Renaissance and expressed the innovative spirit in art, manifesting itself mainly in the first half of the seventeenth century in English literature as metaphysical poetry. On the other hand, according to the view that Renaissance in England, unlike in the rest of Europe, lasted until the middle of the seventeenth century, one would consider metaphysical poetry to be the last phase of British Renaissance, its last manifestation of literary innovation, a literary extravaganza co-existing and conflicting with the classical style and later being rejected and suppressed by the rising neoclassicism.

The dominant poetic figures of this first half of the century were John Donne – with his intellectually ingenious love and religious verses representing metaphysical poetry – and Ben Jonson, with his drama and poetry modelled after classical tradition. Many of the later seventeenth-century poets were classified, again inappropriately, as disciples of either Donne (the "School of Donne") or Jonson (the "Sons of Ben"), that is, as followers of either metaphysical innovation or traditional classical models.

The first half of the seventeenth century preceding the Puritan period is dominated by the genre of poetry next to which being drama but it is this period that saw also some minor prose writers and some poets of secondary to metaphysical position in the history of British literature. But prose writings such as the philosophical work *Leviathan* by Thomas Hobbes and the prose fiction *The Pilgrim's Progress* by John Bunyan take prose of the period onto the level of high aesthetic esteem.

Other authors of prose works are Robert Burton (1577-1640), an Oxford scholar, once famous for his vast *Anatomy of Melancholy* (1621), a compendium of both scientific and literary information; Jeremy Taylor (1613-1667), a clergyman in the Church of England and writer of *Holy Living* (1650) and *Holy Dying* (1651) which made him be known as "Shakespeare of Divines"; and Izaak Walton (1593-1683), a London tradesman and student, and the author of *The Compleat Angler* (1653) and of the brief lives of John Donne, George Herbert, and other contemporaries.

Along with biography, autobiography emerges as a very important seventeenth-century genre with some 200 works composed as compared to only 14 in the previous century. Autobiography, sparked off also by the Calvinist-Puritan stress on calling the self to account, marks the rise of self-disclosure and self-analysis in a confessional manner. A famous religious autobiography would be *Grace Abounding to the Chief of Sinners* (1666) by John Bunyan, in which the reader follows a conventional "conversion narrative" consisting of calling, conversion, and ministry, which is a narrative of the self passing through temptation and liberation, failure and success as to discover the "love and mercy of God" and transcend struggles into success and ecstasy. A more secular autobiography is *Religio medici* (1643) by Sir Thomas Browne (1605-1682), a more self-centred narrative, but his experience is attempted to be idiosyncratic rather than exemplary; also, concerning its text, sentences and paragraphs are constructed on the principle of parataxis rather than hypotaxis.

Drama would be a strong literary presence on literary scene in the second half of the seventeenth century during Restoration in the form of the comedy of manners, whereas until 1640s, a very popular type of this genre was the masque, encouraged by Queen Anne of Denmark, the king's wife, who was also an active participant. A type of courtly entertainment, the masque would be performed by the court for the court glorifying the nobility and monarchy. The status of Ben Jonson contributed to its popularity too, the playwright being responsible for 21 of 33 main masques performed at court between 1605 and 1640, among which his *Pleasure Reconciled to Virtue* (1618) in which *virtus* and *voluptas* as opposites come together at the Twelfth Night. Other authors of masque were Chapman and Beaumont. Essentially a drama piece, the masque goes actually beyond the limits of the literary work and represents a remarkable union of genres: apart from text (by writers), it includes music (by composers), dance (by choreographs), and stages sets (by architects).

Concerning the lyric poetry, apart from the great metaphysical poets John Donne and George Herbert, there were some minor poets who continued writing until the second decade of the seventeenth century and later. These poets followed the Elizabethan spirit in poetry until the separation occurred between the literature of the age of Elizabeth and that of the reign of James I and Charles I, and the Elizabethan style was replaced by the metaphysical more self-conscious artistry of intellect.

Among those who kept the Elizabethan idealism alive in poetry was Thomas Campion (1567-1620), a physician and poet who composed both words and music for several song-books; Michael Drayton (1563-1631), once acclaimed for his spiritual, pastoral and historical poems; and the Scotch poet William Drummond of Hawthornden (1585-1649), known for his pamphlets as well as elegies showing the influence of Spenser's and Sidney's pastoralism. Another poet of the period, who continued the pastoral form and whose writings *Britannia's Pastorals* (1613) and *The Shepherd's Pipe* (1614) were influenced by Spenser, was William Browne (c.1590-1645).

Ben Jonson, who continued writing drama and non-dramatic poetry at the beginning of the seventeenth century, shows in both genres the revival of the classical spirit. His lyric poetry is less emotional then intellectual, emphasising the strength of mind in the manner of the epistles and satires of Horace, as well as the classical virtues of common sense, clearness, brevity, proportion, and rejection of all excess. These qualities appear also in the lyrics which abound in the plays of the Jacobean playwright John Fletcher (1579-1625), who collaborated with Francis Beaumont (1584-1616) until Beaumont's retirement and early death in 1616. Fletcher continued working, both singly and in collaboration with other writers, producing until his death about fifty plays which, by the middle of the 1610s, secured him a popularity equal to that of Shakespeare, influenced the tragicomic writings of his contemporaries, and remained a major part of the King's Men's repertory until the closing of the theatres in 1642.

A more devoted to classicism poet and a better disciple of Ben Jonson was Robert Herrick (1591-1674), a true member of the "Sons of Ben". They were also known as "royalists" or "Cavalier Poets", a group of writers attached to Court, who admired and imitated the works of Jonson but who could also imitate Donne. Herrick's literary reputation rests on *Hesperides*, a collection of secular lyric poetry, and *Noble Numbers*, a collection of religious lyrics. Other cavalier poets, active mainly before the Civil War, were Thomas Carew (1595-1640), Sir John Suckling (1609-1642), Colonel Richard Lovelace (1618-1659), George Wither (1588-1667), and others who followed the classical principles of Jonson in poems that also owed much of their facile and light-hearted spirit, devoted to the poetic treatment of conventional love relations, to the great school of British metaphysical poets. Suckling, for example, more attached to Donne, could imitate both, just like Lovelace. Other poets and writers are Edmund Waller (1606-1687), Abraham Cowley (1618-1667), Sir William Davenant (1605-1688), Samuel Butler (1613-1680, epic writer in *Hudibras*, 1663), Richard Crashaw (1612-1649), and Thomas Traherne (1637-1674), famous for his poems but especially his prose work *Centuries of Meditations* which contains meditations, confession, autobiography, and didactic treatise.

Apart from the co-existence of innovation of the metaphysical poetry and tradition of the revived classical models, or John Donne versus Ben Jonson, dominating the literary scene in the first half of the seventeenth century, the rest of the century saw the literature of the Puritan period and that of Restoration, as well as the further Continental and English advancement of the genre of prose.

Puritanism was a religious and then political movement (culminating in the mid-century Interregnum) rather than a literary one, though it had some – negative rather than positive – repercussions on literary development in Britain and then in America. The literary expression of the Puritan outlook is better revealed in the works of Andrew Marvell and John Milton, and both are also to a lesser or greater extent under the influence of both the metaphysical innovation and classical tradition.

Restoration as a literary period – following the political event of the restoration of monarchy in England in 1660 – reveals the revival of drama, the receptiveness to contemporary French influences and the consolidation of the dominance of classical principles, in consequence being seen as a period reflecting the beginnings of neoclassicism in Britain, as the first phase of English neoclassicism whose dominant literary figure is John Dryden.

With regard to literary genre, the century on the whole keeps the balance between the three main genres of poetry, drama, and prose with their various subgenres or subtypes such as satire, epic, comedy, picaresque, sonnet, and so on, as to exhibit a decline of drama, supremacy of poetry, particularly the metaphysical poem, and the advancement of novel, particularly the picaresque one.

Important subgenres or literary species include satire and epigram in verse, pastoral play and tragicomedy in drama, and essay, paradox, and meditation (mainly religious) in prose. Some of these strengthen the role of tradition, others represent innovation and experimentation; some are borrowed from classical antiquity, others from contemporary French literature – for example, essay from Montaigne – and Italian literature – for instance, paradox from Ortensio Lando.

Such a diversity is impressive and would provide interesting matters of critical concern but there are metaphysical poetry, the Puritan period and its literature, the literature of the Restoration period, and the condition of prose, including picaresque, with their major authors and representative texts, which play the most important roles on the seventeenth-century literary scene and are traditionally subject to individual and more detailed critical attention, as we shall see in the following.

2.2 Metaphysical Poetry, Its Alternatives and Aftermath

The dictionary definition of "metaphysics" refers to a type of theoretical philosophy of being and knowing, and the term "metaphysical" as based on abstract general reasoning, over-subtle and incorporeal. Similarly, the poetry termed "metaphysical" stands for exact and careful thinking, the development of the concept as a poetic image which is explored and extended, and which offers to the reader the intellectual pleasure to discover the hidden meaning in the poem.

The general characteristics of the poetry termed "metaphysical" in the seventeenth-century English literature are considered in relation to the general cultural attitude of the European Baroque. Moreover, in the present state of terminology, "metaphysical" and "Baroque" are accepted as synonyms to describe a period of intense emotional attitudes, complexity and confusion, in which the poetry of John Donne, George Herbert, Henry Vaughan, Richard Crashaw, Abraham Cowley, and Andrew Marvell received the highest level of prominence.

The term "Baroque" (from the old Portuguese noun *barroco* meaning an "irregular pearl") was initially applied to the European architectural style of the late sixteenth century to the early eighteenth century, and then to the literary style during the period between the decline of Renaissance in Europe in the 1580s and the rise of the Enlightenment in the 1680s. In European cultural background, the Baroque poetry was the dominant literary style from the late 1500s to the late 1600s. Its concern with the relation between reality and appearance, its attempt to exceed the rational limits of the background, and especially the general extravagance of its poetic themes and techniques were determined by the Reformation and Counter-Reformation, the conflict between religion and Humanism, the new teachings of science which conditioned a doubt in the validity of appearance, a doubt that expresses itself as an obsessive concern for appearance along with a more general religious and spiritual concern.

By contrast with the classical tradition, the literary concerns of the Baroque poets gave rise to a number of their characteristic strategies, such as the startling conceit, the dramatic contrast, the hyperbole, the concentration of language, the complex syntax, the development of paradoxical argument, and the apparent contradiction in some of amorous poetry in that the sensuous and physical love was treated in most rational terms. Hence the form of irony and ambiguity, and of musical or sculptural effects, and especially the irrational confusion of senses that the poetic style of the Baroque literature may sometimes reveal due to the poet's attempts at exceeding the limits of the background.

Although unified by a creative spirit which rejects the classical tradition, the complexity of concerns of the Baroque poetry makes it not a definite style but a group of poetic styles or trends, one of which is "Marinism", or "Secentismo", founded by Giovan Battista Marino in Italy, and another is "metaphysical", developed by John Donne in England. In this respect, John Donne's poetry belongs at once to the more particular trend which is "metaphysical" as well as to the general classification "Baroque".

"Metaphysical" is the traditional term which came to name a number of English writers of the seventeenth century, who formed a school of poetry which revolted against the conventions of Elizabethan love poetry, in particular the Petrarchan conceit, and their similar methods and thematic concerns allow their consideration within the framework of one literary system, one literary trend, which is the metaphysical trend in British poetry.

Metaphysical poets did not manifest as critical voices whose theories would strengthen the literary validity of their art and confer to it continuity in literary history, as was the case of the poet-critics Wordsworth or Coleridge, for example, regarding the romantic literary practice. There were other writer-critics who acclaimed or, on the contrary, derogated this school of poetry.

The first written mentions of the term have been attributed to John Dryden and Dr. Samuel Johnson, both advocates of the neoclassical principles. The former used the term in derogation to accuse John Donne of affecting "the metaphysics, not only in his satires, but in his amorous verses, where nature only should reign; and perplexes the minds of the fair sex with nice speculations of philosophy, when he should engage their hearts, and entertain them with the softness of love" (*A Discourse Concerning the Original and Progress of Satire*, 1693). The latter, in *Lives of the Poets* (1781), gave to the term its present use to designate a special poetic manner, the critic claiming that "about the beginning of the seventeenth-century appeared a race of writers that may be termed the metaphysical poets" because the images or imagery that they used were relevant to different spheres of experience, such as philosophy, geography, or astronomy.

The present criticism discusses metaphysical poetry in relation to the Baroque style as well as to the Elizabethan one, revealing the existence of both similarities and differences between the general Baroque, the general Elizabethan, and the particular metaphysical. Concerning the concept of love, the metaphysical poets extended the poetic treatment of the experience of love, where Donne, among others, "displays a range of mood more varied and a concept of passion more complex and profound than any of his predecessors". Moreover, continues Margaret Willy, in reaction against "the Petrarchan tradition favoured by Elizabethan sonneteers – the faithful lover for ever pining, prostrate and spurned, at the feet of a disdainful mistress – Donne's love poems often strike a defiantly disenchanted note. Conventional sentiment and diction are displaced by a testy aggressiveness (...). Prosaic adjectives and verbs (...) are paralleled by the audacious conceit (...). Human love is enlarged, intensified, and dignified by its cosmic context, as it echoes and is echoed by the activity of sun and moon, sea and floods, tempest and earthquake, the very air itself" (Kirkpatrick).

The critical tradition from Dryden to present focuses on "imagery", and the characteristic image of the Elizabethan and later Baroque (including metaphysical) poetry is "conceit", which is an extended metaphor or a metaphor which surprises by the apparent dissimilarity of the things compared. Etymologically, conceit is a poetic device which derives from a concept rather than observation, and this use of ingenious intellect, or "wit", to create imagery links actually all the Baroque styles. Two main types of the conceit are often distinguished, namely the "Petrarchan conceit" and the "metaphysical conceit". The latter is also referred to as the "Baroque conceit" by some critics, whereas others consider them as two distinct figures of speech, yet always differentiated from the Petrarchan one.

Highly popular among the sixteenth-century sonneteers, such as Sir Thomas Wyatt and Edmund Spenser, the Petrarchan conceit was an ingenious but exaggerated comparison applied to the beautiful but cold and cruel mistresses, and to the suffering of their worshipful lovers. In his Sonnet 130, Shakespeare parodied some of Petrarchan conceits – "My mistress' eyes are nothing like the sun; / Coral is far more red than her lip's red (...) " – and, in the seventeenth century, Donne and other representatives of the metaphysical school, exploiting the knowledge from philosophical, theological and natural sciences, shifted the comparison in the Petrarchan conceit between the subject and a rose, a garden, a ship, or another object, to the more complex, startling, paradoxical and highly intellectual analogies.

With the metaphysical poets, the conceit had truly become a "concept", or "conception", not a poetic device in itself but an instrument of persuasion, not a simple poetic metaphor but a means of definition in an argument. The metaphysical conceit is conceived less by emotional states than in the mind of the poet, being defined by Dr. Samuel Johnson as "wit", which is "a kind of discordia concors" (Johnson's inversion of Horace's phrase concordia discors, "harmony in discord"), meaning for Johnson "a combination of dissimilar images, or discovery of occult resemblances in things apparently unlike. (...) The most heterogeneous ideas are yoked by violence together."

The metaphysical conceit receives its validity and importance as concept, as a combination of the intellectual with the sensuous, whereas the Baroque conceit emphasises the sensuous level. Compared to the Elizabethan use of the conceit, the metaphysical poets endeavoured to create a more intellectual, less verbal representation of their wit in the text, as in "more matter and less words" desiderate which reveals their attempt to achieve conciseness of expression though it may lead to a certain irregularity and even roughness in versification.

The Elizabethan style of the second half of the sixteenth century, which was highly artificial and rhetorical, gave way in the first half of the seventeenth century to a kind of writing which would approximate the poetic to a more direct, even colloquial speech. In this respect, a major difference in matters of the use of original conceits is that in metaphysical poetry the conceit is used for persuasion, whereas in Elizabethan poetry it is used for decoration.

The metaphysical poems, both religious and erotic, are characterized by concentration and logical coherence; they represent a type of poetry dense with meaning, which focuses on idea or argument, and forces the addressee in the poem and the reader to follow and accept that idea or argument. English metaphysical poets created a learned, argumentative imagery, and achieved in their lyrics a peculiar blend of passion and reason, feeling and mind reconciled in a single act. This peculiar fusion of passion and thought, or "*feeling thought*", as T. S. Eliot put it, is considered to be essential to the reading of metaphysical poetry being one of the essential ingredients of the metaphysical conceit.

The concept of wit together with the use of conceit is central to the metaphysical poetic discourse in which a thought represents an experience and modifies the poet's sensibility. In order to express accurately the experience, metaphysical poets appeal to human mind and analytical thinking rather than to senses, and reveal in their work a great number of characteristic features regarding, on one hand, the themes and subject matter of poetry, and, on the other hand, the style and structural organization of the text.

Concerning the thematic level of a metaphysical text, poets perceive a harmonious pattern of the universe, in relation to which stands the significance of the human experience in its double hypostases: religion and love. The chief subjects are God, love, death, and human frailty, which are expressed and made explicit by the use of *carpe diem* ("seize the day") and *tempus edax* ("devouring time") motifs.

Concerning the style, the main features of the metaphysical poetry are concision and concentration in poetic expression, which means a conscious tendency towards economy in language. The poet is too busy arguing an issue in terms of reason and leaves outside whatever seems irrelevant.

Concerning the techniques of textual organization, there is always in a metaphysical poem an argument upon which the entire text is based. The argument is linked to an idea which is usually stated at the beginning and which is to be developed and explicated step by step in the text. The argument or the need to argue arises from this point at the beginning of the poem, where an actual position or situation is vividly imagined, and an idea about existence or a moment of experience is created. The poet deliberately attempts to explain the idea and persuade the reader, and, in this sense, persuasion is also one of the most important elements in the whole organization of a metaphysical poem. The basic structural devices such as rhythm and metre are also used to enforce the meaning, to express and shape emotions through logical reasoning, their function being "that of a stimulant, not a narcotic to the intellect" (Bennett 18).

Concerning both the thematic and structural levels of the metaphysical poetry and what unites these levels in a coherent poetic discourse is the use of the startling imagery, which is often borrowed from different fields of human experience (philosophy, geography, astronomy, technical and natural sciences). The seventeenth century on the whole was a period of transition characterised by a philosophical, scientific and geographical spirit of enquiry. The new philosophers and scientists displaced an accustomed view on world and bewildered their contemporaries, just as metaphysical poets did by reflecting in their works the ideas and events which had become matters of public interest and imagination. John Donne's *The Good-Morrow*, for instance, refers to the lovers' eyes as hemispheres, and the experience of love is expressed through the images of latitude and longitude, maps, and discoveries of new worlds.

> The images or imagery result from a twofold perspective involving the famous metaphysical wit – representing a means of creating imagery, or the ability of the poet to make apt comparison and to associate ideas in a natural but unusual and striking manner so as to produce surprise joined with pleasure – and the similarly famous metaphysical conceit – representing the textual expression of the wit.

In other words, the conceit results from the poet's use, during aesthetic activity, of the wit in the form of an unusual, much elaborated, audacious and far-fetched comparison, metaphor or simile, with an apparent dissimilarity of the things compared: for example, the souls of parted lovers and the action of the compass in Donne's *A Valediction: Forbidding Mourning*, or, in another of Donne's poems, the flea that, in uniting the blood of lovers, becomes their "marriage bed, and marriage temple".

Both wit and conceit constitute the source and essence of the metaphysical imagery which represents the whole form of a poetical text, and, as such, they create in the reader a surprised recognition of the validity of the relationship presented between seemingly unrelated things.

Conceit, especially, is that poetic device by which metaphysical poets achieve also the reconciliation between thought and passion, the equilibrium between intellect and feeling in which emotion is curbed by the rational, and the rational is illuminated by emotion. The metaphysical conceit appears to be the intellectual equivalent of emotion, the instrument of persuasion in an argument.

A metaphysical poem, however, despite its rational and intellectual argumentation, is not a pure piece of analytical and abstract thinking; its logic of thought goes hand in hand with emotion, and almost every poem starts from a personal experience, there always being a connection between the abstract and the concrete, a unique blend of reason and passionate imagination. It is this blend that underlies the unity of existence, where, Joan Bennett observes, "the same flame that lights the intellect warms the heart; mathematics and love obey one principle (…) one law is at work in all experience" (144).

The metaphysical texts, as lyric poems, represent brief but intense meditations, characterised by the striking use of wit, irony and wordplay. Beneath the formal organization, containing stanza form, rhyme and metre, is the underlying structure of the argument in the poem, which reveals that metaphysical poetry is concerned with the poet's personal experience – intelligent, scholarly, serious – as well as with the whole experience of man, or rather with the profound areas of human experience such as art, learning, relation with God, pleasure, romantic and sensual love, and others.

The term "metaphysical" was first used derogatorily; the conceit was thought to be far-fetched; the poetic expression was regarded as impudent colloquialism; and metaphysical poetry on the whole was viewed in its own and later periods with disapprobation and complaint. Metaphysical poetry was restored to its dignity and its true literary value was fully asserted at the beginning of the twentieth century by, among others, Thomas Stearns Eliot in his essays on the seventeenth-century English poetry (in particular, in *The Metaphysical Poets*, 1921). Eliot himself, as well as William Butler Yeats and Ezra Pound, as representatives of the twentieth-century modernism, found in the metaphysical poetry a kind of literature which marked the transition to modern sensibility, and a kind of poetry capable of expressing a large range of experience, feeling, and thought on the basis of its experimental attempts to free the poetic discourse from any restriction imposed by the poetical conventions. They saw metaphysical poetry as being difficult, and this difficulty, thinks T. S. Eliot, is very much comparable to that of modernist poetry which considers the complexity of our world and the variety of aspects of human experience – in this respect, reasons Eliot, the "poets of the seventeenth-century possessed a mechanism of sensibility which could devour any kind of experience".

The chief developers of the metaphysical trend in British poetry are John Donne, George Herbert, Andrew Marvell, Richard Crashaw, and Henry Vaughan (1621-1695), whose subtle, ironic, mysterious and distinct love and religious lyrics represent the best English literary records of intelligent, acute and sensitive minds that were able to achieve the fusion of feeling and reason, passion and thought, which are reconciled in a single act of poetic discourse.

Some poets, like Donne and Marvell, wrote both love and religious poetry; others, like Herbert, were almost exclusively religious poets. In all cases, however, they attempted to achieve poetic innovation and experiment with both subject-matter and method.

A country priest, Herbert, as a religious poet, in most of his 167 poems, which were published as the collection *The Temple* after his death in 1633, speaks about the relationship between the individual and God, where separation from divinity brings confusion, frustration and alienation, as in *Denial*. More often, his poems end in a sense of hope and reconciliation, of harmony with God, which leads in turn to the harmony of the poet and his work, as in *The Collar*. Herbert is actually individualized among his contemporary poets less by his religious concerns than by his production of shape poetry, which is considered to be his main contribution to the poetic originality of the period. This type of poetry intends to harmonize form with content and feeling, which is shape with meaning: the poem *The Altar*, for example, represents by its typography the shape of an altar, or the poem *Easter-Wings*, with its two stanzas, resembles a pair of wings. Yet this type of poetry on the whole is not quite original given the European tradition going back to the *Greek Anthology*, which is the tradition of the "emblem poetry" fusing visual and verbal levels, and language both describing and representing the image.

Emblem poetry, more complex than Herbert's pattern poems, consists of three parts: a motto (a single line, usually proverb or sentential), a picture (contains the idea from the motto, usually an engraved image), and verse (brings out the relationship between the two, usually a poem). Herbert himself might be said to have written emblem poems, for instance *Hope*, in which he alludes to anchor as symbol of hope.

Revived later by William Blake, the seventeenth-century emblem poetry consists of secular emblem – offering moral lessons – and Christian emblem created for meditative and devotional purposes. Francis Quarles (1592 – 1644) produced it in his *Emblems* (1635) and *Hieroglyphikes of the Life of Man* (1638); Henry Vaughan wrote in an emblematic mode in his third collection, entitled *Silex Scintillans* (1650).

The first half of the seventeenth century represents the period of flourishing of the metaphysical poetry. Yet apart from Donne's and Herbert's metaphysical poems one should also consider other important authors and works – such as Ben Jonson's drama and poetry, Francis Bacon's prose, King James's translation of the Bible, some of John Milton's major poems – as well as the writings of some minor prose writers and religious poets of both Jacobean and Caroline periods. It was the first half of the seventeenth century that saw the culmination of the long series of the sixteenth century translations of the Biblical texts in what is called the "King James Authorized Version" of the Bible. This version, which replaced all other English versions for both public and private use, was the result of the work of about fifty scholars divided into six groups, who started the translation in 1604 and completed it in 1611. The translators followed the previous versions, checking them by comparison with the original Hebrew and Greek texts. They attained the greater correctness while preserving the accumulated stylistic excellences of some three generations of predecessors, offering to British nation a genuine masterpiece of English prose style which combines the imaginative atmosphere with the genuine religious spirit.

2.3 The Puritan Period and Its Literary Expression

The next part of the seventeenth-century was the turbulent period of the "Commonwealth Interregnum" which lasted from 1649 to 1660. Politically, the period was ruled by the Puritans led by Oliver Cromwell, the Lord Protector of England. The Puritan period emphasized the idea of community service, preaching a doctrine of spiritual equality among men. Its programme concerning the abolition of church courts would end the dependence of church upon monarchy and would damage the political stability, which proved itself by bringing the Civil War and by leading to the abolition of monarchy and the House of Lords in 1649 and Episcopacy three years later.

After the death of Oliver Cromwell in 1658, the Puritan government of the Interregnum became unstable. The inability of Richard Cromwell, Oliver's son, to rule the country and the rise of the democratic movement of the time, which came to actively oppose the interests of the new rising nobility and bourgeoisie, led the Parliament to compromise with the Royalists and decide upon the restoration of monarchy: Charles Stuart, son of Charles I who was executed in 1649, was called back from Holland and crowned King of England.

The general consideration of Puritanism as conservative and thwarting the development of modern thought and science is often counter-positioned in relation to Protestant origins of many innovative scientific and philosophical ideas which proved themselves major intellectual doctrines of the century, in particular that of Francis Bacon. His doctrine "knowledge is power" attempted to build a body of knowledge which would help to improve men's position and in doing so it rejected the normative authority while proposing new scientific methods of acquiring and testing knowledge by reason and experiment. Such a doctrine imposed theories on cultural and, in particular, literary development by the middle of the seventeenth century.

The prose productions of the period, which consisted mainly of political pamphlets, historical writings and philosophical speculations, developed a new style of language which came to represent concreteness, clarity and simplicity. If things are more important than words, than prose had to be functional rather than allusive or persuasive, and the language of ordinary men had to break through academic field.

As far as the other two literary forms, poetry and drama, are concerned, the "Golden Age" of Elizabethan literature and the flourishing of the metaphysical poetry early in the seventeenth century were followed by a total decline during the Puritan middle decade of the century. The decline concerned first of all drama and theatrical representation; during the reign of James I theatres were already placed under the direct control of the crown, and later, in 1642, the Parliament decided the abolition of all playhouses, which proved a major disadvantage for dramatic production.

The literary works produced during the years of Commonwealth were, among others, John Milton's *Defence of the English People* (1651), Thomas Hobbes' *Leviathan* (1651), Abraham Cowley's *Poems, Davideis, Pindaric Odes* (1656), and some translations of French texts.

Disregarding strict periodization, the spirit of Puritanism found its supreme expression in poetry in the works of John Milton and Andrew Marvell, and in prose fiction in the writing of John Bunyan, although by the chronology of their texts, the three writers belong to other periods. For instance, Milton's *L'Allegro, Il Penseroso*, and *Lycidas* came in the previous Caroline Age and his *Paradise Lost* in the next period after Interregnum which is the Restoration period; similarly, Bunyan's *The Pilgrim's Progress*, perhaps the most famous English Christian allegory ever written, also came in the next period of Restoration. However, the poetic work of John Milton, the most representative poet of Puritanism, and, next to Shakespeare, the greatest of English poets, along that of Andrew Marvell, an active supporter of the new government of Cromwell's England, as well as the prose work of John Bunyan are first in line to receive special critical consideration in any study on the literary expression of the Puritan outlook in literature.

The information about the life of John Bunyan (1628-1688) is largely drawn from his *Grace Abounding* (1666), an autobiographical work reflecting his abandoned life, experience of sin in youth, and the later conversion, deaconry, and preaching. Bunyan's preaching was a success from the start, making him extremely popular throughout the country, but preaching without a license caused him two imprisonments, one in 1660 and another in 1675.

Bunyan's most famous work, *The Pilgrim's Progress*, was written in two parts, the first published in 1678 and the second in 1684 (the combined edition of the two parts in one volume came in 1728), and it is said that he had begun the work during his first period of imprisonment and probably finished it during the second.

The full title of the text is *The Pilgrim's Progress from This World to That Which Is to Come*, clearly a religious work and the theology expressed in it is largely Puritan. The textual version of the author is the main character Christian, previously called

Graceless, who, at first, with "a great burden on his back", asks "What shall I do to be saved?" and sets off in a quest leaving behind his wife and children, which prompts the idea that salvation is a private matter. Each individual being must tend to save his/her own soul forging a way forward as a journey which is both external and internal. The external one, in which the protagonist is accompanied by helpers as well as adversaries, displays a realistically imagined landscape, actual and symbolic, full of people and motion of life. His internal journey presupposes human intercourse and Christian talks to everyone, listens to characters telling their life-stories, recapitulates episodes, but more importantly is that his conversations and debates with other people stimulate thinking, soul-search, and especially an analysis of the qualities needed to defeat sin and death. His journey is thus a pilgrimage to acquire knowledge and self-knowledge, where at the end, Christian reaches heaven, the Celestial City; a brief episode is added in which Ignorance is sent to hell; consequently, the balance of the system of values is restored and the dreamer wakes and the book ends.

Unlike Bunyan's earlier work, *The Pilgrim's Progress*, according to its major thematic and narrative components, may be considered to be a text of prose fiction or a novel, but it is the term "allegory" which is mainly applied to describe it, as it follows the progress of Christian through the world in search of salvation. On the one hand, the allegorical technique employed here makes the work be representative for the human condition in general, since for all humans life is a journey and all might sooner or later pass through the Slough of Despond, Doubting Castle, Vanity Fair, and the Valley of Humiliation, places where the human soul suffers and is tested. Universal in its appeal, *The Pilgrim's Progress* was firstly aimed at reaching the common reader, hence the naturalness of the language and the directness of the point of view. On the other hand, the thematic arrangement of *The Pilgrim's Progress* relies heavily on the tradition of the picaresque writing, and in this almost picaresque story, its characters are not only moral types but also represent individuals who tell stories of their lives, for which flashbacks are often used, and present a familiar, verisimilar world in a narrative manner prefiguring the ways of fictional expression in the eighteenth- and nineteenth-century novels of realist concern. To say nothing that the scene of "Vanity Fair", a world-adversary where everything is for sale, gives the title to a famous Victorian realist novel, to which it is thematically connected, particularly with regard to their moral message. Like later in Thackeray's novel, each episode in Bunyan has a moral significance and supporting its ethical didacticism is the introduction of personified moral types, for example Mr Wordly-Wiseman, but the story never loses its grasp of everyday reality and relies heavily on the concept of verisimilitude.

Apart from various religious writings, of which Bunyan's *The Pilgrim's Progress* and Milton's *Paradise Lost* are the best examples, the turbulent years of the mid-century Puritan Commonwealth saw also the flourishing of political literature in English, of which the pamphlets, usually containing personal attacks, and the different forms of propaganda, in general aiming to reform the country, were most commonly produced. Of the latter type of the political literature, the work entitled *Leviathan*, written by Thomas Hobbes, is claimed to be one of the most important writings. Hobbes was an important seventeenth-century philosopher who also contributed to the fields of theology, history, ethics, and even geometry, but it is his work *Leviathan* on political philosophy that he is best remembered for.

Apart from pamphlets and propaganda, the political unrest during the Puritan period saw also the flourishing of a number of works which were the precursors of the modern newspapers. Such journalists as Henry Muddiman, Marchamont Needham, and John Birkenhead represented the views of different parties; they were often arrested and their opinions suppressed but it was their work that gave rise to British journalism.

2.4 The Restoration Period and Its Literature

The last period of the seventeenth century was the "Restoration Age" between 1660 and 1700, which followed the Puritan rule and started from the restoration of the Stuarts to the throne of England in 1660. The period included the reign of Charles II between 1660 and 1685, followed by the reign of James II (1685-1688) and the reign of William and Marry (1689-1702). On the general social level, the Restoration was a historical and cultural period distinguished from other periods not only by the restoration of monarchy but also by the appearance of two clearly defined political parties as the ancestors of the traditional British Whigs and Tories, and by an aristocratic reaction against both some Protestant sects (including Non-Conformists and Dissenters) and Catholicism in favour of the Established Church. The Whigs opposed the succession to the throne of James, Duke of York, because he was a Catholic, and advocated the foundation of a limited monarchic institution. They came to represent the interests of aristocracy and later middle class, industrialists and others who desired political and social reforms. The Tories, on the other hand, were against the exclusion of James, and in general represented the interests of the country clergy and gentry.

The period bears its significance to the restoration of Charles II who on his return to London in 1660 received a most popular welcome since the majority of English population never reconciled with the execution of Charles I and it optimistically believed that the institution of monarchy was not to determine the end of the Protestant independence. The optimism in the religious freedom of Protestantism – won against the royal and Episcopal absolutism in the early 1640s – seemed unfounded by 1685, when James II, Charles's brother, a conversed Catholic, followed as King. The fear and resentment of English people facing a new Catholic rule led to the repudiation of James II in 1688, by which the Catholic monarchic rule was removed once and for all. The establishment of the Protestant succession to the throne became definite in 1689 by what was known as the peaceful "Glorious Revolution", when a resolution stipulating the obligation of all the succeeding kings and queens to belong to the Anglican Church was achieved. The first on the English throne in this line were Mary, James's Protestant daughter, and her Protestant husband William of Orange, who ruled between 1689 and 1702.

In literature and thought, the main representative of the Restoration period was John Dryden, a poet, playwright and theoretician of early neoclassicism, but the period had also Milton's *Paradise Lost* (1667), John Bunyan's *Pilgrim's Progress* (1658), and John Locke's *Essay Concerning the Human Understanding* (1690). The period saw also the foundation of the Royal Society in 1662, the re-opening of the theatres with the accession of Charles II, and the rebirth of arts and literature on the whole.

In literature, Restoration was a period of poetry and drama and less prose produced by both men and women writers. Except the prose fiction (with *Oroonoko, or the History of the Royal Slave* (1688), an attack on the colonial problem of slavery, as the most famous novel) and drama (with *The Rover* (1677), based on Thomas Killigrew's *Thomaso or The Wanderer*, as the most successful play) of Aphra Behn (1640-1689), who is considered to be the first professional woman writer in England, professional not by choice but economic necessity, much of the Restoration women writing is essentially that of amateurs. This is the case of Anne Killigrew (1660-1685), the niece of the playwrights Thomas and Sir William Killigrew, or the poetry of Katherine Philips (1631-1664), or the work of the pioneer feminist Mary Astell (1666-1731), whose best-known work, *A Serious Proposal to the Ladies for the Advancement of Their True and Great Interest* (part one in 1694, second part in 1697), is concerned with women's prospects in social and family life, and advocates their need to reorganize their mission in public and private affairs, to help each other and become aware of the necessity of their intellectual development.

On the general literary level, there are two main aspects generally brought into discussion: first, concerning the literary doctrine, Restoration was the period of the revival and institutionalization of the classical doctrine, which make Restoration represent the beginnings of neoclassicism in Britain; second, concerning the literary practice, and due to the reaction against the rigid Puritan rules now replaced by the refinement and sophistication of the court, the Restoration literature was characterized by pleasure-seeking and valiant heroism, a kind of hedonistic atmosphere which manifested itself mainly in dramatic comedy, and became the stylized version of sophisticated upper class ethics in which elegance, abstractness, and, in particular, wit represented the ideal of the Restoration literature. Defined by John Dryden, in the preface to his poem *Annus Mirabilis*, as "the faculty of imagination in the writer", wit became the reflection of a new respect for reason and clarity as well as the main criteria of aesthetic evaluation of the literary text. For both literature and thought, there was, according to Andrew Sanders, the necessity of a tradition "to be re-established which was both responsive to the recent past and a reflection of new tastes and fashions" (Sanders 266).

In this respect, John Dryden, in his *An Essay of Dramatic Poesy*, urged his fellow writers to follow classical and contemporary, in particular French, doctrines in thought and to revive the Elizabethan drama of Shakespeare and Jonson in order to imitate it, along with the contemporary European models, in literature.

The growth of British literature in the next eighteenth century reveals that the first aspect was a triumphant accomplishment since it successfully came to dominate as neoclassicism the English cultural background for a long period which ended around the 1780s. Concerning the second aspect, though the writers of Restoration attempted to recapture the status of drama as a major literary tradition, and produced a huge amount of dramatic works, they never succeeded in reviving it, the eighteenth-century English literature consisting mainly of neoclassical, satirical and philosophical, poetry, and, with the weakening of neoclassicism by 1750s, also pre-romantic poetry, at the same time witnessing the rise and consolidation of the British novel writing tradition.

To revert to the second half of the seventeenth century, except poetry (lyric, satirical, political, and religious verse) and critical essay, the dominant genre of the Restoration literature, which flourished from 1660 to 1700, was drama, generally referred to as "Restoration comedy" and, in particular, as "**comedy of manners**". Restoration drama represented the rebirth of English drama which started with the re-opening of the theatres in 1660, after the public stage performances had been banned from 1642 onward for eighteenth years by the Puritan regime. There were, of course, evasions of the law, with performances offered in secrecy in private houses or inns located some miles out of town, but it was only upon the restoration of monarchy that theatres in England actually re-opened.

In August 1660, Charles II issued patents for two companies of players, followed by many others that were provided with fine playhouses, and performances immediately began. Since Charles II and many members of the Royalist party stayed in France during the greater part of the Protectorate, French influence was felt primarily in the theatre. There were the newly established neoclassical standards for tragedy of Corneille and Racine, the drama of Moliere, the opera of Quinault, and the French versions of the plots of Calderon and Lope de Vega which supplied the British plays with thematic material, leading to the disappearance of the national types of drama. However, apart from this influx of foreign drama, there was also a return to the great masterpieces of Elizabethan and Jacobean periods, particularly by Shakespeare, Jonson, Beaumont, and Fletcher. In every important structural and thematic respect, Restoration drama was far inferior to both Elizabethan and foreign models, lacking many of the admirable qualities of the contemporary French plays and those of the English predecessors.

Restoration comedy is famous for its representation of the polish, artificial, stylized, fashionable, and highly sophisticated society of the city, and for its portrayal of a number of stereotypic and artificial character types that follow a life of pleasure rather than of loyalty and honesty. Restoration comedy is also famous for its explicitly displayed sexuality and the stylish aristocratic ethos of the newly restored King's court, and it attracted as its audience aristocrats as well as their servants, and a substantial part of the middle class segment. The audience was attracted by the crowded and lively plots of the comedies, the introduction of the first professional actresses, and the rise of the first celebrity actors.

The Restoration drama, written now by both men and women, was concerned with general human and social interests, and was represented mainly by comedies – plays generally designated as "comedy of manners" – most of which being French and Spanish adaptations, and some ridiculing the Puritans or provincialism.

The pattern was given by those aristocrats who spent their exile in France and became experts in French gallantry and wit; they were actually called "court wits", among whom Sir Charles Sedley, John Sheffield, Charles Sackville, and others who rejected the provincial values and provincial setting in favour of a metropolitan culture based on courtly and fashionable circles of London. The country people were satirized for their lack of sophistication, whereas London was acclaimed as the place where the superior aristocracy was able to cultivate the stylized wit and sensual hedonism, high passion and noble loyalty. Some of the dramatists attempted to revive the tradition of the heroic tragedy but the Restoration period on the whole was an unheroic age, the concept of heroism being inflated, the writers falling into artificial declamations and reflecting almost nothing but the values of the actual Restoration, the spirit of the age, or rather an idealised world as desired by the "court wits".

The Restoration theatre was a cultural phenomenon of quick rise and decline, its major representative being John Dryden, out of whose twenty-eight dramatic works, the play entitled *Marriage A-la-Mode* (1672) is considered to be the most important and subtle in its social satire, revealing the Restoration attitudes towards youth and age, love and marriage, vanity and affection.

Among other representatives of the Restoration drama, mention should be made of Sir George Etherege (1634-1691) who, in *The Comical Revenge, or, Love in a Tub* (1664), *She Would if She Could* (1668), and *The Man of Mode, or, Sir Fopling Flutter* (1676), attempts to render the Restoration character with his or her conflicting ways of life, torn between wit and virtue, surrender to passion and desire for freedom; William Wycherley (1640-1716) who, in *The Country Wife* (1675) and *The Plain Dealer*, reveals a critical spirit not entirely compatible with the Restoration ethos but reacting against tricksters and bullies, dishonesty, selfishness, cruelty, lust, and obsessive compulsion; William Congreve (1670-1729) whose *Love for Love* (1695) and *The Way of the World* (1700) granted him the status of the true master of the comedy of manners concerning both character representation strategies and the sophistication of the plot construction in the dramatic expression of some dominant Restoration thematic perspectives, such as the contrast between private behaviour and public reputation, strong emotion and artificial loyalty. Other writers who wrote comedies were Sir John Vanbrugh (1664-1726) and George Farquhar (c. 1677-1707).

The Restoration drama, consisting mainly in the comedy of manners, developed a dramatic form which satirizes the follies, hypocrisy, pretension, and, in general, the manners and habits of a social class often represented by stock characters that are rather types than individuals, such as fops, rakes, coxcombs, old persons pretending to be young, city gentlemen whose purpose in life is to make love to their neighbours' wives, stupid and jealous husbands and fathers, dull countrymen, jealous wives, amorous widows, chatterers and gossips, and others who fail to conform to the elegant manners and fashions of a sophisticated society.

Also, in the comedy of manners, the comic mode results from the exaggeration of stylish behaviour, absurdity in fashion style, or deviation from what is accepted as civilized norms of conduct. The comedy of manners could develop in the literature of a society in which there is a leisured class which would create certain standards of politeness, good sense, and sophisticated manners.

In this cultural context, satire became a favourite literary form among Restoration writers such as John Dryden and John Wilmot, earl of Rochester (1647-1680). These playwrights along Etherege, Wycherley, and Congreve used satire mingled with various thematic elements – for example, emotion or exposition of society's hypocrisy and other follies – to develop new viewpoint and a new philosophy of life through new types of character for whom wit counts more than moral qualities, but the wit which goes with self-knowledge receives a positive moral value. Hedonistic London young men in search of money or sex or marriage for money and young women in search of a say in choice of a marriage partner, they represent a new generation repudiating past and choosing freedom of speech and action.

The rules of writing such a drama are yet rooted in the past and the antecedents of the Restoration comedy of manners are to be found firstly in Antiquity – namely, in the new comedy of the ancient Greek playwright Menander, whose style, plots, and characters were imitated by the Latin Plautus and Terence – and, secondly, in Renaissance. In Britain, the first comedy of manners might be considered Shakespeare's *Much Ado about Nothing*, but it was Ben Jonson's comedy of humours that directly influenced the genre of the Restoration comedy. In Europe, the best-known comedies of manners were those of the French playwright Moliere, particularly plays such as *L'École des femmes* (1662) and *Le Misanthrope* (1666).

The Restoration comedy of manners is a type of realistic comedy which displays a witty, satiric atmosphere, laying emphasis on social comment rather than characterization. The plot of the comedy of manners, elaborate, artificial, and often concerned with an illicit love affair or some other scandal, is generally less important than the satire and the witty, epigrammatic, and often bawdy dialogue.

There was no special psychological analysis of the characters but there were some clearly defined stereotypes, such as the "Libertine", both male and female, living according to *carpe diem*, nature, and natural urges such as flirt, passion, and sexual desire; the "Sensible Couple", living according to reason, tradition, and responsibility; the "Discarded Mistress", usually an ex-lover of the male Libertine, who, full of revenge, plans to get back the Libertine; the "Fop" (Sir Fopling Flutter), a comic figure who tries to imitate the Libertine; the "Country Bumpkin", a rich man from countryside coming to city to spend money and time on prostitutes; the "Betrayed Husband", a rich old man married to an infidel younger woman, usually from countryside.

The stereotypic characters are involved in stereotypic situations, or scenes, such as "the Lady and the Maid Scene" or the "Unmasking Scene", which express a number of stereotypic themes, such as "arranged marriages", "passion and jealousy", "pursuit of sex and money", "appearance versus reality", "natural versus artificial", "honesty versus hypocrisy", and others.

Apart from the comedy of manners, another type of play popular in Restoration, though for a short period during the 1670s, was the "heroic drama", also called "heroic tragedy", developed by Dryden and followed by other writers, such as Sir George Etherege and Sir Robert Howard.

Distinguished from the comedy of manners by both verse structure and subject-matter, the heroic drama is composed in heroic verse (closed couplets in iambic pentametre) and focuses on subjects related to national history, mythological events or other important matters, and the hero is of epic significance, powerful and decisive, and often torn between passion and honour. This type of tragedy is characterised by bombastic dialogue, excessive spectacle, elaborate scenery, and grand action, usually the conquest of a country.

The setting is usually a distant land such as India or Mexico, and the main motif is the violent conflict between the hero and a villain, usually a rival in love, or a tyrant, or the father of the heroine who is torn between her love for the hero and loyalty to her father, and whose rival is a violently passionate villainess, sometimes the heroine's best friend; if the hero and heroine are able to overcome the demands of both duty and love, the play ends happily for them and unhappily for the villain and villainess.

The term "heroic drama" was invented by John Dryden for his play entitled *The Conquest of Granada* (1670), in whose Preface to the printed version, Dryden developed a series of rules for this type of drama, arguing that drama was a species of epic poetry for the stage, and that the heroic drama was to other plays what the epic was to other poetry. "Heroic drama" is a form of tragedy, "drama in the epic mode – grand, rhetorical and declamatory; at its worst, bombastic. Its themes were love and honour and it was considerably influenced by French classical drama, especially by the work of Corneille" (Cuddon 408).

The attempt to produce a dramatic entertainment about serious subjects from national history and the failure of the dramatists to create credible powerful and military dominating heroes were the reasons for the attacks on the heroic drama by, among others, George Villiers, the second Duke of Buckingham, whose satire *The Rehearsal* was successful enough to make the heroic drama largely disappear from the English literary scene.

Although the Restoration drama attempted at reviving and imitating the Elizabethan dramatic tradition, it actually manifested a violent break with the Elizabethan drama in matters of both thematic context and theatrical representation, and even concerning the size of the theatre.

The Elizabethan theatre was very large, with seats for 2000 people, and the building was hexagonal, whereas the Restoration theatre held about 300 spectators, the stage was mostly rectangular, it had a roof, and candelabrums were used for artificial lighting. Unlike in the Elizabethan theatre, in the Restoration one, there were actresses on the stage, the costumes were more elaborate, the scenery was painted on canvas or panels, thus making possible the quick change of the scenery. Also, in the Restoration theatre, the audience became homogenous, for it was a kind of drama of the upper-class for the upper-class, and in the plays representing the life of the upper-class the audience watched themselves.

In this respect, the Elizabethan theatre had a larger variety of subjects, but the Restoration theatre was more geographically and historically accurate, introducing a strong element of realism, yet it was this unilateralism of the thematic concern, among other things, such as sexual explicitness, which contributed to a growing disinterest in the Restoration drama in the next eighteenth century.

However, the succeeding periods in the history of British literature saw some attempts to revive the Restoration drama, in particular its comedy of manners, as to mention just the late eighteenth-century Oliver Goldsmith's *She Stoops to Conquer* (1773) and Richard Sheridan's *The School of Scandal* (1777), the late nineteenth-century Oscar Wilde's *The Importance of Being Earnest* (1895), and the twentieth-century Noel Coward's *Hay Fever* (1925).

Unlike drama, the poetry of the Restoration period did not manifest such a violent break with the Elizabethan tradition, and the metaphysical style, which dominated the poetic production of the first half of the seventeenth century, being largely a continuation of certain conflicts which began to disturb the Elizabethan *status quo*, continued to influence the poetry of the Restoration period, which relied on concentration and straightforwardness, paradox and antithesis.

There was a search for the "golden mean" which, starting with the Restoration period, would juxtapose the internal conflicts of the metaphysical poets upon the philosophical certainties and satirical comments in the poetry of some neoclassical writers of the late seventeenth century and the next eighteenth century.

On the other hand, the rising in Restoration neoclassical spirit manifested as a strong reaction against the cultural extravagances of the Baroque and metaphysical poetry. Instead, it revived and institutionalized the classical principles, which makes Restoration, the last part of the seventeenth century, to be the first of the three parts of the neoclassical period in British literature. As a part of British neoclassicism, the Restoration period was followed by the "Augustan Age" (also referred to as the "Age of Reason"), in the first half of the eighteenth century, and by the "Age of Johnson" which, between the 1750s and 1780s, represented the decline of neoclassicism.

The eighteenth century in Europe, in general, is called the "Age of Enlightenment", a term often used to name also most of the eighteenth-century history of Britain, including the "Augustan Age" and the "Age of Johnson" which came before the rise of romanticism in the 1780s.

The Restoration period gave the beginnings of neoclassicism in English literature, or, in other terms, the beginnings of Enlightenment, which is to be considered as reifying a major literary change which occurred during Restoration and which resumed an earlier Renaissance element of tradition – represented by Ben Jonson – reflecting the revival of and reliance on ancient classical values which emphasize order, reason, and good sense.

As part of the general eighteenth-century European cultural movement called "Enlightenment", the British Age of Reason (the Augustan Age), representing the eighteenth-century neoclassicism, started in the second half of the seventeenth century in the Restoration emphasis on the power of reason, empiricism, science, rationality, clarity, regularity, normative restraint, elegance, decorum, stylized poetic diction, urbanity, owing much of its theoretical input to both empiricists and rationalists, both John Locke's and Rene Descartes' philosophical works. Apart from empiricists and rationalists, of equal importance for the consolidation of the neoclassical doctrine in Britain were the leading French ideas from, among others, *L'Art Poétique* by Boileau and *Réflexions sur la poétique d'Aristote et sur les ouvrages des poétes anciens et modernes* by Rene Rapin.

The beginnings of Enlightenment and neoclassicism in British cultural background, which took place during the Restoration period as the result of some major Continental influences, were also the direct consequences of some major changes in the native literary taste which occurred in that period, and the neoclassical doctrine itself should be regarded primarily as a new literary attitude that came to influence the rise of the English novel in the eighteenth century and to dominate the poetic production for over a hundred years during the late seventeenth century (represented in the best possible way by John Dryden) and most of the eighteenth century (dominated by the work of Alexander Pope and Samuel Johnson).

2.5 The Picaresque Tradition in European and English Literature

The seventeenth century continues the brilliant tradition of the picaresque novel in Spain with Francisco de Quevedo's *La Vida del Buscon don Pablos de Segovia* and Luis Velez de Guevara's *El Diablo Cojuelo*. Nonetheless, this kind of fiction has also spread to other cultural areas: to France, with Charles Sorel's *Histoire Comique de Francion* (1623-1633), Paul Scarron's *Le Romance Comique* (1651), and Francois de Fenelon's *Les Aventures de Telemaque* (1699); to Germany, with Hans Iacob von Grimmelshausen's *Simplicius Simplicissimus* (1668); and to England, with John Bunyan's *The Pilgrim's Progress* (1678).

As a result of the translation of the four main Spanish picaresque novels into French, German, and English, the picaresque fictional pattern began to emerge in other cultural backgrounds of the seventeenth and eighteenth centuries and gave types of national picaresque narrative. In this respect,

[each] of these novels is a unique fusion of existing conventions and an imaginative response to specific historical circumstances, but within the novel writing traditions of their respective countries, they all performed similar functions. By breaking down the traditional separation of styles and expanding the range of acceptable subject matter to include the morally serious treatment of nonaristocratic characters, they constituted one of the most important stages in the transition between earlier literary prose and the modern novel, which itself became the dominant mode of fictional expression in eighteenth- and nineteenth-century Europe. (Bjornson 3)

Apart from performing similar functions, the seventeenth- and eighteenth-century picaresque novels maintain similar elements of their thematic and narrative pattern: the form of a fictional autobiography; the linear, chronological narration; omniscient, usually autodiegetic, narrator; the protagonist as a low-born subject, a rogue with no fixed social status and obligations, a vagabond with no fixed occupation or profession, sometimes an offender against social/civil and moral law.

They represent quest narratives and narratives of travel, adventure, ordeal; they are pictures of society, as well as life-novels about the picaro(a) seeking self and freedom from social laws and conventions, and, paradoxically, a role in society and social advancement at the same time with defying the milieu. Just as the novel in its incipient stage parodies and plays with various other genres and forms, the seventeenth- and eighteenth-century picaresque fiction offers to quest, ordeal, travel and other types of narrative "new ironic or parodic or tragicomic forms" (Dunn 15).

The seventeenth-century picaresque novels emerge in other cultural and literary contexts, in particular German, French, and English, marking – as would also happen in the eighteenth century – the universalization of the subgenre, as well as its novelty and transformation of the picaresque content. At the turn of the sixteenth century, Nashe already added the historical concern to the established pattern of the picaresque thematic elements, whereas more drastic innovation – by adding the element of reflection on the human condition and especially a more detailed observation of and focus on individual experience of the character – would emerge in the eighteenth century in novels such as *Gil Blas* and *Moll Flanders*.

These new picaresque tales represent new steps in the general process of development and consolidation of the genre of novel as a literary tradition. This is due to their characters' life experience, which consists mainly in physical and spiritual pilgrimages, and culminates in changes in the exterior condition and sometimes inner world of the characters. These novels are often the equivalents of Renaissance conduct books insofar as one of the recurrent themes is the making of the gentleman.

But in a complex and busy existence the gentlemanly ideal is difficult to discover; and the struggle for survival in the contemporary world is also hardly conducive to good manners and quiet consideration of others.

In terms of the general pattern of the picaresque fiction, the character's experience of life consists of a long journey from home into the crowded and exciting background of contemporary society. The journey is instrumental in the fulfilment of the character's desire for adventure and action, but also acts as the source of corruption.

In the view of M. M. Bakhtin's conception on the historical advancement of the novelistic genre (Bakhtin 10-59), the narrator follows carefully his character's growth (also biological) as it becomes more complex, and presents his experience at the same time with the influences of the background. The character's adventures and wanderings provide the narrator with the possibility of rendering the spatial (social) multiplicity, which is chiefly static and consists of the contraries of human existence as determined socially.

Some of the seventeenth-century novels which continue the picaresque tradition are centred on the pedagogic idea governing the process of character formation, for example Fenelon's *Les Aventures de Telemaque*. Others, for instance Sorel's *Histoire Comique de Francion* and Scarron's *Le Romance Comique*, fashion a burlesque design drawing on the picaresque tales of adventure, bringing together, and also satirizing, the travel scheme and the adventurous form of the picaresque and the pastoral elements.

Scarron, on the one hand, satirizes the false intellectual and spiritual values of his contemporary social environment, and tells, at the same time with a remarkably coloured picturesqueness and humour, the story of two lovers who find refuge among some itinerant actors.

Sorel, on the other hand, when his character becomes a shepherd and lives for a while among simple people, praises the pastoral values and creates the image of an uncorrupted existence away from the court and town, from acquiring and spending. Thus, Francion's passionate quest for Nays, whom he truly loves, is mingled with his yearning for a lost innocence, for a prelapsarian paradisiacal life in which man existed in harmony with nature. Sorel's critical outlook on reality, the same as Quevedo's and Guevara's, transfigures the external world, which becomes less interesting in itself and is turned towards comicality and caricature.

Sorel's novel follows closely the picaresque mode of writing: its protagonist passes through different social media and meets different sorts and conditions of man, and he is presented in his general development from childhood to maturity; its narrative consists of events which succeed each other and are united by the thematic implications of initiation and education of the main hero, who experiences adventures and trials; its structure is thus a linear movement with no special or distinct narrative levels of the general narrative framework.

The same thematic and structural perspectives of literary organization are more or less preserved in Grimmelshausen's work, which marks the continuation of the picaresque tradition and provides a new step in the consolidation of the genre of novel as a literary tradition. The aspect of novelty represents the fact that the character formation principle in the novel is linked to the changes which take place in the external world. That is to say, the character's growth and development take place at the same time with the evolution and consolidation of the world. The world's foundation changes and the character has to change with it; the hero thus loses his private features and becomes subject to such issues as reality and human possibilities, freedom and the problem of creative initiative.

The character's development and change are placed on a moral level: Simplicius reveals a gradual movement from youth's naïveté and idealism, through a dissolute life, to the final moral regeneration and desire to leave the world full of injustice and cruelty and become a hermit.

An account of a more personal spiritual pilgrimage is John Bunyan's *The Pilgrim's Progress*, a direct development from his previous work, *Grace Abounding* (1666, an autobiographical representation of the awakening of his soul to sin, his conversion, and his later ministry). *Pilgrim's Progress* is a picaresque tale and an allegory, as well as a moral and theological book about the search for salvation.

Such religious themes co-exist in the century with the pursuit of knowledge and the belief in the perpetual renovation of knowledge, as Francis Bacon, in *Novum Organum* (1620), promotes *viva activa* and philanthropy directed at personal and social reformation. Bacon also argues that knowledge no longer comes only from books but also from observation and experiment, and from the pursuit of inductive method as a process from individual observation to general laws.

The Pilgrim's Progress can be labelled a novel, but it is actually an allegory which traces the progress of Christian through the world in search of salvation: "Christian's progress, accompanied at first by the martyred Faithful and latterly by the redeemed Hopeful, represents that of the individual believer blessed by the three theological virtues of faith, hope, and charity"; he is also "blessed with a gathering certainty of his election to eternal salvation and he forges a way forward aided simply by his understanding of Scriptural promises" (Sanders 246-247).

The Pilgrim's Progress is thus an interesting departure from Bunyan's earlier work in its allegorical illumination of spiritual experience; its allegory draws on Biblical images, Christian typology, and popular retellings of stories of virtuous conduct. Yet *The Pilgrim's Progress* relates to the rise of the English novel and reveals intertextual connections also with picaresque fiction and the romance, and, to an extent, with the Bildungsroman too. Bunyan's work is a precursor in the development history of the Bildungsroman through its focus on the protagonist's spiritual progress, an important element in later novels of formation.

The Pilgrim's Progress is also a novel in its continuation of the picaresque tradition: in this quasi-picaresque story, the characters are intended to represent moral qualities and vices, and their names are only moral tags (Christian, Faithful, Obstinate, Hopeful, Madam Wanton), although, strikingly enough, they actually acquire individuality through speech. The naturalness of the dialogue makes the allegory deeply rooted in the actual and the familiar: such scenes as those of the "vanity" and the trial of Christian and Faithful are fully compatible with scenes which the later writers of fiction would emphasize in rendering their protagonists' process of development.

Actually, with its masterful delineation of character and its realism in the observation of human behaviour, *The Pilgrim's Progress* marked a new and important step in the development of the novel and influenced a huge body of the eighteenth- and nineteenth-century English fiction. Its thematic focus on the spiritual experience of moral improvement of a human subject is crucial in the process of character representation as textualized by later novelists, particularly those who relate to the tradition of realism, among whom the producers of the realist novel of formation.

3.

MAJOR LITERARY VOICES

Keywords: metaphysical poets, John Donne, *The Good-Morrow*, *The Ecstasy*, *The Canonization*, *Song*, *A Valediction: Forbidding Mourning*, *Holy Sonnets*, George Herbert, *The Altar*, Andrew Marvell, *An Horatian Ode*, *The Garden*, *To His Coy Mistress*, John Milton, *L'Allegro*, *Il Penseroso*, *Lycidas*, *Paradise Lost*, John Dryden, *Absalom and Achitophel*, *An Essay of Dramatic Poesie*

Among the major writers, who necessitate a special critical consideration in the overall study of the seventeenth-century British literary experience, John Donne, George Herbert, and Andrew Marvell are exponents of the metaphysical trend in poetry, John Milton represents Puritanism, and John Dryden is the spokesman of Restoration.

3.1 The Metaphysical Poets I: John Donne

The most important and influential of all English metaphysical poets is John Donne (1572-1631). He was born in Bread Street, London, in 1572, into a prosperous and devout Roman Catholic family at a time in England when Catholics were persecuted. The fact that he belonged to a Roman Catholic family made Donne's life uneasy as he was to play the role of an outsider plagued by religious doubts, some of which based on personal experiences. In 1593, for example, Donne's brother Henry died of a fever in prison after being arrested for helping a proscribed Catholic priest, an event that made Donne question his faith.

Donne's father, John Donne, was a well-to-do ironmonger and citizen of London but who died suddenly when Donne was four, leaving the three children to be raised by their mother Elizabeth (who married six months later a Catholic physician), the daughter of John Heywood, a famous epigrammatist and a relative of Sir Thomas More. First educated at home by Catholic tutors, John Donne at the age of eleven, together with his younger brother Henry, went to Hart Hall, University of Oxford, where he studied for three years, and then spent three more years at the University of Cambridge, but at that time Donne took no degree at either university because he could not take the Oath of Supremacy required at graduation. Donne was admitted to study law as a member of Thavies Inn (in 1591) and Lincoln's Inn (in 1592), and it seemed natural that he would embark upon a legal or diplomatic career.

It was during this period of residence in London that Donne wrote his first book of *Satires*, considered one of Donne's most important literary efforts. Although not immediately published, the volume had a fairly wide readership through private circulation of the manuscript. Same was the case with his love poems from the volume of *Songs and Sonnets*, which are assumed to have been written at about the same time as the satires.

Having inherited a considerable fortune, John Donne spent his money on women, books, theatre, and travels. Among his friends were Christopher Brooke, a poet and his chamber-fellow at Lincoln's Inn, and Ben Jonson, who was part of Brooke's circle of literary associates. In 1596, Donne joined the naval expedition that Robert Devereux, second Earl of Essex, led against Cádiz in Spain, and the following year joined an expedition to the Azores, where he wrote *The Calm*. Upon his return to England in 1598, Donne was appointed private secretary to Sir Thomas Egerton, Lord Keeper of the Great Seal, afterward Lord Ellesmere.

Donne began a promising civil career, in 1601 being elected Member of Parliament for Brackley, Northants, an Egerton seat. In the same year, he secretly married Lady Egerton's niece, seventeen-year-old Anne More, daughter of Sir George More, Lieutenant of the Tower, and thereby ruined all chances of fulfilling his career. Donne was dismissed from Egerton's service and imprisoned for some weeks together with his friends Samuel and Christopher Brooke who had aided the couple's clandestine affair. For the next dozen years, the poet had to struggle hard to support his growing family, getting help from Anne's cousin who offered them refuge in Pyrford, Surrey, and from Lady Magdalen Herbert, George Herbert's mother, and Lucy, Countess of Bedford. It was not until 1609 that reconciliation took place between Donne and his father-in-law, and Sir George More was finally induced to pay his daughter's dowry.

Meanwhile, Donne made a living as a lawyer, serving chiefly as counsel for Thomas Morton, an anti-Catholic pamphleteer, later Bishop of Durham. It is said that Donne may have collaborated with Morton in writing pamphlets which appeared under Morton's name from 1604 to 1607. Donne's main literary accomplishments during this period were *Divine Poems* (1607) and the prose work *Biathanatos* (posthumously published in 1644) in which he argued that suicide is not intrinsically sinful.

As Donne approached forty, he published two anti-Catholic polemics, *Pseudo-Martyr* (1610) and *Ignatius His Conclave* (1611), which were a kind of public testimony of Donne's renunciation of the Catholic faith. *Pseudo-Martyr*, in particular, which argued that English Catholics could pledge an oath of allegiance to James I, King of England, without compromising their religious loyalty to the Pope, won Donne the favour of the King. Also, in return for patronage from Sir Robert Drury of Hawstead, Donne wrote *A Funerall Elegie* (1610) on the death of Sir Robert's fifteen-year-old daughter Elizabeth, the elegy winning for Donne and his wife an apartment in Drury house. In the poem, the death of Elizabeth Drury is likened to the physical and moral decay of the entire world, and her entry into Heaven signifies the hope for the world's regeneration.

Earlier in 1607, John Donne had refused to take Anglican orders, but King James I persisted in the view that Donne was unfit for confidential employment and urged him to enter the Church. In 1615, Donne reluctantly entered the ministry and was appointed Royal Chaplain later that year. In 1616, he was appointed Reader in Divinity at Lincoln's Inn after finally receiving from Cambridge the degree of Doctor of Divinity two years earlier. As a person of Church, Donne proved to be a pluralist, and his style, full of elaborate metaphors, religious symbolism and flair for drama, together with his wit and wide knowledge, established him as one of the greatest preachers of the period. Just as Donne's fortunes seemed to be improving, his wife, Anne Donne, aged thirty-three, died on 15 August, 1617, after giving birth to their twelfth child, a stillborn, and only seven of the children survived their mother's death. Struck by grief, Donne wrote his seventeenth "Holy Sonnet" entitled *Since She Whom I Lov'd Hath Paid Her Last Debt*.

According to Donne's friend and biographer, Izaak Walton, Donne was thereafter "crucified to the world" and the time for love songs was over, but he continued to write poetry, producing many of the famous *Holy Sonnets* (1618). In 1618, Donne went as chaplain with Viscount Doncaster in his Embassy to the German princes, writing before the journey *Hymn to Christ at the Author's Last Going into Germany*, which already suggests Donne's apprehension of death. The poet returned to London in 1620 and was appointed Dean of Saint Paul's in 1621, a post he held until his death.

Donne's private meditations, *Devotions upon Emergent Occasions*, written while he was convalescing from a serious illness, were published in 1624. In the same year, Donne was made Vicar of St Dunstan's-in-the-West. On March 27, 1625, James I died, and Donne preached a sermon before Charles I. Donne would have certainly become a Bishop in 1630 if not prevented by his ailing health (Donne was suffering from infections of the mouth). Obsessed with the idea of death, Donne preached what was called his own funeral sermon, *Death's Duel*, just a few weeks before he died in London on March 31, 1631. The last of Donne's writings was *Hymne to God, my God, In my Sicknesse*, written just before his death.

John Donne received during his lifetime the status of one of the major English poets of the first half of the seventeenth century, his poems being read in literary circles before they were printed, but they exercised their influence mostly after they appeared in book-form when collected by his son John and published posthumously in 1633. Almost the entire metaphysical poetry in English literature has been associated in the minds of its readers and most critics with the poetic work of John Donne – hence the name of the "School of Donne" given to metaphysical poetry in Britain – since a great number of Donne's literary concerns, major themes, and poetics techniques occur in all English metaphysical poetry.

Among Donne's most famous poems dealing with the theme of love, *The Good-Morrow* is a good example of metaphysical poetry in that the poet, making use of the dramatic tone, tries to persuade the reader of a matter that seems essential for a certain moment in his experience.

In the first stanza, the lyrical I, the voice of the poet in the poem, expresses the awareness of his inadequate status prior to falling in love. He discovers that he has been childishly engaged in some "country pleasures" which offered to him mere sexual gratification. The pleasure of real love, he understands, is different from all the previous experiences which were illusions and dreams, for they offered just physical gratification, which is not love but delusion.

In the second stanza the lyrical I meditates on his present love experience, making the necessary distinction between the physical pleasure and the true beauty of spiritual love. Now he welcomes the "good morrow" of their "waking souls" that have no fear of unfaithfulness; it is the physical pleasure which involves jealousy and fears, whereas the true love is free from such thoughts.

The conceit makes itself present in this stanza in the striking declaration that each lover is a world but through love the lovers create a single world of their own, a world made up of the union of their souls: "worlds on worlds have shown, / Let us possess one world; each hath one, and is one". The Platonic idea of love is employed in the last stanza in that the physical beauty reflects the inner beauty, and the two lovers, each representing a universe, manage to complete each other and create one perfect world derived from the strength of their true feelings. The two lovers mirror each other – "My face in thine eye, thine in mine appears" – and the metaphysical conceit is developed here by the comparison of the eyes of each partner with the hemispheres "without sharp North, without declining West".

The "declining West" symbolises a falling away of their present love, which is contrasted to the characteristic of "sharp North" suggesting an extremely cold and static condition, and meaning that their love is free from extremes and any possibilities of decay. Finally, the poet draws on the alchemical notion of equally mixed substances which cannot disappear or change, and if anything perishes it is because of being imperfectly mixed. The conclusion is that the two lovers enjoy a perpetual ecstasy which holds them together, neither of them falling away from exhaustion but becoming immortal through their non-perishing love.

The ecstasy of the lovers is the central concern in the poem entitled *The Ecstasy*, which discusses the nature of love in its both spiritual and physical manifestation, where the term "ecstasy" refers not to the sensual delight but to the movement of the soul outside the body. The poem develops the theme of a full relationship between man and woman, which is possible by the fusion of two separate identities into a perfect whole and the acknowledgement of the interdependence of body and soul in passion, of the fact that love, however liberated from their bodies the lovers are, cannot exist indefinitely in abstraction but must "take a body too".

The poem opens with a pastoral scene, the two lovers sitting together on a riverbank of violets. The scenery is presented in erotic terms in that the riverbank is "like a pillow on a bed", "pregnant" and swelled with water, and the "violet's reclining head" suggests the springtime. To a Renaissance reader, the image of violets symbolizes faith, love, and truth. Another familiar to the Renaissance readers detail is the lovers' hands being closely entwined as they look deeply into each other's eyes, people believing that the spiritual love is reflected through the light emanating from the eyes, but the metaphysical tradition considers the union of their hands and the reflection of their eyes as the physical unity of the lovers.

Referring to the souls of the lovers liberated from their bodies, the poet compares them to the two equal armies. As in a battle between them the outcome is uncertain, the interaction between the two lovers' souls leaving the bodies is unpredictable as well. During such a state, the bodies of the two lovers lay as still as the stones on tombs, suggesting the insignificant nature of the physical body without the presence of the soul. The souls of the lovers interact peacefully, merge, speak a mutual language, and if there might be somebody who is purified by love, as a totally rational mind he might understand the language of the souls and might take away a new, purer refinement of love. The lovers experience ecstasy out of the movement of their souls outside the body and their subsequent merging represents an act of purification, the state of ecstasy which makes them be aware of the true nature and purpose of their love:

> This ecstasy doth unperplex,
> We said, and tell us what we love;
> We see by this it was not sex;
> We see we saw not what did move.

Referring to the souls of the lovers leaving the bodies, the poet develops the idea of love as divine revelation, the lovers existing, according to Margaret Willy, in "a mystical state of clarified perception unhampered by senses of reason". The state of ecstasy which the two lovers experience makes them understand that it is the spiritual rather than physical desire which motivates them, and just as all separate souls contain a mixture of different unidentified elements, love takes these "mixed souls" and mixes them all again, so that their constituent parts become an inseparable unity.

Like a violet, which is poor and weak in its growth but when transplanted becomes strong and "redoubles still, and multiplies", the union of the souls grows with a new and stronger energy, and remedies the defects of each. The fused souls of the lovers become a single, united, "abler soul", which, transcending the "defects of loneliness", is, unlike the body, perfect and unchangeable.

Why, then, the lyrical I asks, "our bodies ... do we forbear?" The answer is that the souls of the lovers are the guardians which control the flesh, the "intelligences" which guide the bodies like the controlling angelic intelligence which, in Ptolemaic astronomy, guides the planet. Also, the lovers should be grateful to their bodies for their first meeting and the subsequent union of their souls: "soul to soul may flow, / Though it to body first repair". Like the spiritual influence which may work through air, the union of souls can come about through the union of the bodies.

The body and soul are thus complementary, but it is the flesh that subordinates itself to the union of the spirits. However, the body should not be considered worthless but rather an element in the mixture in which the inferior is made more valuable by the unity with the superior. Moreover, the body and soul are both necessary aspects for a successful love relationship, since a disembodied, pure spiritual love is like "a great prince [that] in prison lies".

Having achieved the understanding that the true love manifests spiritually as well as physically, the souls decide to return to their bodies and offer instructions on love to others by their own example. The lesson is possible, once more, only if both the spiritual and physical elements reveal themselves, since "Love's mysteries in souls do grow, / But yet the body is his book". Apart from a mild expression of egocentrism, the special relationship of the lyrical I with his lover becomes a universal symbol of true love, complete and permanent, since any observer would notice little change in the nature of their love when their souls return to their bodies.

The theme of love takes in *The Canonization* new thematic perspectives in the form of a dramatic monologue drawing on analogies from mythical animals to Roman Catholic religious practices. In the first stanza, the speaker impatiently interrupts a person who has shown concern and has criticized him of threatening the chances of social advancement because of his relation with his mistress. The speaker asks that person to talk of any other subject except the poet's love, telling his friend to get a place near the Archbishop, or the Duke, or the King, wherever it pleases him, but let the poet love. This sudden break displays irony because, as the poem unfolds, the speaker is the one who will not hold his tongue, and after this sudden interruption, the poet's friend turns into a silent listener, having no other possibility to enter the discussion. Contrary to his friend's emphasis on social advancement, the poet expresses scorn for those who are interested in social positions rather than in the value of genuine love.

In the second stanza, the speaker asks to be allowed to love his mistress neither to please her nor to please himself, but on the premises that their love harms no one. In order to express the idea that no person can be injured by his love, the poet develops a parody on some typical Petrarchan conceits: the poet in love does not cause flood to anyone; no one is drowned by sighs as strong as the tempest; he does not cause a spell of warm weather; and he does not cause the death of plagued people with the heat. The poet and his mistress being in love, the people interested in injuring each other can still find reasons to quarrel.

The poet invites everybody to call him and his mistress whatever they like, and he is not offended even by being called a "fly" because flies always follow each other and are always together, and, at the same time, the fly is a symbol of the transitory life. The two lovers may be called "tapers" as well, and they will die down like burned candles after they consume themselves; there is here an allusion to the old superstition that every act of intercourse subtracts a day from one's life ("to die" in the punning terminology of the seventeenth century was to consummate the act of sexual intercourse).

As the poet continues to persuade his friend (and the reader) about his feelings, he finds time to meditate on the nature of love by developing an imagery based on symbolic beings. The eagle and dove are symbols of earthly wisdom and strength, and heavenly purity, respectively. The Phoenix bird is a symbol of immortality and desire rising from its own exhaustion. Eagle and dove are also alchemical terms for the process leading to the rise of Phoenix. The Phoenix riddle is explained here through the theme of love since lovers finally become one sexless, hermaphroditic being. By love they awaken and get up as if from bed, and ascend upwards as if from grave. The lovers resurrect, as Phoenix does, from their own ashes. In this respect, the poet argues, their love does not fit tombs but poetry; he and his mistress will shape in their bedroom fine verses out of their amorous sighs, and the people – making love or reading these verses – will come to regard them as saints and "all shall approve / Us canonized for love".

The last stanza represents a hyperbolic conclusion in that the poet imagines other lovers seeking to model themselves on their love. The lovers being one another's hermitage or solitary retreat are reflected into each other's eyes. They will see the miniature of countries, towns, courts in the eyes of their mistresses. The lovers are thus above the world for they have reached God. This idea is linked to the seventeenth-century belief that God is perfection and one should aspire to achieve perfection by reaching God.

The poem also postulates the belief that each person represents one half of a whole, and by finding each other's second half, the lovers form an ideal pair, a complete and perfect wholeness. This perfect unity of lovers constitutes the perfect love relationship, and only the couples sharing the non-perishable feeling of love and having found the ideal counterpart may reach God. The lovers in the poem have done so since they are close to God, are canonized, and represent the ideal model of the male-female relationship that everyone who is in love should follow.

The term "canonization" as applied in this poem reveals the metaphysical wit opening unexpected thematic perspectives; likewise, in the poem called *Song*, the reader is likely to expect music, harmony, or else audibly pleasant, or read an ode to love and women, but the "song" refers to nothing like that. At first the poem's message seems lyrical and romantic: to go and catch a falling star is a romantic thing to offer, and the lines 3 and 5 propose similar traditional romantic activities which evoke wonder and pleasure in contemplation. But these activities alternate with other suggested ones (lines 2, 4, 6) which create a sharp anti-romantic sentiment.

From this contrast one may understand that these suggestions have nothing in common with the traditional love poems and popular songs, but rather represent parody on Petrarchan devices which would show the impossibility of measuring the poet's love for his mistress. The result is the impossibility of all proposals: it is impossible to catch a falling star, it is impossible to make a mandrake pregnant, and it is impossible to tell who created the devil's cleft foot. Likewise, to hear the mermaid's singing can be delightful, but impossible; to be untroubled by envious thoughts would be delightful, but again impossible.

By trying desperately to find out if there is any possibility of making someone honest, in the second stanza, the poet argues that there is actually no honesty and faithfulness in the world: if you have an inclination to see strange sights or invisible things, search for ten thousand days and nights till you get old. When you return from the quest, you are able to tell all the strange things you have seen and at the same time you will be disillusioned that nowhere you could find a "woman true, and fair". The speaker knows cynically that a faithful woman is never beautiful and vice versa.

In the last stanza, the poet entertains himself for a moment with the possibility of a true and fair woman to exist and imagines visiting her as if on a pilgrimage to Virgin Mary because such a person is extremely rare, representing an ideal. However, with a bitter mockery, the poet assumes that even such a woman, though "she were true when you met her", would betray him two or three times. The poem has a dramatic tone, presenting an atypical view on love, and as it unfolds, the poet surprises the reader, whose expectation fails, as fails the possibility for the reader to face the wit.

An atypical poetic treatment of the theme of love is also offered in the poem entitled *The Indifferent*, in which the poet speaks of the vices and cruelty of women but not men, the poem being thus thematically connected to *Song*. In *The Indifferent*, the lyrical I experienced love with as many as twenty women, and could love any woman, blonde or brunette, who prefers loneliness or prefers companionship, born in the countryside or in the city, yet all are vicious to the poet's mind and "not true". The poet views them as thieves who wish to rob him and from whom he wants to be free: "rob me, but bind me not, and let me go".

The metaphysical wit reveals itself in the poet surprising the reader by presenting an atypical and contrary to our expectations view on women and love – a cruel attitude towards women, in general, who are considered vicious – and, as a "heretic in love", he surprises Venus as well, who "heard not this till now", but even the goddess of love finally accepts it:

> Alas, some two or three
> Poor heretics in love there be,
> Which think to 'stablish dangerous constancy,

and designates that the poet, since he will be true, "shall be true to them who are false" to him.

Donne's most popular poem is *A Valediction: Forbidding Mourning*, presumably addressed to his wife on the occasion of his trip to the Continent in 1612. The poem contains an example of what is perhaps the most famous English metaphysical conceit: the poet develops an analogy between the legs of a compass and the souls of the lovers, trying to persuade his beloved one that their love is inseparable like the pointers of the compass though they indicate different directions, and thereby not to mourn at his departure, which is a temporary separation. Again, as in Donne's poetry in general, the conceit is here the instrument of persuasion, of definition in an argument, and never merely a poetic device in itself.

In the opening lines of the poem, the lyrical I likens the separation of the two lovers to the soul of a dying man separating from his body, and, by referring to the water element ("tear-floods") and the element of air ("sigh-tempests"), the poet implores her to remain stoic, not to surrender to the sorrow for his departure and not to reveal to people their private issues. The "virtuous men pass mildly away" because they are confident in their relationship to God and, in the same manner, the bond of lovers will dissolve quietly and temporarily like the soul of a dying man separating from his body but then joining the divinity.

This comparison is to be regarded as another of the poem's conceits in that the lovers' relationship is likened to the sacred, religious faith. The separation is painful for the staying ones rather than for those who go away, yet there is no meaning in fearing it since love and faith are unshakable.

Mourning and tears provoke in vain floods and tempests, and the poet asks her not to release them because the only effects of the "tear-floods" and "sigh-tempests" would be the profanation of the sanctity of their love, and the public display would be inappropriate for the unique bond between them. To tell everybody of their private issues is compared to the "moving of th' earth" which brings "harms and fears" and affects everybody, and people think of it as an omen of misfortune. An earthquake is a common phenomenon, an image Donne associates to the useless outpouring of emotions. Compared to earthquake, the movement of the planets ("trepidation of the spheres") is more powerful and, though it should create a greater impact, it is "innocent".

According to the Ptolemaic system of the universe, circles and spheres are perfect shapes and represent a perfect relationship based on harmony; according to Aristotle, the motion of the celestial bodies is not straight and finite but circular, and therefore eternal and unalterable. Donne once again elevates their love to a superhuman status, which cannot be affected by anything earthly.

Next stanza creates a contrast between their exceptional love and the "sublunary" love of the others. The inferior love of the "sublunary lovers" is ordinary and subject to change, and such lovers, "whose soul is sense", cannot admit separation because they need physical love to compose their relationship. By contrast, the poet suggests that he and his lover share a purely spiritual love, "a love so much refined" that is almost indefinable. The reason can free itself from any connection with a sensory experience, and, their love being "inter-assured of the mind", the lovers have developed rational souls.

Donne points again to the extraordinary nature of their love, which is free from caring about "eyes, lips, and hands to miss", which is from the need of the physical proximity of one's beloved person.

Next stanza refers to the perfect union of the lovers, the lyrical I claiming that he has found in his lover a soul-mate: the phrase "our souls … are one" reveals the extraordinary relation which both of them share, the perfect connection of the two lovers, a perfection that reminds of the divine love. The poet emphasises the stretching of the lovers' resources in that the love continues to exist in spite of the separation or other circumstances. The separation and the distance between them cause no harm to their love; on the contrary, as the result of the temporary separation, their devotion might become stronger. The reference to gold in this stanza points again to the uniqueness of their relationship which is precious and rare.

The last stanzas contain a more direct persuasion about the vainness of the mourning at his departure, where the instrument of argumentation becomes one of the most striking English metaphysical conceits. The lyrical I compares himself and his lover to the compass, an instrument associated with precision and certainty. It is an instrument whose accuracy depends on the collaboration of both pointers working in a tandem. Likewise, collaboration, confidence and reliance are the most important elements of a successful love relationship. In spite of the apparent differences between the souls, and even if "they be two" like "stiff twin compasses are two", they are identical ("twin") and interdependent since the soul of his lover, though "fixed" and "in the center sit", and "makes no show / To move, but doth, if the' other do", similar to the movement of the compass.

To further persuade his lover, the poet proves his idea by the circle made by the compass. The soul of the lover who remains alone is the fixed pointer ("the fixed foot") of the compass and the speaker who departs is the other pointer of the compass, the one that "doth roam", and when he does so the soul of his lover, "though it in the center sit", "leans and hearkens" after him, and "grows erect, as that comes home". The lyrical I asks his lover to be that "fixed foot" for him, which provides strength, stability, and firmness to their relationship, meaning someone who makes their "circle just". Without the firmness of her soul, the poet is not able to precisely complete the circle, which is to complete the journey and make his way back home:

Such wilt thou be to me, who must
Like th' other foot, obliquely run;
Thy firmness makes me circle just;
And makes me end where I begun.

In the last stanza, the poet ends his act of persuasion by adding, in the Neo-

Platonist tradition, the image of a spiral motion as the movement of the soul similar to that of the circle, symbolizing again the unity of their souls. The image of the circle denotes the regained unity but also the perfection and infinity which cement the notion of their elevated love. The circle represents also the journey that the two lovers endure as a trial of separation but they support each other spiritually and eventually merge in a perfect spiritual and physical union. Moreover, the circle reminds of the wedding ring, suggesting once more their unity on earth and in the name of God.

Apart from the poetic treatment of love and the relationship between man and woman in all their complexity, an important part of Donne's poetry addresses religious themes, namely in a series of poems generally designated as *Holy Sonnets*. Most of the nineteen sonnets were probably written between 1609 and 1611, and all of them follow the standard Italian sonnet form of three quatrains, each with a distinct but related image, and concluding couplet.

Written at a time of personal spiritual crisis and a larger cultural crisis for the country, Donne's sonnets represent a turning to God and are characterized by a deep sense of repentance and a desire to reach redemption and God. Like his love poems, "Donne's religious verse insistently suggests an emotional relationship, that of the sinner to a loving but severe God" (Sanders 199).

In the Sonnet 5 ("I am a little world made cunningly"), the poet likens himself to a world composed of body and soul, and, because he is sinful, his both body and spirit must perish just like the northern and southern parts of the world die. Considering himself a "world", in his remorse, the poet addresses the astronomers and explorers who discover new worlds, asking them to find new oceans to weep or any water to wash away his sins. He begs God to give flood so that he can suffer and reach salvation. He is committed to the sins of lust and envy, two of the seven deadly sins. As washing and drowning are of no use for him, he begs Lord not to burn him in the fire of lust and envy but in the fire of zeal which heals while it burns, bringing redemption.

Thematically connected to this one is the Sonnet 7 ("At the round earth's imagined corners") in which the poet reflects on the unworthiness to be admitted to Heaven of all those people (including the poet himself) who will have to face God in the Judgement Day. The poem opens with the striking image of "round earth's imagined corner" in which the entire round earth resembles the shape of the Christian church and is seen as a Christian universe where the "imagined corners" formed by North, South, East, and West suggest the Christian cross. The sound of the trumpets will raise the incorruptible dead, and those who are alive when Christ returns will be redeemed.

The poet expresses his inner conflict in that he has many sins and he believes that when his time comes, it may be too late for him to be forgiven by God. Therefore, he wants to be taught how to repent, because, if he learns it, repentance would be equal to the pardon of Christ who, by His sacrifice, promised forgiveness to all.

The Sonnet 14 ("Batter my heart") represents the most striking example of all Donne's daring paradoxes. Like the rest of the cycle of *Holly Sonnets*, there is a distressed sinner showing to be fearful of his damnation. Similar to the beginning of many of his love poems, the sonnet starts with a forceful assertiveness addressing yet not a woman or friend but God: "Batter my heart, three-personed God". The poet struggles to bring God into his life and calls upon God to reveal Himself more powerfully to him, yet no matter how hard the poet tries, he cannot escape the bonds of life. Explaining his need for renewal in the first two quatrains, the vigorous expression of emotion in the first quatrain changes into a calm and rational declaration in the second, turning the poem, in the manner of the Italian sonnet, in the direction of the desired resolution between the octave and the sestet, but at the end of the third quatrain, the emotion breaks again through the form.

Reason and love for God represent two sides of the scale by which the poet "balances a plea for a violent physical stirring of his passion against an evident intellectual pleasure in the display of theologically resolved paradoxes" (Sanders 199). The poem culminates in the intellectual paradox that one never achieves freedom unless he or she is captured by God and ends in the most daring of the paradoxical juxtapositions in that the poet asks God to "ravish" him into the condition of spiritual chastity.

The conceit of the "Divine Rape" which ensures chastity might emerge as a blasphemy given its sexual imagery, which can be regarded as a meaning in itself. When not to be taken literally as sexual assault, "to ravish" means an assault "to win someone's heart", and the poet's desire for the violence of the God's ravishment becomes an ideal of devotion, as it is the only assault God can make in order to capture the poet's mind and soul:

> Take me to You, imprison me, for I,
> Except you enthral me, never shall be free,
> Nor ever chaste, except You ravish me.

John Donne's religious and love poetry reveals the use of paradoxes, puns, and startling parallels as well as of a subtle logic aimed at achieving a realistic, ironic, sometimes cynical, even aggressive, and often passionate treatment of the complexity of human motives.

John Donne's fifty-five various poems from the collection of *Songs and Sonnets* (which is the title under which they were first published in 1633) reveal the sense of human dignity and the idealized view of both spiritual and sexual love, and are characterised by an opening which should arise the reader's attention, sometimes by asking a question, which is followed by the argument which is ingeniously developed in terms of ideas derived from philosophy and sciences in a dramatic or rhetorical form.

Like his Baroque contemporaries Theophile de Viau (1590-1626) in France, Luis de Gongora (1561-1627) in Spain, and Giovan Battista Marino (1569-1625) in Italy, John Donne carried in England the characteristics of the late Renaissance period to extreme, to a cultural extravaganza transmitting an exaggerated sensibility subjected to wit in a period when language became more refined, the feeling more crude, and the difference between poetry and prose grew sharper. Donne's poems express the revolt against the poetic conventions of his age, in particular against Spenserian and Petrarchan sonnet writing schools, their highly regular metres and harmonious cadences.

Instead, Donne preferred to violate the canons of rhythmical organization, to write freely divided lines, to express at full the complexity of emotion. Donne sought the allegory, epigram, the pastoral poetry, mythology, the fantastic, Platonism, all combined with passion and dramatic turns, the secular and the religious, and in this complexity of poetic expression anticipating the modernist poetry of T. S. Eliot and others centuries later.

3.2 The Metaphysical Poets II: George Herbert

Another important English metaphysical poet dealing with religious subjects is George Herbert (1593-1633), a priest characterized by diligence and humility, which are traits reflected in his poetry which, on the whole, expresses the conflict between the religious and secular life. George Herbert was born in Montgomery, Wales, on April 3, 1593, as the fifth son of Richard and Magdalen Newport Herbert. After his father's death in 1596, George Herbert and his six brothers and three sisters were raised by their pious mother, a friend and patron to John Donne who dedicated his *Holy Sonnets* to her.

Herbert was educated at Westminster School and Trinity College at Cambridge, where, in 1620, he was elected to the prestigious post of the Public Orator of the University, being responsible for giving speeches of welcome in Latin to famous visitors and writing letters of gratitude, also in Latin, to acknowledge gifts of books for the University Library. This brought him to the attention of King James I who granted him an annual allowance and seemed likely to make him an ambassador. George Hebert, who had originally gone to college with the intention of becoming a priest, became much involved in the life at the court, and, in 1624 and 1625, was elected to represent Montgomery in Parliament. In 1626, Herbert was ordained and became Vicar and then Rector of the parish of Bemerton and neighbouring Fugglestone, not far from Salisbury. In 1629, Herbert married his stepfather's cousin Jane Danvers. He served faithfully as a parish priest and his generosity and good will won him the affection of his parishioners. Being long in ill health, Herbert died on March 1, 1633, forty years old.

George Herbert's literary activity starts with two sonnets written and sent to his mother in 1610, in which the poet argues that the love of God is a worthier subject for verse than the love of woman. Herbert continued writing poems, mainly religious with a few exceptions such as in 1626, when, at the death of Sir Francis Bacon (who had dedicated his translation of *Certaine Psalmes* to Herbert the year before), Herbert contributed a memorial poem in Latin. Shortly before the end of his life, when realizing the eminency of his death by consumption, Herbert sent a collection of his poems in manuscript to his friend Nicholas Ferrar to judge whether to burn them or publish them.

The book was *The Temple*, containing religious poems in common language and rhythms of speech, which was published after his death to enormous popular acclaim and running to thirteen editions by 1680. Herbert also wrote a volume for parish clergy, called *A Priest to the Temple; or, The Country Parson*, which was also published after his death in 1652 and which contain prose advices to country clerics showing the intelligent devotion with which Herbert undertook his duties as priest.

The poetry of George Herbert is largely religious on the thematic level and, on the structural level, is memorable for the poetic techniques of the so-called "shape poetry", of which Herbert was an imitator. In this poetry, the shape of the text enhances and even represents the meaning of the poem. The typographical shape of *Easter Wings*, for example, is that of a flying bird, a shape which reinforces the poem's meaning that man's fall and rise are likened to the motion of a lark's wings while flying. The beginning of the poem – "Lord, who createdst man in wealth and store," – is a direct reference to God, revealing the text's religious thematic concern. The Almighty God created the human being and gave Heaven to him, but the man unwisely lost it. The humans continuously decayed until the first coming of Christ, and the decay and subsequent suffering of mankind were the effects of the original sin.

The poet longs for God's help to rise and he wants to be resurrected as Christ was. This spiritual elevation is important for him because as he gets older, he becomes more sensitive and fragile. The poet suffers from being sinful, and God punishes sin by illness and shame. Shame was the first knowledge of mankind, for it was shame that Adam and Eve experienced after they ate the forbidden fruit. Realizing their nakedness, they could not face the angels, and the human being's woes in general came to the world after the consumption of the desirable forbidden fruit. The suffering and remorse make the poet grow thinner than ever, but this illness does not definitely suggest weakness since it may also stand for a corporeal lightness which would help him rise and emerge into the spirit of God. The final point in this "shape poem" is that through deep suffering and remorse one is granted the hope of reaching purification and attaining God.

The poem called *The Altar* is another example of the shape poetry and, as the title suggests, it is the representation of an altar. The broken Altar is made of heart and cemented with tears because the poet feels remorse. Again, the poet suggests, in order to reach salvation one should regret, mourn, and repent. God gives shape to the heart, and the poet's art is unique, but a heart without love for God is just a stone. Only after the poet's "hard heart" meets the frame of religion and love for God, he is able to praise divinity with all his heart. It is a blessing to possess a sensible heart full of love for God since God created every single part of the poet's heart which bears the name of God and praises the divinity. As long as there is a chance of not committing any sins, all the elements which form his heart will be praising God. The poet's wish is to sacrifice himself for God and become blessed to "sanctify this Altar to be thine".

The religious concern of Herbert's poetry takes in *Love (III)* new thematic perspectives in that the lyrical I performs a kind of symbolic voyage from sin to salvation. At the beginning of the poem, he is welcomed as guest in an inn, but his soul "drew back, / Guilty of dust and sin". The poet is the heir of Adam's Fall, therefore sinful, feeling unworthy to enter the place and be there though the innkeeper named Love claims that he is. The guest is ashamed of his sin, but Love takes his hand, implying that he knows everything, and makes the traveller come to the realization that he should repent in order to be worthy of the place and its host.

The lyrical I discloses that he searches for salvation; he is aware of being sinful and should repent, and he does not want to carry his shame. The innkeeper replies that Satan is to be blamed and, by serving God, one can reach salvation. The metaphysical conceit in the poem is represented by the innkeeper being actually Jesus himself, and the poet-traveller is a guest attending the last supper of Christ.

In the poem entitled *Jordan (I)*, Herbert drops aside the techniques of the shape poetry along with his general thematic concern with God and religion, and focuses on the theme of poetic beauty. As the poem begins, the poet challenges the idea that only unreal matters are true sources for a beautiful poem, asking "Is there in truth no beauty?", the issue behind this question being that truth may also carry beauty. In the second stanza, the poet criticizes the pastoral poetry, arguing that the shadow of "groves" and "arbors" makes more obscure a weak craftsmanship, while the direct poetry is divine because it discloses its meaning openly to the reader.

In the last stanza, the poet concludes that pastoral poets ask riddles, and those who understand them only guess the meaning. The poet emphasizes the idea that he does not envy shepherds who sing their secular songs, for he writes for his God, his King. The poem declares that false poetry is the secular one, like pastoral lyrics, and that divine love poetry and devoted poetry are true and beautiful.

The elegance of Herbert's poetry is as much the result of art as it is an expression of a cultivated spiritual humility. He insists that he would make "Humility lovely in the eyes of all men", and his work is pervaded with references to religious service and Christ, which are expressed through the voice of a lyrical I assuming the position of a suffering servant.

Today, George Herbert is remembered chiefly for *The Temple* book, the poems in which influenced the style of other poets, including Samuel Taylor Coleridge, and several of them have been used as hymns, in particular *Teach me, my God and King* and *Let All the World in Every Corner Sing*.

3.3 The Metaphysical Poets III: Andrew Marvell

The religious thematic component of the metaphysical poetry in Britain receives its supreme artistic expression also in the poems of Andrew Marvell (1621-1678), who, similarly to Milton, is regarded by many as a spokesman of Puritanism. Andrew Marvell was born at Winestead-in-Holderness, Yorkshire, on March 31, 1621, in the family of reverend Andrew Marvell and his wife Anne. When Marvell was but three years of age, the family moved to Hull, where his father was appointed lecturer at Holy Trinity Church. Marvell was educated at the Hull Grammar School, and, in December 1633, he matriculated at Trinity College, Cambridge, being elected to a scholarship in April 1638 and graduating BA in 1639.

Two poems by Marvell, one in Greek and another one in Latin, were printed in 1637 in the *Musa Cantabrigiensis* (a Cambridge volume congratulating Charles I on the birth of a daughter). Marvell's mother died in April 1638, his father remarrying in November of the same year. Marvell remained a few more years at Cambridge, leaving it for London only after his father's death by drowning in 1641. It is uncertain what Marvell did in the years that followed. It is possible that he held a clerkship in his brother-in-law Edmund Popple's trading house from 1640 to 1642. It is known that he travelled abroad in France, Holland, Switzerland, Spain, and Italy between 1643 and 1647, learning languages, and perhaps deliberately avoiding the Civil War. On his return to England, he probably moved to London literary circles and had friends among Royalists.

In the early summer of 1650, Marvell wrote *An Horatian Ode: Upon Cromwell's Return from Ireland*, perhaps the greatest political poem in England. From 1650 to 1652, Marvell tutored young Mary Fairfax (later Duchess of Buckingham), daughter of Sir Thomas Fairfax, retired Lord General of the Parliamentary forces. It is assumed that at the Yorkshire seat of the Fairfax family, Nun Appleton House, Marvell, during a period of about three years, wrote most of his lyrical poems, among which *The Garden*, *To His Coy Mistress*, *The Definition of Love*, and perhaps his most profound work, *Upon Appleton House*, a poem crucial to his development both as man and poet, and in which he examines the competing claims of the public service and the search for personal insight.

Marvell had befriended John Milton by 1653, when Milton wrote a glowing recommendation for Marvell for the post of Assistant Latin Secretary to the Council of State, a post he eventually secured in 1657. Marvell, who had initially been a supporter of the King, under the Commonwealth became an adherent of Oliver Cromwell. Meanwhile, in 1653, living at Eton, Marvell tutored Cromwell's nephew and ward, William Dutton. In September of 1657, Marvell was appointed assistant to John Milton, Latin Secretary for the Commonwealth. Marvell was paid a salary of £200, same as Milton's, though his was not a life pension. In his quiet way, he seems to have been helpful after the restoration of monarchy in 1660 in saving Milton from an extended prison term and possible execution. In 1659, Marvell was elected Member of Parliament for his hometown of Hull, which he continued to represent until his death.

During the last twenty years of his life, Marvell was engaged in political activities, taking part in embassies to Holland and Russia. He continued his literary activity, writing political pamphlets, satires (for instance, *Last Instructions to a Painter*) and prose works (for example, *The Rehearsal Transpros'd*), in which he attacked the financial and sexual corruption at Court and in Parliament, as well as the arbitrary royal power, and set new standards of irony and urbanity in literature. Marvell died on August 16, 1678, in his house in Great Russell Street from medical treatment prescribed for a tertian ague.

The majority of Andrew Marvell's poems were not published until the posthumous *Miscellaneous Poems* of 1681. The poems were printed from papers found in his rooms by his housekeeper who gave herself out to be his widow and who signed the Preface by the name of "Mary Marvell" in order to get £500 which Marvell kept for two of his friends. This volume did not contain the satires, which appeared later in *Poems on Affairs of State* (1689-1697), the authorship of some of which being still disputed by critics.

In the tradition of the metaphysical poetry, Andrew Marvell develops his poetic discourse based on strong persuasive principles, each text containing conceits which help the argumentative purpose. Sometimes a whole poem can be considered to represent a single conceit, as is the case of *On the Drop of Dew*, in which a subtle analogy is progressively created between a drop of dew and the Christian soul aspiring to dissolve itself "into the glories of th' Almighty Sun".

Andrew Marvel expressed in his poetry not only religious and love themes, which are representative for metaphysical tradition, but also themes of public interest, and here as well his voice is that of a metaphysical poet. The best example is the political *An Horatian Ode: Upon Cromwell's Return from Ireland*, written on the occasion of the return of Cromwell from his military campaign in Ireland in May 1650, and the anticipation of another campaign against the Scots. It is a "Horatian Ode" because it is a neo-Roman public poem in which Marvell imitates the oblique method of argument used by Horace in his *Odes*. The inevitability, the rapid change of events and the complexity of the public issues are successfully suggested by the structural organization of the poem, particularly the metre which Marvell uses: an essentially iambic octosyllabic couplet (two rhyming lines with four stresses each) with short interludes of hexasyllabic (six syllable) couplets.

As in other of his works, in this poem, Marvell remains an intellectually detached historian, producing ambiguity of imagery and meaning concerning the nature of contemporary events, and thus opening the perspective of multiple readings of the text. Regarded as the greatest poem of the Civil War, at first reading, the text suggests a formal ode to the glory and extraordinary vitality of Oliver Cromwell, the fulfiller of tradition and the breaker of moulds. Modelling on the metaphysical pattern, Marvell relies on classical references to argue about the historical necessity of Cromwell and the inevitability of his destiny in a period of English history when only a strong leader could save the country from chaos.

However, still a constitutional monarchist at the time when the poem was written, Marvell places a careful tribute to Charles I as a representative of an honourable but dying order, and it is this praise of the King which led some critics to argue that the poem is actually a covert attack on Cromwell, a kind of "crypto-royalist" poem. The King's bleeding head is seen not as a threat to the newly born Republic but as a sacrifice prophetic of its "happy fate" akin to the ancient Rome. The ancient workmen who dug the foundations for the temple of Jupiter at Rome discovered a bloody head, considered an omen that Rome would be the head (*caput*, hence the name of the temple, *Jupiter Capitolinus*) of an empire. England under Cromwell, the poet implies, holds promises no less inferior to those of ancient Rome, for it has been set apart for a special destiny evident in the personal triumphs of those who remain faithful servants to Commonwealth and in the military triumph over the rebellious Ireland and Scotland, and, if it is God's will, over the Catholic France and Italy.

Cromwell outclasses Roman precedents and receives the role of a Christian hero, a man made by peculiar circumstances of his modern times, who is an elemental force, a lightning, beyond the limits of the human control, and who acts like an agent of divinity, according to the will of God. Unusual for the Christian expectation is here the lack of any evidence of peace since the leader is stirred to turn from the arts of peace to those of war, being, like lightning, destructive and without mercy, and bringing not peace but sword.

Influenced by the classical poets Horace and Lucan, and sharing the former's sense of the ambiguity of power in the state, Marvell implies that the martial courage is inglorious when shown in pursuing peace, the political power asserted by force ceases to remain balanced, and it is this objective evaluation of Cromwell which makes the poem a study of the ambiguities of power rather than a simple, formal eulogy of the Puritan leader.

Another of Marvell's most popular poems is The Garden, in which the poet uses nature as the starting point for certain philosophical speculations – where nature, reflected in the mind, assumes a life of its own – which go far beyond what the poem seems to promise. The Garden is regarded as the culmination of Marvell's lyric poetry, his most complete poetic expression of the fusion of soul and body into an ecstatic state defined by critics as "Platonic", "Plotinian", "Christian", or "Hermetic". The garden is a natural Paradise, a pre-Fall world in which the poet's identity is dissolved, and the human corruption is separated from the natural goodness.

The poem begins with the idea that people try in vain to win laurels since the narrow shadows of these crowns do not reflect the efforts that were done to obtain such an honour. Therefore, it is regretful that a man tries so hard and receives so little reward that may offer just a short moment of glory.

In the second stanza, the poet turns to the "sacred plants" which are Sweet Solitude and her sister, Innocence, realizing that it was a mistake to look for them in the company of people. Such sacred plants can only grow among the plants in nature. He understands that society, considered to be a refined order, is nothing but rude and vulgar in comparison to solitude. Not many people understand that the beauty of the garden is incomparably more overwhelming than the beauty of a lover. Cruel lovers, emphatuated in their feelings, cut on trees the names of their mistresses in order to make people pay attention to their emotions, and those who injure the trees are far from the understanding that there is nothing more beautiful than the green garden representing nature.

The fourth stanza expresses a change in the attitude: when people exhaust their passion, Love comes to its end, and even the gods Apollo and Pan, who fall in love with mortal beauties, know that after passion ends, their beloved ones would conveniently turn into plants, meaning that all passions eventually turn to nature.

The fifth stanza represents the climax of sensuality since the poet becomes a passive beneficiary of the delicious natural harvest of different fruits. In this stanza, the poet expresses a hedonistic idea in that the garden is a fertile Paradise where fruits offer themselves to be tasted, and, at the same time, the garden could be the place for important scientific discoveries, as it was the case of Newton who discovered the theory of gravity. The garden is thus the background where scientific and pleasurable things co-exist. Even the Fall of Man mentioned here does not bear anything painful: the Fall results from the amorous outreaching of melons and the embraces of flowers.

The human being is happy and the mind savours the pleasures in nature. Human mind is likened to an ocean, and every experience of the mind creates a new sea. In the garden, mind forgets everything and contemplates nature. This passage of the poem typifies metaphysical poetry in its astonishing leap from the concrete to abstract, from objects to thoughts which do not only reflect things but also reflect upon them. The creative mind finds the strength to annihilate all existing creation into the freshness of "green thought in a green shade".

The seventh stanza develops allegorically the image of the Paradise possessed by the solitary Adam. The Paradise is described as a garden and its inhabitant finds delight in every aspect of the place. The harmony and peace of solitude in nature are disturbed by the God's decision to create Eve. The intrusion of "the mate" ends the "happy garden-state". The reference to time in the final image of the poem suggests subtly that Eden having no seasons is separated from a corrupted and transitory world by the consequences of the primordial sin, the Fall.

Regarded by some critics as an expression of the Horatian Epicureanism or as a mystical ecstasy by others, *The Garden* celebrates the contemplative garden – the "garden of the mind" of classical philosophy, or the Garden of Eden, or the enclosed garden of the *Song of Songs* – and reflects on the abyss between the withdrawal into meditation and the life of man in the actual world as to finally subvert the seriousness of the theme of contemplation by pervasive irony.

Andrew Marvell's most popular poem is by far *To His Coy Mistress*, written in the manner of another popular poem, which is Catullus' invitational lyric *Vivamus, mea Lesbia, atque amenus*. Marvell's poem is thematically divided into three parts which blend together the eternal archetypes of love, time, and immortality. Concerning the poetic treatment of love, throughout his argumentative discourse, by alternating hedonistic and pessimistic states, the poet develops an arithmetical recital of the lady's beauty, attempting to persuade his beloved to give up her timidity and yield to his advances. Time is an important factor for either the fulfilment or lack of accomplishment of their seemingly physical love, and the poet advocates sensuality as a means of defeating time.

In this invitational lyric, the time equals to eternity unless the act of making love is a present experience. In proffering his invitation, and in developing the image of the incompatibility between time-consuming coyness and the relatively short time of enjoying the pleasure of making love, the speaker in the poem relies on two classical motifs – *carpe diem* and *tempus edax* – the motifs on which Marvell structures the entire poem.

In the first part, there is a comic demonstration of the folly of resisting seduction and the issue of time is ironically treated in the expression of the fulfilment of love: the speaker presses the lady to yield before the extinction of passion on the Day of Judgment, unless a hundred years would be needed to praise her eyes, two hundred for each breast, and "thirty thousand to the rest". Also, to highlight his invitation and emphasise the urgency of sexual fulfilment, the poet refers ironically to the growth of his "vegetable love", which represents the lowest level of the Renaissance doctrine of the three souls (vegetative, sensitive and rational). The temporal reference termed "long love's day" is either the day designated for settling personal disputes or the day devoted to making love; in both cases, the phrase combines two opposite qualities: "long" suggesting eternity, the indefinite duration, and "day" meaning the shortness of time devoted to the consumption of the erotic experience.

Time is likened here to eternity and is a pleasant view, unlike the philosophical realism of the second part in which the tone is harsh, the eternity is a desert, and the psychological distress is vivid in the anxiety caused by the anticipated failure to fulfil the sensual desire. Time does not redeem but destroys the physical beauty and the energy of desire; its "winged chariot" rushes the lovers towards the prospect of "Deserts of vast eternity" and grave.

The entire poem argues against the idea of resistance to desire, but only the third part offers the most profound argumentative speculations on time and love, expresses the reassertion of love and pleasure, and culminates in the hedonistic idea of enjoying the pleasures of life and trying to devour time instead of being devoured by it. The solution for reversing the irreversible is to concentrate on present sexual gratification, which would result in speeding up the time. The poet understands the impossibility to stop the devouring time and insists that the lovers' energy spent on making the sun stand still might be better spent on forcing it to run after them. The poem, although briefly, desperately holds out the possibility of a physical triumph over decay and the changes determined by the passing of the time:

> Let us roll all our strength and all
> Our sweetness up into one ball,
> And tear our pleasures with rough strife
> Thorough the iron gates of life:
> Thus, though we cannot make our sun
> Stand still, yet we will make him run.

The life and work of Andrew Marvell are both marked by extraordinary variety and range, as is the history of his reputation. Gifted with a most subtle and introspective imagination, he turned his talents in mid-career from incomparable lyric explorations of the inner life to satiric writings on the issues involved in one of England's most crucial and turbulent political periods. Famous in his time as a satirist, patriot, and rebel against tyranny, Marvell was virtually unknown as a lyric poet. The century which followed Marvell's death also remembered him almost exclusively as a politician and pamphleteer, and even if his poems were published in 1681, they were neglected in the centuries to come (except, perhaps, by some of the nineteenth-century American writers who appreciated and started a gradual revival of Marvell's work).

It was not until after World War I, with Sir Herbert J. C. Grierson's *Metaphysical Lyrics and Poems of the Seventeenth Century* and T. S. Eliot's *Andrew Marvell*, that English history has lost Andrew Marvell as a public figure against the modern high estimation of his lyric poems. Starting with the second half of the twentieth century, Andrew Marvell's lyrics have received much more critical attention than the work of any other British metaphysical poets, even more than that of John Donne.

3.4 John Milton: The Voice of the Century

John Milton (1608-1674) was born on December 9, 1608, in Cheapside, London. His mother, Sarah Jeffrey, was the daughter of a merchant sailor, and his father, John Milton, was a prosperous scrivener and lawyer, Puritan but broad-minded, contributing to his children's education with a love induced for music, reading, and learning. Milton's father was also a fairly well-known composer who contributed to a collection of madrigals in honour of Queen Elizabeth. At the age of twelve, Milton started his education at St Paul's School, and at sixteen, in 1625, he entered the Christ's College, Cambridge, where he remained for the next seven years. During this period, he wrote seven or eight poems in Latin, Italian, and English, among which *On Shakespeare* (1630), but never at that time seriously considered a career in writing but rather for ministry or politics.

To his college years belongs also the poem entitled *Ode on the Morning of Christ's*

Nativity, a Christmas hymn which shows the influence of Spenser and the contemporary pastoral poetry; a number of conceits in the poem reveal the influence of the poetic school of Donne. At Cambridge, Milton was expelled for a term after starting a fistfight with his tutor. Also his eyesight, bad since childhood, was made even worse by all his study, and he frequently suffered terrible headaches. From the very beginning of his literary career (the first literary texts are two successful paraphrases of Psalms 114 and 136, written at the age of fifteen), Milton trained himself a bilingual writer – English and Latin – but we ought to count also his Italian sonnets and songs.

After finishing his formal schooling and leaving the university in 1632, Milton had given up his original plan to become a priest due to the growing influence of the High-Church party, and adopted no profession but spent six years at leisure in his father's home, a country estate at Horton, twenty miles west of London. Here Milton devoted his time to further pursuing his studies in Greek, Latin, and Italian languages, and in Greek, Latin, French, Italian, and English literature, writing, during this period of time, *L'Allegro* and *Il Penseroso* (1632), *Comus* (1634), and *Lycidas* (1637). Like many well-off young men would do at that time, in the late 1630s, Milton toured the Continent, travelling in France and Italy, and meeting the jurist and theologian Hugo Grotius in Paris and the astronomer Galileo Galilei in Florence.

Milton returned to London in 1639 and set up a school having his nephews and a few other children as pupils. In 1640, Milton began a campaign of pamphlets against the authority of the bishops whom many people at that time resented, but the Civil War, which began in 1642, silenced his literary work for about twenty years.

In 1642, John married Mary Powell, aged seventeen, who belonged to a Royalist family, while Milton himself was a supporter of Parliament. Mary Powell grew bored with the life of a poet soon after the honeymoon was over and went back home where she stayed for three years. Concerned with the Puritan cause, Milton wrote a series of pamphlets against Episcopacy, on divorce, in defence of the liberty of the press, and in support of the regicides. These works are some of the greatest English prose declarations ever written dealing with political and religious questions, among which *Of Reformation* (1641), *Apology for Smectymnuus* (1642), *The Doctrine and Disciple of Divorce* (1643), *Areopagitica* (1644), *The Tenure of Kings and Magistrates* (1649), *Eikonoklastes* (1649), two 'defences' of the English people (*Pro Populo Anglicano Defensio*, 1651, and *The Second Defence of the People of England*, 1654), and *A Treatise of Civil Power in Ecclesiastical Causes* (1659) are the most important works.

Meanwhile, in 1646, Milton published a collection of poems but politics was still his main occupation. Milton also served as the Secretary for foreign languages in Cromwell's government. After the death of Charles I, Milton published *The Tenure of Kings and Magistrates* supporting the view that the people had the right to depose and punish tyrants; however, though loyal to Puritanism, he disapproved of Oliver Cromwell's dictatorial ways after declaring himself Lord Protector of the Commonwealth. Though a Puritan in his thought, morally austere and conscientious, some of Milton's beliefs were unconventional to the point of heresy and came into conflict with the official Puritan stand.

In his 1643 *The Doctrine and Disciple of Divorce*, for example, Milton argued that a true marriage was of mind as well as body, and that the chastity and modesty were more likely to find themselves "chained unnaturally together" in unsuitable unions than those who had in youth lived loosely and enjoyed more varied experiences.

In the meantime, Milton's eyesight illness aggravated and, in 1651, he became blind. His wife died in May 1652, shortly after giving birth to the couple's third child. Milton remarried in 1656 and had another daughter in 1657, but both his second wife and daughter died in 1658. During this brief second marriage, Milton began work on *Paradise Lost* and Andrew Marvell began working for him as a secretary, remaining a loyal friend to Milton even after the restoration of monarchy. Almost at the moment when Charles II returned to England, Milton wrote *A Readie and Easie Way to Establish a Free Commonwealth* (1660). After the restoration of Charles II to English throne in 1660, Milton was arrested as a defender of the Commonwealth, but was soon released.

He might have been easily hanged for his many services to the Commonwealth, but Andrew Marvell and several other people of influence spoke out on Milton's behalf. Except the public burning of *Eikonklastes* and the first *Defenso* in Paris and Toulouse, Milton escaped from more punishment after the restoration of monarchy, but became a relatively poor man and in fear of his life.

In the 1660s, Milton moved with his third wife to Burnhill Row and, except a brief visit to Chalfont St Giles in 1665, he spent there the remaining years of his life to avoid the Plague. The Great Fire of London and the Plague delayed the publication of *Paradise Lost* until 1667, when it was an instant success, and none of Milton's other works reached such a widespread popularity in his lifetime. *Paradise Regained* and *Samson Agonistes* were published in 1671, and Milton spent most of the rest of his life writing poems which were dictated to his daughter, nephews, friends, and disciples. Milton died on November 8, 1674, in Chalfont, St Giles, Buckinghamshire, and was buried beside his father.

3.4.1 *L'Allegro* and *Il Penseroso*

Among John Milton's works of youth, *L'Allegro* and *Il Penseroso* already announce some major characteristics of his more mature poetry, such as the concern with the music of the lines rather than their visualizing power, and the poet's ability to create an imagery suggesting vast, limitless space.

The two poems are read and discussed as a single poetic utterance, representing two sides of the poet's soul, two ways of living; in fact, they represent a synthesis of the human active and passive states, and, for this, the poems are complementary rather than competing ones. The poems are idealized visions of the pleasures of rural life viewed in two contrary moods, respectively of light-hearted joy and reflection. Each poem is highly dependent upon the other and neither of them stands adequately alone. The poems were written during the period which Milton spent at Norton, in a green wooded and well-watered region of the country, and the poems show a deep feeling for nature. Termed "pastoral" poems, they are partly descriptive and chiefly poems of sentiment, revealing less a landscape than feelings and states of mind.

L'Allegro (the "cheerful man"), written in 1631, depicts a day spent in the countryside in cheerful activities, where the poet banishes Melancholy, invokes

Euphrosyne, one of the Three Graces, the Goddess of Joy, and other allegorical figures of cheerfulness and merriment, and eulogizes the active and joyful life and the more cheerful side of literature. Such a philosophy of existence is contrasted two years later in *Il Penseroso* (the "contemplative man"), which depicts a similar day spent in countryside but this time in contemplation. The lyrical I is now a contemplative being, withdrawn into a life of thought, and the poet praises the virtues of study and philosophical speculation.

Each of the two poems begins with the dismissal of the opposite state, reflecting contrasting emotions: "Hence, loathed Melancholy / Of Cerberus and blackest midnight born" (*L'Allegro*) and "Hence, vain deluding Joys, / The brood of Folly without father bred" (*Il Penseroso*). In the former, the poet, a cheerful person, dismisses the melancholy; in the latter, the poet, a contemplative person of deep thoughts and meditation, dismisses the mirth, but in both poems Milton deliberately exploits the ambiguity of both terms "melancholy" and "mirth".

The parallelism of the opening parts turns into a relationship of qualitative progression within the framework of the artistic detachment from the dimensions of the real world, with necessary differences in this respect. *L'Allegro* develops a pastoral picture of the rustic existence with its Ploughman, the Milkmaid, the Mower, the festival of marriage, where a simple, common experience represents the secular source of pure pleasure. Supported by a great number of mythological allusions, the poem invokes Euphrosyne, the goddess of beauty and delight, the "goddess fair and free", the "heart-easing Mirth", who is summoned to bring with her "Jest and youthful Jollity".

On the contrary, *Il Penseroso* creates images of some "lonely tower" having existence only in the poet's mind, and the poem hails the "divinest Melancholy" which represents, in association with darkness and shadow, a different source of pleasure in the blessed state of peace, quietness, retired leisure, and "mute silence". The poet finds the desired intellectual experience in the books of those who have reached the final gratification of immortality.

The poems focus on different kinds of experience but there is an uninterrupted flow of harmonious sound which unites them. The differences, in this respect, regard, for example, the approach to the Orphic legend. In *L'Allegro*, Orpheus hears the music given to him from the "hidden soul of Harmony". In *Il Penseroso*, the soul of Orpheus makes the music which "forces hell, grant what love did seek", and the poet, called into a new life, reproduces the song in a kind of new creation. The progression from *L'Allegro* to *Il Penseroso* is also noticeable in the two kinds of dream desired by the poet: in *L'Allegro*, the dream is closely linked to common experience, described as "Such sights as youthful poets dream / On summer eves by haunted stream", whereas in *Il Penseroso*, the poet wishes "some strange mysterious dream".

Structurally, the poems, written in the graceful Elizabethan octosyllabic couplet and containing altogether 328 short lines, represent forms in rhyming couplets, each line having four accents. Both poems are permeated with a coloured imagery reduced to grey, brown, and light black, and developed through a sophisticated treatment of musical effects.

Thematically, the common concern of these two poems is the search for felicity and pleasure with respect to the two opposite states of the human mind, and the final preference is for Melancholy, which represents the solitary state. Love is curiously excluded as a source of pleasure, except the vague allusion in one of the poems to a fair lady living in a neighbouring castle. There is no much expression of the tragic element in the poems, no conflict between desire and duty, no reflection of sin, evil, or pain. The mankind is nothing but a passing spectacle without strong passions and feelings.

However, the poems render a susceptible complexity of expression in the progression from the daylight to night, ranging from careful observation of the countryside to meditations on human destiny through mythic projections. The final part of *Il Penseroso* makes the transition from the profane to the sacred and the mysterious – the underlying theme of both poems – where the poet hopes to hear "more than is meant to meet the ear".

Nature might be a source of pleasure by the sunrise, the spring, the lark's song, the rustic life, the stories told at night (*L'Allegro*), but there is no deeper pleasure and joy than those of the solitary meditation at sunset of the Penseroso who, in "some high lonely tower", reads his books of science and philosophy, letting "gorgeous Tragedy / In sceptered pall come sweeping by" (*Il Penseroso*). The theme of "the quest for created solitude" – in order to find the ultimate and intimate joy and pleasure in the solitary existence of contemplation and study – discloses Milton's ambition to be considered a poet-prophet, and, by being complementary, the two poems show the progression from the common earthly experience in *L'Allegro* to the intellectual experience in *Il Penseroso*, from the profane to the sacred, and the end of the latter poem represents the final step of the condition in which the poet expects the sacred music of anthems to

> Dissolve me into ecstasies,
> And bring all heaven before my eyes.
> And may at last my weary age
> Find out the peaceful hermitage,
> The hairy gown and mossy cell,
> Where I may sit and rightly spell
> Of every star that Heaven doth show,
> And every herb that sips the dew
> Till old experience do attain
> To something like prophetic strain.

Other literary texts written by Milton in the years of his youth are the celebrated sonnets and the poem entitled *Lycidas*, which, together with *L'Allegro* and *Il Penseroso*, would have secured him a prominent place in English literature had he not written anything else at all.

3.4.2 *Lycidas* and Sonnets

Lycidas is a pastoral elegy in which the idyllic existence of the shepherd represents the background to lament the loss of a friend. As its subtitle suggests, the poem uses the unfortunate drowning of a friend as the starting point for its lyrical movement, and "by occasion foretells the ruin of our corrupted clergy, then in their height". The season presented in the poem is spring, but the usual cheerful atmosphere of this time is unexpectedly harsh, and the lyrical I plucks the unripe berries, showing his suffering and anger at the cruel and unjust world in which his friend, Lycidas, has prematurely ended his life. The poet asks the Muses to help him to glorify the greatness of his friend who, a poet too, deserves to be honoured. The lyrical I is not willing to accept his own death either, but when his moment comes, he hopes to receive similar honours.

The poet is first of all a man and therefore not immortal, but by being glorified and elegized, he may become eternal in the memory of the others; moreover, the poet who glorifies another one also receives eternity in his elegy through the act of artistic creation.

The poet, himself a shepherd, sings a funeral song for Lycidas, his fellow shepherd and poet with whom he has shared his pastoral duties. Following the conventions of a pastoral elegy, the lyrical persona recounts his and his friend's experiences of the past, when they could listen to the sounds of the nature and write poems, and even Apollo in his chariot would listen to them. Now things have changed, and even nature mourns the death of Lycidas. In turn, the poet expresses anger with nature deities that could not intervene when the sea took his precious friend, yet he understands the futility of it since Calliope, the Muse of epic poetry, could not save Orpheus.

In his anger, the poet argues of the uselessness of the pastoral poetry written by shepherds, and goes further by attacking the idle and ungrateful Muses that desire only to be famous. Fame cannot be achieved by every mortal, but only by a "noble mind"; it stimulates "clear spirits" that live "laborious days", but when the time of reward comes, "the blind Fury" destroys "the thin spun of life". The poet blames Neptune for letting death happen but at the same time justifies the god for wanting Lycidas who has become "precious now", and finally accepts the inevitability of death.

Expressing no benevolent attitude towards Christian clergy and condemning its carelessness about spiritual issues and its inability of being a "pastor" that should "feed" spiritually the flock, the poet, however, turns to claim that the body of Lycidas should receive Christian burial, for one may not find his place in nature but have his real home in the Christian world, touched by the grace of God.

For this reason, the mourning of the shepherds should stop, because "Lycidas sunk low, but mounted high". "Shepherd" and "pastor" are the traditional names for a Christian priest, and Milton combines the idea of mourning for his friend with a consideration of what a priest ought to be and what are the priorities of being a priest and a poet. In the final stanza, the death of Lycidas is likened to the setting of the sun into the ocean, and the experience of death and resurrection of Christ creates a parallel to the death and re-birth of the day and the length of human life. The poet has been singing the whole day and now, when the sun ends its daily movement, he would prepare himself for tomorrow and other new songs, suggesting the renewal of the poet himself and his further step into eternity.

The issue of time related to human destiny is also a major concern in Milton's sonnets, among which the most celebrated ones are *How Soon Hath Time* (1632), and *When I Consider How My Light Is Spent* (1652). The two sonnets are thematically connected in revealing a personal understanding of the issue of time in relation to the destiny of mankind, in general, and the poet, in particular. The common to both poems image is that of God the "taskmaster", people having certain purposes to accomplish in life and for which they ought to strife. *How Soon Hath Time* reveals the poet's anxiety of not fulfilling his task, the labour of his poetical gift, given the temporal limits of human existence.

In *When I Consider How My Light Is Spent*, written many years later on the subject of his blindness, the poet considers his talent "useless" and his blindness a punishment for not accomplishing the task. However, his anxiety disappears when, as if in a state of epiphany, the poet realises the importance of the faith and devotion to God. His blindness is "his yoke", the burden which he must bear, but the handicap cannot prevent him from serving God by his belief, which is of spiritual essence and thus far superior than any physical activity, work, or "exact day-labour". God "doth not need / Either man's work or his own gifts", and those "who best / Bear his mild yoke, they serve him best" and "They also serve who only stand and wait".

With Milton, the pastoral poetry and the sonnet writing tradition, both representative of the Renaissance literature, had newly flourished in the seventeenth-century English literature and placed the poet in the glorious line of Shakespeare, Spenser, and Sidney. It is also another genre, that of epic poetry, which is revived by Milton in modern period and which places him, as the producer of *Paradise Lost*, in another line, this time of the great ancient writers Homer and Virgil.

3.4.3 *Paradise Lost* and the Epic of Puritanism

The narrative poem *Paradise Lost* is the culmination of Milton's literary efforts as a Puritan writer, and represents the result of his ambition to compose an epic poem to rival the *Iliad* by Homer and *Aeneid* by Virgil. The poem was originally issued in ten books, in 1667, and in twelve books in the second edition of 1674. The chief sources of the poem are the Bible (as interpreted by Patristic and Protestant authorities), the classical writings of Homer and Virgil (from whom Milton developed a conception of the literary pattern of epic), as well as Spenser's *The Faerie Queene* (a text which influenced Milton's use of language and imagery). Like Spenser's text, Milton's *Paradise Lost* is a synthesizing poem by which Milton establishes his status as an epic poet as well as a moralist and theologian.

Milton is a Christian Humanist using much of the resources of the European literary tradition – biblical, classical, medieval, Renaissance – especially the biblical text and Jewish and Christian learning but also motifs, themes and imagery from various ancient myths, pagan classical writings, medieval romances, folk legends and stories, all of which are used to accomplish a clearly defined moral and, above all, Christian purpose.

Paradise Lost textualizes the theme of Fall and Expulsion from Eden, which was a matter of Milton's concern since the 1640s, and that of religious conflict on which the troubled times in which Milton lived left their mark. At the beginning of Book I, Milton states his thematic concern and indicates the ambitious and comprehensive nature of his task –

Of Man's first disobedience, and the fruit
Of that forbidden tree, whose mortal taste

> Brought death unto the world, and all our woe,
> With loss of Eden, till one greater Man
> Restore us and regain that blissful seat

– while also describing himself as an epic poet of high moral status having a high moral task and seeking divine instruction and inspiration for its accomplishment:

> And chiefly though, O Spirit, that dost prefer
> Instruct me, for thou know'st;
> (…) What in me is dark
> Illuminate, which is low raise and support;
> That to the height of this great argument
> I may assert eternal providence
> And justify the ways of God to men.

Apart from an exploration of the moral consequences of the Fall and the failure of the humankind to live according to divine law, another major theme in the poem is that of rebellion, which is reflected in the revolt of Satan and his followers against God and in the disobedience of Adam and Eve against divine order. Milton sets himself the task of justifying God's creational will to his seventeenth-century readers, and, in discussing issues like obedience and the forms of government, Milton also speculates on freedom, social relationships, and the power of authorities.

Apart from various religious issues, the poem confronts political problems too, which, at the time of the poem's composition after the Civil War, the Commonwealth, and the restoration of monarchy, were of real urgency to both Milton and his readers. Milton felt that he could best serve God by following his vocation as a poet and his poetry would serve England by providing it with noble religious ideas in the highest poetic form. Milton sought to write poetry, which, if not directly or openly didactic, would serve to teach delightfully. The body of his work emerging from two main impulses – one religious, the other political – witnesses Milton's development as a Christian poet and national bard. It is with *Paradise Lost* that Milton becomes the Christian singer of an epic poem, a poet concerned with universal issues of general human interest as well as of English national interest between 1640 and 1660.

In writing *Paradise Lost*, Milton, like Pope in the Age of Enlightenment, was not only justifying God's ways to humans in general, but also God's ways to English people. In his attempt "to justify the ways of God", Milton was telling his contemporaries why they had failed to establish a good society by deposing the King and why they had welcomed back the monarchy. Like Adam and Eve falling from the ideal into the human condition, Milton's contemporaries failed through their own weaknesses, sins, lack of faith, extreme passion, and greed. God is not to be blamed for humanity's expulsion from Eden, nor is He to be blamed for the trials and corruption that befell England during the time of the Commonwealth under Oliver Cromwell. For Milton, the failure of the Puritan Revolution was an equivalent of the Fall, English people failing to govern themselves according to the will of God instead of being governed by royal despots. England had the opportunity to become an instrument of God's plan but ultimately failed to realize itself as the "New Israel".

Milton's ambition was to produce "such a work as the world would not willingly let die", a work as a Christian epic which would rank with the great epics of Antiquity and Renaissance, and whose narrative movement containing the story of the Fall of

Man is a "sad task" but

> Not less but more heroic that the wrath
> Of stern Achilles on his foe pursued
> Thrice fugitive about Troy wall, or rage
> Of Turnus for Lavinia disespous'd,

Milton believed that every important period in the course of a nation's history, and Puritanism would presumably represent such a period in English history, produces an epic or epics (*Iliad* and *Odyssey* for ancient Greece, *Aeneid* for the imperial Rome, etc.) to reflect some historically defined thematic perspectives and contain mythic or religious elements. In this respect, *Paradise Lost* is truly an epic, for its mythic component is represented by Christian tradition and its historical and political component refers to Puritanism, a movement which is religious and at the same time political. Offering epical resonance to the fusion of mythology and history, *Paradise Lost* is a true epic of the Puritan period, a text which is religious as well as national, Christian as well as English.

Paradise Lost is more than a work of art; it is a moral and political treatise, a poetic explanation for the course that English history had taken. One should not, however, rely heavily on political in relation to religious issues in the interpretation of the poem, or regard the text only as an allegory on the events taking place in the mid-seventeenth-century England. The poem has an intrinsic literary value in itself, noticeable in the mythic projection of the human existence, the fight between good and evil, the conflict between authority and the rebellious desire of freedom, and the struggle of the individual to assert his personal identity.

Paradise Lost tells the biblical story of the Fall of Adam and Eve – and, by extension, all humanity – with God the creator of mankind and Satan who is thrown out of Heaven to corrupt humankind. Milton attempted at poetically rendering the story, told in Genesis, of the Fall of Adam and the loss of the Garden of Eden to clarify some of the paradoxes of the human status and demonstrate the moral tragic ambiguity of the human being. With his heroic poem, Milton would also explore a cosmic battle in Heaven between good and evil, where the supernatural creatures, including Satan and God, merge with humans and act and react with humanlike emotional states. As in other epics, such as Homer's epics or *Gilgamesh*, Milton opens the discussion on the origin and nature of divinity and man and man's relation to divinity, presenting his own and his culture's views on the meaning of good and evil, the mankind's relationship with the Absolute, and the destiny of man as individual and species.

In point of literacy, there is no other epic poem containing such a variety of styles and voices, as one may observe in Satan's proud speech in Book I, God's teasing of Adam about his wish for a mate in Book VIII, Eve's trancelike speech describing her dream to Adam in Book V, or her gentle tone of the penitential "Forsake me not thus, Adam" in Book X, revealing the beginning of her and Adam's moral recovery. Remarkable is the voice of the poet himself, as in the description of the ideal nature in the account of Eden in Book V, or in the emotional and elegiac tone of the concluding passage of the poem in Book XII, in which Paradise has become lost, uninhabitable, hot and frightening, the angels guarding it leading Adam and Eve, "our lingering parents", to the eastern gate and down to the "subjected plain".

At the end of the poem, after the Fall, the Paradise is lost, the ideal existence of innocent idleness changes into daily work, which is the daily agricultural labour as a punishment for the Fall, the eternal spring gives way to the procession of the seasons, but it is this procession of the seasons which suggests recovery, the cycle of perpetual death and rebirth, and it is this daily labour which establishes a note of satisfaction in human accomplishment.

Moreover, although Adam and Eve, staying "hand in hand", look back at Eden for the last time and some "natural tears they dropped", the "subjected plain", meaning the actual world, "was all before them" awaiting to be conquered by them, this concluding passage suggesting a newly rising spirit of hope and companionship in spite of despair, the impossibility of complete communication and love between the individuals, their loneliness and "their solitary way":

> They looking back, all th' eastern side beheld
> Of Paradise, so late their happy seat,
> Wav'd over by that flaming brand, the gate
> With dreadful faces throng'd and fiery arms.
> Some natural tears they dropp'd, but wip'd them soon;
> The world was all before them, where to choose
> Their place of rest, and Providence their guide.
> They hand in hand with wand'ring steps and slow
> Through *Eden* took their solitary way.

Milton achieves a remarkable employment of the character representation strategies, creating complex personalities to Adam, Eve, God, and Satan, and developing subtle changes in the moral attitude on a cosmic scale involving four great backgrounds of action: Heaven, Eden, Hell, and the familiar postlapsarian world. Here Milton, operating as a poet rather than moralist or theologian, achieves also a remarkable development of the poetic imagery, in particular the one which is related to Paradise, the lost world of felicity, and another which works on a theological level and is related to Heaven and Hell, and the opposition of one to another. This opposition means an eternal war between good and evil, where evil spirits are hold off by good ones, and evil is submitted to good and the hope of redemption.

In *Paradise Lost*, in general, Milton the poet, moralist and theologian creates a new version of the biblical myth, a poetic pattern of the cultural transfer regarding Bible and the seventeenth-century English Puritanism, of which another remarkable example would be Byron's *Cain* in the context of English romanticism. Like Byron more than a century later, Milton follows the general narrative movement of the biblical story but modifies it according to the values of his period and presents his own point of view within its thematic pattern. Adam is the first created man, the father of all mankind, but has no heroic destiny. His love for Eve is out of control and prevails over his love for God, and by his free will, he decides to disobey God instead of separating from his mate. Eve, the mother of all mankind, is impulsive, egotistical, easily flattered, and it is her vanity which is the source of her disobedience. Eventually, Adam and Eve acquire the knowledge of good and evil, understand their having corrupted all humankind and that each generation of their descendants must spiritually struggle to regain the Paradise.

God is the Absolute, the just ruler of Heaven, the creator of earth and humans.

God is all seeing, though He seems to pay less attention to things further away from His light. He is surrounded by angels who praise Him and whom He loves. Displaying a sense of humour, God laughs even at the follies of Satan but when Satan falls taking many of Heaven's population with him, God decides to create a new being, the man, and a beautiful place for him in hope that someday the human being would receive the Heaven.

Called Lucifer in Heaven before turning away from God, Satan is one of God's favourite angels, and, before falling from Heaven, it is his *hybris* ("excessive pride") – and *hamartia* ("tragic flaw"), the fault of presuming to be greater than God – which is the source of Satan's disobedience, separation from God and eventual fight. After being defeated in the War of Heaven, Satan, surrounded by some angels and reigning as king in Hell, becomes the principle of evil in the universe, antagonistic to God, embarking on an eternal fight against God and goodness for the souls of human beings and seeking revenge:

> All is not lost; th' unconquerable Will,
> And study of revenge, immortal hate,
> And courage never to submit or yield.

In the later, romantic period, Byron, in his work *Cain*, develops a similar image of Lucifer – "a shape like to the angels / Yet of a sterner and a sadder aspect / Of spiritual essence" – and makes the fallen angel a distinct hypostasis of the Byronic hero, which, together with Cain and Shelley's Prometheus, represents the aspect of rebelliousness of the English romantic hero.

In Milton's work, at first an angel with a single defect, which is pride, throughout the story Satan turns more and more morally distorted. As represented by Milton, Satan is negatively defined by his standing in opposition to the ideas of Christian heroism displayed through the poem. However, despite being the source of all evil, some critics cannot avoid claiming that Satan is a rather sympathetic figure, the most beautiful of the angels, a powerful creature rising from the fire burning in Hell, and, similar to Byron's Lucifer, a courageous spirit, a rebel, and a symbol of revolt and energy:

> He above the rest,
> In shape and gesture proudly eminent
> Stood like a tower; his form had yet not lost
> All her original brightness, nor appeared
> Less than Archangel ruined, and th'excess
> Of glory obscured: as when the sun new ris'n
> Looks through the horizintal misty air
> Shorn of his beams, or from behind the moon
> In dim eclipse disastrous twilight sheds
> On half the nations, and with fear of change
> Perplexes monarchs. Darkened so, yet shone
> Above them all th'Archangel: but his face
> Deep scars of thunder had entrenched, and care
> Sat on his faded cheek, and under brows
> Of dauntless courage and considerate pride,
> Waiting revenge.

Milton's Satan becomes the opponent of God, and, by forcing the direction away from God, Satan becomes a creator himself – the creator of evil – the principle which is opposed to the principle of good which is created by God. As one of the two main principles of the world, Satan becomes the necessary antithesis for the equilibrium of the universe, a divine Faust who, by the acquired supreme knowledge, places himself in the frame of an eternal existence, independent and firm, ready to confront the absolute divinity. At war on Heaven, God shows His true almightiness but Satan pushes his army to fight and make "a heaven of hell, a hell of heaven". Hell reflects Heaven, and many symbols and structures from Hell echo those from Heaven: Satan has twelve friends drawn from pagan mythology and kings of the past, similar to Christ and the twelve apostles; the same architect who worked in Heaven is used by Satan to build a large and glorious temple in Hell; in both Heaven and Hell, there is a similar hierarchy of the king and angels. In most of these cases, Hell is a distorted image of Heaven, the places being the reverse of each other: Hell is dark, whereas Heaven is full of God's grace and luminous light; physically, the angels of Heaven are beautiful and glorious, those from Hell have become hideous and repulsive; psychologically, Satan's and his angels' pride and stubbornness are the reverse of God's goodness and His angels' obedience and respect.

It is shown that the physical degradation of the angels is due to the distance from the glory and blessings of God. The distance is also responsible for the suffering of the fallen angels, their physical pain, and their spiritual decadence which equals their physical corruption. Hell itself is described as a disfigured body, whose "womb" is torn open to expose the "ribs" of metal ore which are necessary to build Satan's temple, and even the natural phenomena which occur in Hell, such as the eclipse of sun, symbolise the natural as well as spiritual decay.

The representation of Hell as reflecting Heaven, a dominant theme in *Paradise Lost*, is then extended to the idea of earth reflecting both. Critics focus on various political implications of Milton's dualism of Heaven and Hell, where in the latter, like in Dante's Hell, characters and institutions are considered to be subtle references to political issues in Milton's period. Images and symbols used by Milton in his work may assist the knowledge of his contemporary historical and religious background. The glory of Hell compared to the light of an eclipsed sun, for example, might refer to the end of monarchy in England and the death of King Charles I, the "Sun King". The actual sources of Milton's poem are yet much more numerous and diverse, ranging from Greek mythology and epic poetry to Egyptian and Canaanite religious traditions, from the Hebrew Bible to the New Testament and apocryphal texts, from the theological works of the Church Fathers to the texts of popular legends, which reveals that *Paradise Lost* is the work of a poet as well as a religious enthusiast and scholar.

On the structural level, *Paradise Lost* strikes the modern reader with its peculiar syntax, difficult vocabulary, and complex style. Like Shakespeare, Milton contributed to the development of English language, the enrichment of its vocabulary, and to the poetic tradition in English with regard to rhythm, sound, and stylistic techniques. One of these would be Milton's use of the double discourse, meaning literally two sentences spoken at the same time. In the first sentence, for example, which is "Of man's first disobedience, and the fruit of that forbidden tree", Milton develops an alliteration in that the repeated "f" sound does not only add to the aesthetic of the utterance but it connects the "f" words to present a different idea than the sentence itself expresses, which is "first ... fruits" are "forbidden".

Dr. Samuel Johnson, the most authorized critical voice of the eighteenth century, argued that Milton's imaginative writing represents "an uniform peculiarity of diction, a mode and cast of expression which bears little resemblance to that of any former writer; and which is so far removed from common use, that an unlearned reader, when he first opens the book, finds himself surprised by a new language". Also, Milton "had formed his style by a perverse and pedantic principle. He was desirous to use English words with a foreign idiom. Of him...may be said...that he wrote in no language, but has formed what Butler called a "Babylonian dialect", in itself harsh and barbarous, but made by exalted genius and extensive learning the vehicle of so much instruction and so much pleasure, that, like other lovers, we find grace in its deformity". Johnson's point of view is not strictly an expression of antagonism directed at Milton's style and the damage it might have done to English language, because Milton's "call is obeyed without resistance, the reader feels himself in captivity to a higher and nobler mind, and criticism sinks in admiration".

Johnson's opinions are expressive of the complexity and paradox which are characteristic of both Milton's poetry and the critical approach to Milton's writings. As a writer, Milton was recognized early, but his personality and works have continued to arouse discussion, in particular concerning the level of poetic technique with regard to the use of English language and the poetic style and diction.

Like Johnson, T. S. Eliot, in an article published in 1936, attacked the Puritan poet and claimed that the imitation of Milton's style led to a deterioration of English language "from which it has not wholly recovered"; that Milton's sensuousness had been "withered by book-learning"; and that Milton's poetry "could only be an influence for the worse". Some years later, however, Eliot reconsidered his opinions in another essay, in which an ambiguity of attitude arises from the peculiar blend of criticism and praise.

For Andrew Sanders, Milton projects the thematic and structural elements of his ambitious scheme of Paradise Lost on a new cosmic scale, for which the appropriate language would be also new, as well as sustained and weighty, and to some extent artificial:

Even the structural parallels with the epic poems of Homer and Virgil, such as the battle in Heaven, the formal debates, and Satan's exploratory journey through Chaos, are given a new cosmic context. Milton deals with what are ostensibly incomprehensible perspectives stretching outwards and upwards in time and space, and his language, remote as it frequently is from everyday discourse, both challenges earth-bound concepts and relocates received images. (231-232)

John Milton is one of the few English poets who identified himself with Puritanism but his vision "floundered amid the evident divisions, schisms, and uncertainties of the England of the Interregnum" (Sanders 233). Milton had so strong a personality that he cannot be taken to represent anyone except himself, as *Paradise Lost* is taken to represent a literary work unprecedented in English literature.

Concerning the thematic perspectives of Milton's work, a historical glance at English literature reveals that Milton has become a factor of influence on the later generations of writers and his work a source of inspiration for, among others, Alexander Pope, John Keats, Lord Byron, and J. R. R. Tolkien. Concerning the character representation strategies, Milton's reinterpretation of the biblical story – which made William Blake state, in *The Marriage of Heaven and Hell*, that Milton was "a true Poet, and of the Devil's party without knowing it" – and, in particular, the creation of a powerful and sympathetic portrait of Lucifer influenced the creation, more than one century later, of a number of romantic characters, such as William Blake's Urizen, Percy Bysshe Shelley's Prometheus, and Lord Byron's Cain and Lucifer, which are some of the most famous romantic rebels acting against imposed standards and divine authority.

Certain more or less subjective or righteous critical views have not denied John Milton's pre-eminence in English literary history, his work being admired and recognized by every new generation of writers and critics, perhaps to a much greater extent than Milton himself stated in *The Reason of Church Government* (1641): "By labour and intent study (which I take to be my portion in this life), joined with the strong propensity of nature, I might perhaps leave something so written to after-times, as they should not willingly let it die".

3.5 John Dryden and His Critical Theory and Literary Practice

John Dryden (1637-1700) was born on August 19, 1637, in Aldwinkle, Northamptonshire, England. He received a classical education at Westminster School and Trinity College, Cambridge, and then moved to London in 1657 to commence his career as a professional writer. His first play, *The Wild Gallant* (1663), was a failure when first presented, but Dryden soon found more success with *The Indian Queen* (1664), which he co-authored with Sir Robert Howard and which served as his initial attempt at founding a new theatrical genre, the so-called "heroic tragedy" or "heroic drama". The term "heroic drama" was actually invented by Dryden himself for his later play entitled *The Conquest of Granada*.

Meanwhile, the young playwright's reputation grew quickly and in 1668, only ten years after he had moved to London, Dryden was appointed Poet Laureate of England (he was later stripped of the title on religious grounds when William and Mary came into power).

In 1668, Dryden agreed to write exclusively for Thomas Killigrew's theatrical company and became a shareholder. Both his first offering, *Tyrannick Love* (1669), and the successful follow-up, *The Conquest of Granada* (1670), are the best examples of the Restoration heroic drama. However, perhaps sensing the failure of his short-lived genre, Dryden turned his creativity to comedy and produced *Marriage A-la-Mode* in 1672, a brilliant battle of the sexes, one of his most famous plays. Meanwhile, Dryden still managed to produce a number of successful works in the genre of heroic drama, including *The Indian Emperor* (1665) and *Secret Love* (1667), which mixed heroic tragedy with contemporary comedy. Dryden's relationship with Killigrew's company continued until 1678, when he broke with the theatre (which was floundering in debt) and offered his latest play, *Oedipus*, a drama he had co-authored with Nathaniel Lee, to another company.

In his later years, Dryden turned to poetry and solidified his reputation as the leading writer of the day with such masterpieces as *Absalom and Achitophel: A Poem* and *Religio Laici*. Dryden continued to write for the theatre, producing such plays as *Don Sebastian* (1689), the story of a king who abdicates his throne after discovering that he has committed incest, and *Amphitryon* (1690), a brilliant retelling of the classic myth. He also adapted a number of Shakespeare's plays, writing, among others, *All for Love* (1678), a retelling of *Anthony and Cleopatra*, another of Dryden's heroic plays which is nowadays one of the best-known and most performed of all Dryden's plays. They totalize more than 20 comedies, tragedies, and operas.

Around that time, the first French opera, *Cadmus and Hermione* by Quinault and Lully, performed in Paris in 1673, crossed the channel almost immediately and influenced Dryden in his attempts to write an English opera. Apart from this, he also wrote the libretto for several operas, including *The State of Innocence* (1677), an adaptation of Milton's *Paradise Lost*, and *King Arthur* (1691), with music by Purcell.

Dryden's desire for ecclesiastical authority and order led him to join the Catholic Church in 1685, when James II ascended to throne, and, as a consequence of this, he spent the last eleven years of his life in relative poverty and in a climate of strong anti-Catholic attitude. During the last years of his life, Dryden had to earn a living for himself and his family, so he resumed plays and poems and started translating from the great Latin poets, and from Boccaccio and Chaucer. Two months before his death, Dryden produced *Fables Ancient and Modern*, prefaced by one of his greatest critical essays. John Dryden was made Poet Laureate and Historiographer, and as a sign of supreme recognition, when he died in London on May 12, 1700, Dryden was buried in Westminster Abbey in the Poets' Corner, next to Chaucer.

The literary activity of John Dryden includes poetry as well as drama of which almost thirty plays for the stage. Dryden is also one of the founders of British literary criticism, highly acclaimed for the critical study entitled *Of Dramatic Poesie, An Essay* (1668), "his most shapely critical manifesto", "a set piece written at a time of enforced theatrical inactivity during the Plague of 1665" (Sanders 257). Dryden also produced a number of translations, including the works of Virgil. He actually wrote in all important contemporary literary forms – comedy, tragedy, heroic play, ode, satire, translation, and critical essay – and every important aspect of the social life in his time (political, artistic, philosophical, and religious) finds expression somewhere in his writings.

John Dryden as a poet, dramatist, and literary critic would dominate the literary efforts of the Restoration period and English Neoclassicism at its beginnings. The dominance was strong in spite of the many contemporary attacks from, among others, Gerald Langbaine (1657-1692) in *An Account of the English Dramatick Poets* (1691) on grounds of plagiarism. Dryden's importance as comic dramatist is rather small compared to that of a man of letters and poet, and much of the importance of Dryden's poetry lies in his occasional pieces. As a poet, Dryden is totally impersonal; he is not concerned with personal feelings but achieves a poetic comment on matters of public concern, writing at best in the tradition of verse compliment, in addressing particular people on particular occasions.

Dryden first important poem was *Heroic Stanzas on the Death of Oliver Cromwell* (1659), oratorical in tone and already showing the creation of a new type of poetic language – precise, musical, and dignified – which remained a model for the whole

Augustan poetic style. Expressing a drastically changed political view, as well as Dryden's support of the established authority and his ideological fear of disorder, *Astrea Redux*, a poem in heroic couplets written the following year, celebrates the return and coronation of Charles Stuart.

Another poem showing Dryden's concern with social and public events is *Annus Mirabilis*, written in 1666, which describes and celebrates that year's main events, two national defensive victories: against the havoc by the Great Fire of London and against the Dutch naval attack. Using classical and mythological images, such as fire as a ravaging monster and the king and his admiral as succeeding Greek heroes, Dryden intended to write a heroic work in the form of a modernized and domesticated ancient epic.

The line of historical poems continues with a number of satirical pieces, the most notable of which being *Absalom and Achitophel* (first part in 1681), perhaps the greatest political satire in English. Dryden created his satirical poems in the form of satirical character sketches, and he expressed his own critical view of what he was writing in *A Discourse Concerning the Original and Progress of Satire*, which prefaced one of his translations in 1693.

Absalom and Achitophel is "a party poem, one designed to please friends by advancing their cause and to provoke enemies by ridiculing theirs"; also, taking at its basis the biblical story of the rebellion of Absalom, the poem is "both a histoire a clef and a witty deflation of those, generally humourless, Protestants whose first recourse in argument was to refer to biblical precedent of justification" (Sanders 258). Also, *Absalom and Achitophel* answers the contemporary to Dryden social affairs concerning the political controversies about the succession to English throne. Charles II's brother, James, as the legitimate heir to the throne, was unpopular because of his Catholic faith, and the Whigs encouraged Charles's illegitimate son, the Duke of Monmouth, to claim the throne on the grounds of being a Protestant. The Whigs were led by the Earl of Shaftesbury and the Duke of Buckingham (the latter satirized Dryden in the mocking play *The Rehearsal* written in 1671). Dryden took the side of the Tories in the dispute on the basis of his allegiance to the established power and legitimacy.

Working on the biblical story of the rebellion of Absalom against his father David and applying it to the contemporary events, Charles II was alluded to as King David, Monmouth as Absalom, Shaftesbury as Achitophel (Absalom's chief adviser) and Buckingham as Zimri, a name Dryden took from 1 Kings, 16, where Zimri is represented as the murderer of King Elah of Israel and a man who "did evil in the sight of the Lord". Although the story is developed in biblical terms, Dryden follows attentively the contemporary persons and events. The whole text is based on parallelisms which create certain ironic humour, as in the case, for example, of the comparison between Charles, the "Merry Monarch", and King David.

The poem contains a small amount of narrative action but its literary validity lies firstly in the creation of a series of masterful portraits, in which even the villains have admirable qualities. Shaftesbury as "the false Achitophel", for instance, meant to be the personification of evil, is also a "daring pilot", "pleased with danger", a genius gone wrong, a complex and brilliant character in that "great wits are sure to madness near allied". All the character portraits are complex and balanced with a mixture of contempt and admiration, meaning that Dryden managed to give each side in the conflict the full benefit of expression, the reader getting a real insight into the essence of the political debate of the late 1670s and early 1680s.

Absalom and Achitophel appeared a week before Shaftesbury was tried on the charge of high treason, but was acquitted, and a medal was struck by the Whigs to celebrate the victory. This event resulted in Dryden's another satire, *The Medal* (1682), which, in its turn, was answered by Thomas Shadwell's satire *The Medal of John Bayes*, a brutal work which made Dryden take his revenge in probably the finest of his shorter satirical poems, *Mac Flecknoe: Or a Satire upon the True-Born-Protestant Poet, T. S.* (1682). The theme of *Mac Flecknoe* is the choice of Shadwell by his father, Richard Flecknoe (an Irish priest and untalented poet), as his heir and successor to the kingdom of nonsense in prose and verse.

Like much of Dryden's work, this satire was written on political and personal grounds, this time more personal since it is a verse mock-heroic satire as a direct attack on another poet of his time, Shadwell, whom he links with the Roman Catholic Richard Flecknoe. The literary value of the poem lies in the use of the heroic couplet as a device for expressing humorous contempt, and in the form of verse compliment, which aims at expressing a strong personal reaction which may be found to be insulting:

Shadwell alone my perfect image bears,
Nature is dullness from his tender years;
Shadwell alone of all my sons is he
Who stands confirmed in full stupidity.
The rest to some faint meaning make pretence
But Shadwell never deviates into sense.

Mac Flecknoe was followed by a second part of *Absalom and Achitophel*, to which Dryden contributed only two hundred lines. Shadwell reappears here as Og and is portrayed with disgust in relation to his double crimes of dullness and treason.

The satirical poems based on historical, political, and personal experience reveal Dryden's unmistakable style with its argumentative quality, but only with *Religio Laici* (1682) he established himself as a master of verse argument. This poem, written in heroic couplets, shifts Dryden's concern from political and general social to religious issues, as the poem discusses such matters as the wisdom of staying within the Church of England and the necessity of revealed religion.

The Hind and the Panther (1687) was his second poem of religious discussion, written to defend the Roman Catholic position in a debate which engaged the whole nation at that time. The poem is written in the form of a beast fable, with animals representing different religions and sects, and Dryden expending considerable ingenuity in translating the religious situation into animal terms. However, the fable soon gives way to argument and here Dryden, more than anywhere, expresses more elaborately and in greater detail his opinions on religion and politics in a masterful flow of the couplets which neatly respond to each turn of thought. Even if many of the detailed points made by the animals refer to contemporary history and are not grasped by the modern reader, the skill with which the verse argument is conducted can be recognized by further generations of readers.

As a dramatist, Dryden produced both heroic tragedy and comedy, of the former type his most famous play being *The Conquest of Granada* and of the latter *Marriage A-la-Mode*. *Marriage a la Mode* is praised as Dryden's best comedy and as one of the best Restoration dramatic treatments of the issues of sex and marriage.

The term "heroic drama" was invented by Dryden for *The Conquest of Granada*, a play which contains the story of the national foundation of Spain, with the hero, Almanzor, a man of great military competence and a strong personality. In the Preface to the printed version of this play, Dryden prescribed the rules of writing in this new genre, and argued about its importance as a new dramatic pattern, claiming that the drama was a species of epic poetry for the stage, and that, as the epic was to other poetry, so the heroic drama was to other plays.

George Villiers, the second Duke of Buckingham, and others reacted against heroic drama in a hilarious burlesque called *The Rehearsal* (1671), a vicious satire of heroic tragedy, which showed the empty and overblown style of the genre and brought a quick end to the form.

However, another of Dryden's heroic plays, *All for Love*, is nowadays one of the best-known and most performed of all Dryden's plays. As part of Dryden's attempt to revive the serious drama after the Puritan rule, the play, written in blank verse, shows the combination of the features of the neoclassical and Shakespearean drama. The play is an imitation of Shakespeare's *Anthony and Cleopatra*, focusing on the last hours in the lives of the hero and heroine, and reveals the author's concern with problematic philosophical, moral and political issues, the results of these investigations coming to form the basis of his later political, satirical, and religious poetic works.

It was not in drama but in poetry and literary criticism that Dryden established a pattern of writing and a number of theoretical principles which determined the character of the neoclassical doctrine and literature in the next century, as he established a new style in prose and poetry which influenced, among others, Alexander Pope, the most brilliant writer among the Augustans.

John Dryden, the second in the line of the most prominent English literary critics, represents the Restoration period in the history of English literary criticism, and, like Sidney's critical work, Dryden's *Of Dramatic Poesie, An Essay* reveals the condition of the contemporary to him literature. Written in the dialogue form borrowed from Plato, Dryden introduces in his text four characters as speakers, who represent ancient Greek drama (Crites) versus modern literary tradition (Eugenius), and the contemporary French dramatic practice (Lisideus) versus English literary practice (Neander). The voice of Dryden in the text is Neander, who expresses critical ideas by comparing Jonson and Shakespeare, the two most important English Renaissance writers, along Fletcher and Baumount.

Working on the seventeenth-century concept of "wit" as the writer's creative power, imaginative flight, and the ability to create unexpected imagery, literature of high aesthetic status, Dryden embarks on a comparative critical evaluation of Shakespeare and Jonson, startling in its approach and concluding reflections.

Dryden's criticism on Shakespeare reveals, actually, only two directions of approach: first, that the great Renaissance writer is a complete Renaissance man, having "the largest and most comprehensive soul", and, second, that Shakespeare is the "greatest wit".

About Jonson, Dryden is able to identify more characteristics, namely that Jonson is (1) subject to training, rules and discipline: "the most learned and judicious Writer which any Theatre ever had", "a most severe Judge of himself as well as others"; (2) promoter of common sense and measure, using to a lesser degree the imaginative faculty, or "wit": "one cannot say he wanted wit, but rather that he was frugal of it"; (3) rational, "saturnine" and less expressive of feelings: "you seldom find him making Love in any of his Scenes, or endeavouring to move the Passions; his genius was too sullen and saturnine to do it gracefully"; (4) satirical in his work: "humour was his proper Sphere, and in that he delighted most to represent Mechanick people"; and (5) educated in the spirit of the ancient tradition and imitative of the ancient models: "he was deeply conversant in the Ancients, both Greek and Latine, and he borrowed boldly from them".

What appears strange and surprising is the subjective and, at the same time, superficial criticism on Shakespeare as compared to the more objective and profound approach to Jonson. In this, one can easily notice that Dryden's preference is for Jonson, "the more correct poet". The Restoration critic Dryden concentrates more on Jonson than on Shakespeare and his critical ideas on Jonson are more systemic and comprehensive than those on Shakespeare.

The question is, then, what has determined Dryden to follow this critical path if in the history of British literature William Shakespeare is considered to be a more important writer than Ben Jonson? Dryden, certainly, does not deny Shakespeare's status, the greatest of English writers, for whom he claims to feel sincere love, but Jonson is a no less important writer, for whom Dryden expresses his sincere admiration:

> If I would compare him [Jonson] with Shakespeare, I must acknowledge him the more correct Poet, but Shakespeare the greater wit. Shakespeare was the Homer, or Father of our Dramatick Poets; Jonson was the Virgil, the pattern of elaborate writing; I admire him, but I love Shakespeare.

In these different attitudes, and especially in considering Restoration – the period in which Dryden wrote his critical text – as the period offering the beginnings of neoclassicism in England, one can find the answer to the question of what might have been the reason for Dryden's critical emphasis on Jonson rather than on Shakespeare.

Moreover, by realising that the characteristics of Jonson, as presented by Dryden, are clear aspects and major principles of the neoclassical doctrine which is on its way of being implemented in English cultural background, one may easily give the answer by saying that Dryden finds and promotes Jonson as an admirable and perfect model found in the Renaissance of a complete neoclassical writer.

In more general terms, it is clear again that John Dryden, in his *Of Dramatic Poesie, An Essay*, a work of art in itself, pleading for European recognition of his native literature and for the synchronization of British with the general European literature, prescribes, with full judicious detachment and open-mindedness, to his fellow writers the ancient classical and contemporary, in particular French, doctrines to be followed in thought and Elizabethan drama of Shakespeare and especially Jonson to be revived, and along with the contemporary European models, to be imitated in literary practice.

In this respect, one might consider Dryden's critical discourse to be, first of all, prescriptive, then dependent on and highly expressive of its literary period, Restoration, as the first part of the larger neoclassical age.

Dryden's criticism is also to be viewed as defensive and subjective. And what he defends through the lens of subjectivity is his national literature, the great aesthetic values of the literary work of Shakespeare and Jonson. This is expressed, among other things, through a sense of national pride revealed in Neander's affirmation that "in obeying your commands I shall draw a little envy upon my self", and, later in the text, when Neander claims that "we have as many and profitable Rules for perfecting the Stage as any wherewith the French can furnish us".

CONCLUSION

THE LITERATURE OF A TURBULENT AGE

The present book is an insight into both the literary practice and critical thinking of the seventeenth-century English cultural background. In particular, it focuses diachronically on English literary phenomenon in the seventeenth century, and it covers some of the most important periods and experiences of English literary history – the seventeenth century, in general, including metaphysical poetry, Puritanism, and Restoration – and in this respect, the reader of the present book learns the characteristics, philosophy and literary theory and criticism, literary conventions and genres, movements and trends, main writers and major works, and the literary interaction and continuity of the given periods. The present book should be useful to a more general reader or anyone concerned with English literature, whose knowledge on particular aspects of the literature in Britain might be enriched by the reading of this book. However, the primary aim of the book regards the needs of students of English in their literature classes, and the book meets the requirements of a teaching aid, while also representing an attempt of academic research in the field of literary history and criticism focused on the "turbulent" seventeenth century.

The seventeenth-century English literature clearly reveals three major parts or periods of its historical advancement, namely (1) **metaphysical poetry** during the first decades of the century, which was followed by (2) **Puritan period** (1649-1660), and finally (3) **Restoration period** (1660-1700), itself part of a longer period called "neoclassicism" which would cover much of the eighteenth century until the rise of romanticism. Such a periodization is convenient – just as it is to name John Donne, John Milton, and John Dryden the dominant literary figures of the century – yet not entirely precise or it is even inappropriate since throughout the whole century the turbulent historical and social scene, the aftermath of Renaissance, the new developments in literary practice, the advancements in thought, and especially the co-existence or rather "battle" between innovation and tradition make it impossible to establish precise dates.

The last decades of the sixteenth century and the first ones of the seventeenth century saw a reaction against the aesthetic principles of the classical art and the whole ancient classical spirit which had been revived and cultivated since the early Renaissance. This cultural reaction which started in Italy and manifested in visual arts, music, and literature is called the "**Baroque**". First in Italy, with "Marinism", or "Secentismo", founded by Giovan Battista Marino, and then in other countries of Europe, including drama in France, Gongora in Spanish painting, Donne and his school of metaphysical poetry in England, the Baroque is unified by a creative spirit which rejects the classical tradition, but the complexity of concerns of the Baroque makes it not a definite style but a group of styles, one of which is "metaphysical". In this respect, John Donne's poetry belongs at once to the more particular one which is "metaphysical" as well as to the general classification as "Baroque". The Baroque rejects the normative prescriptions, rules of composition, reason, measure, common sense and the separation of the genres. Instead, it advocates the freedom of artistic expression, strong emotion, violent action, return to nature, rediscovery of the supernatural, cult of wit, and the intellectual play. In England, the metaphysical writers revolted also against the conventions of the Elizabethan love poetry, in particular the Petrarchan conceit.

Baroque (including metaphysical poetry) is designated as a cultural extravaganza of the period, the highest manifestation of the innovative element in the historical advancement of literature at the beginnings of modernity.

In the aftermath of the metaphysical poetry, the rest of the seventeenth century displays a complex as well as turbulent literary phenomenon encompassing innovation and tradition co-existing and opposing each other throughout the period. This conflict has received the name of "the battle of the books" or "la querelle des anciens et des modernes".

In the literary field, the beneficial outcome of the battle was productivity, creativity, experimentation, innovation, and originality, which ultimately means the advancement of literature through history while developing and acquiring complexity of new thematic perspectives and new means of artistic expression.

The chief developers of the **metaphysical trend** in British poetry are John Donne, George Herbert, Andrew Marvell, Richard Crashaw, and Henry Vaughan. Their subtle, ironic, mysterious and distinctly love or religious lyrics represent the best English literary records of intelligent, acute and sensitive minds that were able to achieve the fusion of feeling and reason, passion and thought, which are reconciled in a single act of poetic discourse.

> The central element in the literary system of the metaphysical poetry is "**imagery**" with its twofold perspective involving the famous metaphysical "**wit**" – representing a means of creating imagery, or the ability of the poet to make apt comparison and to associate ideas in a natural but unusual and striking manner so as to produce surprise joined with pleasure – and the not less famous metaphysical "**conceit**" – representing the textual expression of the wit.

John Donne's ***A Valediction: Forbidding Mourning*** is a canonical metaphysical work of the poetic genre, where each line and each stanza prompt features of metaphysical poetry: (1) a **conceit** in the first stanza compares the separation of soul and body with the separation of "he" and "she", which should remain a private matter not to be exhibited or made a public performance; (2) next stanza relies on **exaggeration** and **irony** when mourning provokes cataclysmic natural effects; (3) next comes an **argument** based on the idea of the spiritual superiority over the physical in love; (4) the argument continues with the idea of mind not sense uniting the lovers, which leads to the metaphysical **rationalization of feeling**, or "feeling thought", in T. S. Eliot's words, and immediately, the concluding idea or point of the argument – that their two souls are one – results in this argument to be exemplified and proven as true by the most famous **conceit** in English literature, which is based on the comparison between a compass and the souls of lovers; (5) the explanation of this comparison requires **intellectual knowledge** which provides the speaker with a superior status, whereas she is on a kind of inferior level; (6) explanation ends and its finality produces persuasion which occurs as the final, ultimate aim of the text; (7) this is better achieved through economy of language as well as a conversational use of language, a language which is alive; (8) finally, mostly related to human intellect, is wit, the faculty of an individual, which is responsible for the production and textualization of all the above features and elements in a metaphysical poem, denoting that wit represents the actual creative faculty responsible for the act of poetic creation.

Since conceit can be viewed as a particular form or materialization of wit, Donne's comparison of lovers to a pair of compasses is indeed the most famous example of both metaphysical conceit and wit, where wit is "an outrageous, fantastic piece of imagination, and yet it is carefully and logically thought out; the image develops in an intellectual precise way, as if it grows in the mind as the poet is writing and has to be analysed even in the act of creation" (Van Emden 3).

The conceit, a type of metaphor created by the power of the creative faculty, which is wit, to develop extended comparison, is "an image which is explored and developed at length, demanding great control and precision on the part of the writer" (Van Emden 3-4). The concept of wit together with the use of conceit is central to the metaphysical poetic discourse in which a thought represents an experience and modifies the poet's sensibility.

In order to express the experience more accurately, metaphysical poets appeal to human mind and analytical thinking rather than to senses, attempt to rationalize the feeling, create the startling imagery prompted by conceit, and make use of wit for argumentation and persuasion just as the earlier, Renaissance poets used it for ornamentation and as it would be used later in seventeenth century, during Restoration, as well as in eighteenth century by Pope and others until the rise of the romantics who will come to proclaim imagination as the supreme creative faculty of the poet in his or her artistic endeavours.

Thematically, the seventeenth-century metaphysical poets perceive a harmonious pattern of the universe, in relation to which stands the significance of human experience in its double perspective: religion and love. The chief subjects are God, love, death, and human frailty, which are expressed and made explicit by the use of carpe diem ("seize the day") and tempus edax ("devouring time") motifs. Concerning the style, the main features of the metaphysical poetry are concision and concentration in poetic expression, which mean a conscious tendency of economy in language. The poet is too busy arguing an issue in terms of reason and leaves outside whatever seems irrelevant. Rationalization of emotion, or "feeling thought", as T. S. Eliot puts, is another important thematic presence in metaphysical poetry induced by scientific advancements as well as by a strong humanist attitude.

Metaphysical poets did not manifest as critical voices whose theories would strengthen the literary validity of their art and confer to it continuity in literary history, as was the case of the poet-critics Wordsworth or Coleridge, for example, regarding romantic literary practice. There were other writer-critics who acclaimed or on the contrary derogated this school of poetry.

In the development of literature, the Baroque, or metaphysical poetry, is regarded in the line of innovation, of which the next important manifestation is the romantic art. Rejecting classicism, romanticism would break the linearity of literary development dominated by tradition and revived the freedom of expression and re-institutionalised experimentation and originality; similarly, the Baroque "represented an oasis of spiritual freedom between medieval scholastics, neo-Aristotelian norms of the Renaissance and the rigours of French classicism" (Ceuca 166).

The most influential among the metaphysical poets is **John Donne**, popular since lifetime with his work circulating in manuscripts and published after death by his son. Donne's *Satires, Elegies, Paradoxes and Problems* of the 1590s and *Songs and Sonnets* roughly between 1610 and 1630 reveal an artistic personality whose poetic gift gave birth to love poetry and religious poetry, as well as satires and paradoxes. His paradoxes and satires rely on play, argument, debate, logical techniques, defence, ornamentation, and persuasion, similar to rhetoric and logic, which is a common discursive practice during Renaissance and seventeenth century. Sidney, for instance, uses these methods to build up a critical defence of poetry in which he also relies on paradox, as in his answer to the second accusation by puritans against imaginative writing.

Donne's love poems break the sixteenth-century tradition in which the poet places his lover on a remote pedestal, approaching her only to be rejected and as a consequence finding inspiration from his frustration of being unable to consume his love. Instead, in his love poetry, the poet, assuming a different identity, wearing a mask, places her next to him in bed and describes and rationalizes the erotic experience exalting love consummated. "I" and "she" of the lovers change into "we" and "us"; their relationship is made universally representative and they are symbols, examples to be followed and become saint-figures, "canonized for love". In his religious poetry of the *Holy Sonnets*, the lyrical I is the poet himself developing a metaphorical expression of the union between individual soul and God in a number of texts which are more conventional in form than his love poems but still relying on various innovative methods and figures of speech such as paradox, where, for example, chastity co-exists with immorality.

In the first half of the seventeenth century, however, the metaphysical poetry of John Donne and others – attempting to achieve originality and experiment – is not an exclusive presence on literary scene but shares it with those who, like **Ben Jonson**, imitate and reflect classical models by which extending the Renaissance revival of and emphasis on ancient classical tradition.

Unlike Donne, who is classified as amateur, writing like others from higher social class not for money bur for purely aesthetic ends, Jonson was a professional writer earning money from writing, especially drama and particularly satires and masques. As a poet, Jonson wrote three collections of poems in which he maintains a strong "I" of himself and a constant attitude to life and poetry, which is primarily moral. His verse can be truly called "ethical poetry", for his choice as its subject-matter is the innate opposition between virtue and vice, and a good poet, in the spirit of humanism, promotes morality, praises virtue, attacks vice, and blames immorality. Then, what in Donne is love, in Jonson is virtue. Unlike in his drama, largely modelled upon ancients, in his poetry, on structural level, Jonson would make some attempts at experimentation, such as with his "broken" couplet involving sound against sense, rhyme against syntax, but he would never achieve the originality, innovation, and complexity which characterize the contemporary metaphysical poetry of Donne and others, or shape poetry, or emblem poetry.

This binary opposition "Donne versus Jonson" led to a famous but inadequate classification of the writers of the period to be designated as the dichotomy of "Sons of Ben" and the "School of Donne", which is, nevertheless, useful to point out the co-existence, in the period, of both traditional and innovative element in literature. The assertion of the revived ancient classical tradition in the seventeenth century owes its success throughout the period not only to the aesthetic conception and literary practice of Jonson and his followers but also to other factors, artistic as well as social, such as education based on Latin and Greek; scholars and writers trained in rhetoric and logic and memorising Ovid, Cicero, and Seneca; and learning classical techniques of composition and figures of speech, and often writing Latin verse as by Jonson, Donne and Milton.

The first decades of the seventeenth century, known as the Jacobean Age (more precisely during the reign of James I between 1603 and 1625), ask for another distinction because they represent also a period of co-existence of older attitudes and forms, rooted in medieval tradition, with new attitudes and forms, rooted in Renaissance spirit. An exponent of the former would be Sir Walter Raleigh who, in the *History of the World* (1614), uses "fall of princes" as the subject-matter of history and, in poems such as *What is Our Life* and *The Lie*, shows a *contemptus mundi* attitude which is again more characteristic of the Middle Ages in their poetic expression of human fall, evil, guilt, and punishment. The latter aspect – signifying reassertion of human dignity, revival of ancient classical tradition, and emphasis on moralising didacticism – emerges in the writings, mostly non-literary, of Francis Bacon and in the dramatic works of Ben Jonson as well as in George Chapman's translations of the ancient Greek epics.

Apart from keeping alive and spreading among his contemporaries the ancient classical models, the great Renaissance writer Ben Jonson extends into the seventeenth century the humanist attitude that a good poet must be a good man, a guide and guardian of morality. The humanist philosophy, born in Renaissance, is actually a strong presence in the seventeenth century, on the whole, and in the works of most of its authors disregarding their appurtenance to either tradition or innovation.

John Donne, for example, is a humanist by (1) assuming his lyrical persona to be an integrated consciousness, a unified self; (2) placing emphasis on individualism, self-analysis, and personal potential; (3) emphasising exploration of the world through the mind, experiment, intellectual curiosity; (4) emphasising the importance of the world of man and of the man in the physical world; (5) acceptance of knowledge, discovery, invention as granted by Divine Power; (6) rationalization of feeling and reliance on argumentation and persuasion; (7) search for knowledge and discovery of the mysteries of existence, as in "my soul ... be thirsty", declares the poet; and (8) a positive and optimistic worldview. The attempts to explore the world by means of experiment, intellect, reason, and scientific curiosity along with the search for knowledge and the discovery of the mysteries of life render the concept of *vita activa* all the way throughout later in Renaissance and seventeenth century, as it can be seen, predominantly, in Frances Bacon, whose merit – grounded in his seventy books, of which the most influential being *The Advancement of Learning* (1605) – would be to have defended and promoted the pursuit of knowledge against all, including Church's, restrictions while strengthening the belief in the perpetual renovation of knowledge.

To revert to literary practice of the period, the Baroque is considered either as the last part of the Renaissance or as succeeding the Renaissance and thus being a particular phase between the Renaissance and the rising, in the seventeenth century, Enlightenment and classicism (neoclassicism) which dominated most of the eighteenth century as well.

Against metaphysical poetry, representing innovation in literature, is neoclassicism representing tradition in literary thought and literary practice and which, following the Puritan period, would rise during the Restoration period and flourish in the next, eighteenth century during the Augustan Age and the Age of Johnson. In other words, as a part of the general eighteenth-century European, philosophical and cultural movement termed Enlightenment, the British Augustan Age or Age of Reason (1700-1750) represents together with the Age of Johnson (between 1750s and 1780s) the eighteenth-century neoclassicism which started actually in the second half of the seventeenth century in Restoration (1660-1700).

Prior to Restoration, the period of **Puritan Commonwealth** creates its own ethos of social and private life as well as its own aesthetics. Sharing this ethos – with its emphasis on individual salvation and a life as test of one's virtue to reach "celestial glory" as the reward – are Milton, Bunyan, and Marvel, who started from a Puritan background to become accomplished authors of the seventeenth century.

A unique phenomenon, difficult to classify, the work of **John Milton** encompasses elements of various contemporary styles, trends, and genres, displaying a distinct manner of writing of a strong literary voice. Milton's individuality is also supported by an impressive background of becoming a poet, which includes years of studies at home, seven years at Cambridge, travels to France and Italy, time devoted to Latin, Greek, Italian, and English as well as to theology, Bible, philosophy, science, and literature. In his prose polemic *Areopagitica* (1644), Milton already displays his conception that good and evil in this world "grow up together almost inseparably" and we must know evil in order to be able to reject it by a deliberate act of will and for this, we must have the liberty to struggle and the liberty of knowledge as well as the free exchange of ideas: "Give me the liberty to know, to utter, and to argue freely according to conscience, above all liberties", claims Milton in *Aeropagetica*. This concept of life finds its later expression in English literature in Pope's declaration of good and evil to be parts of a "stupendous whole" or in Blake's oppositions in his both "songs of innocence and of experience" and "prophetic books". Milton himself produced works with oppositions, such as *L'Allegro* and *Il Penseroso*, meaning cheerful and thoughtful, or Renaissance dichotomy between virtue and pleasure in *Comus*, which also expresses the ethics of *Areopagitica*. The concept of *vita activa* is embodied in his work too, which, in general, shows Milton's involvement in religious and political life of his period. *Lycidas* is a pastoral elegy to the memory King Edward, but the majority of his writings, particularly his eighteen works produced between 1641 and 1660 support the Puritan rebellion and its cause.

Paradise Lost, his masterpiece, would be the epic poem of Puritanism, which Milton believed that would last to represent a major phase in human history and, as every great epoch, it necessitates its own master-work, an epic, the aesthetic representation of its system of principles, values, mentality. Published in 1667 after many years of studies and preparation, this epic without a hero embodies elements of epic as well as drama; Milton actually conceived it originally as a tragedy, given the issue of temptation, the fall of the angels, and the fall of man, and the lack of admirable roles. Fallen angels represent the greatest evil in God's creation and Milton makes evil look both sinister and ridiculous, where they are shown as a mixture of degradation, absurdity, and futility. Stepping in front on the thematic stage is Satan, a pseudo-hero seizing the role to seduce mankind, which denotes the dramatic material of the temptation in Eden. In the tradition of the epic poetry, the involvement of the poet in the poem as narrator is vivid, as it can be seen in Eve's soliloquy or in the rendering of Satan as both a character and a point of view, and the events being directed by the poet as well as retold by him. Milton's purpose in his poem is "to justify the ways of God to men" – assumed later by Pope in *Essay on Man* – which he combines with the aim to render and defend artistically the divine plan to redeem mankind's sin and fall through the sacrifice of God. For this, connected to *Paradise Lost* is *Paradise Regained*, a "brief epic", as it is known, five times smaller (2,065 lines) than the former work (10,565 lines). *Paradise Lost* ends with the expulsion of Adam and Eve from paradise whereas *Paradise Regained* celebrates Christ's rejection of Satan's tempting and allows the possibility of salvation.

John Bunyan's *The Pilgrim Progress* reverses the moment of expulsion from *Paradise Lost*. Here, ordinary characters are introduced, with whom everybody shares the goal to solve the soul. Due to this and also due to its being rooted in everyday reality, but also its universal resonance by its events being recounted by a narrator as the dreamer figure as if borrowed from medieval allegory, Bunyan's work experienced greater appeal with the public, allowing stronger involvement of reader, than Milton's work. The journey of Christian, particularly his internal pilgrimage, is a journey of acquiring knowledge and self-knowledge, and the work ends with the reestablishment of the balance of the value system.

A distinct English writer of the period is Andrew Marvell with an interesting biography – Latin Secretary, political agent abroad, acting MP, active during Interregnum, but also survived the Restoration by proving his loyalty to the returning monarch – and similarly complex literary life. Marvell involved in ethical and state issues strongly believing that a writer must assume a responsible role in society to encourage and celebrate "well-being". This involvement finds its thematic expression in his work through the concern with the dialectic between private and public life, such as in his most famous invitation to love, which is *To His Coy Mistress*. Referred to as a metaphysical poet, Marvell blends, like Donne, lyricism with paradox, feeling with thought, conceit with wit in most of his lyrics, which display a complexity of thematic perspectives and a diverse typology ranging from political poems to love poems, as well as religious poems, pastorals, and satires. An exception against the image of his active and hectic life is *The Garden* in which the speaker rejects the whole ethos of his active life, including society, crown, women, the pleasures of senses, and withdraws into a reverie from which his soul looks forward to its flight to heaven.

Following the Puritan Commonwealth Interregnum, the restoration of monarchy with the return of Charles II to the throne made Marvell and other poets change views and welcome the king's imminent return only a short period after having celebrated or commemorated Cromwell. Edmund Waller is among them; Marvell too, who wrote in 1650 his famous political poem *An Horatian Ode: Upon Cromwell's Return from Ireland*; John Dryden, who gives his name to the last decades of the seventeenth century – "Age of Dryden" – wrote *Heroic Stanzas on the Death of Oliver Cromwell* to mourn Cromwell's death in 1659 and, a year later, he wrote *Astraea Redux* in which, using metaphysical conceit, creates an imagery of the land moving from its place to receive the king in his ship drawing near.

Now, with the return of the king and throughout the **Restoration period**, literature changes its concerns and subjects as if proving the postmodern concept of the individual subject, including writer, to be subjected to power systems and imaginative writing, responding to social events, and to constitute artistic transformation of ideological representations. The king and court are now celebrated, Cromwell forgotten, Puritans lampooned and their values and beliefs subverted in various works, such as *Hudibras* by Samuel Butler. The dominant genre of the period is drama and its main type is the so-called "**comedy of manners**".

Concerning literary practice and critical thinking on literature in the last four decades of the seventeenth century, the period is governed by the impressive figure of **John Dryden**, characterised by a strong historical-literary sense and that of political security. Proud for his national achievements, both social and aesthetic, Dryden writes thematising the glory of nation in the past and in his age, as in the historical poem *Annus Mirabilis*, celebrating two public victories, or the critical treatise *Of Dramatick Poesie, An Essay*, which grounds him the title of the father of English criticism, celebrating artistic, literary achievements of English nation. Dryden's importance in the historical advancement of literature rests mainly on his literary criticism followed by his translations of Virgil's pastorals and *Aeneid*, and other works, his writing of more than 20 comedies, tragedies and operas, as well as on his witty satires, while perfecting **heroic couplet** (iambic pentametre with pairs of rhyming lines aabb) and allowing literary experiment co-exist with his assumed attempts to promote ancient models into his contemporary cultural background. Concerning the thematic progress of his works, most of them and, in particular, his satires are written on personal and political grounds – such as *Mac Flecknoe*, on issues concerning literary endeavours, and *Absalom and Achitophel*, on a political issue involving the succession – and relate to some real characters and events. The former refers to Dryden's actual conflict with Thomas Shadwell, another poet of the time. The latter regards actual political events of the period: Charles II had no children and his brother the Duke of York was to become king as James II, unpopular for being Roman Catholic, in 1685; the Monmouth Rebellion led by James Scott, first Duke of Monmouth, was unsuccessful and the instigator was beheaded for treason on 15 July 1685; eventually, James II, the last Roman Catholic monarch was overthrown by the Glorious Revolution in 1688. Openly supporting the Church of England, showing Dryden's involvement this time in religious life, is his another satire, *Religio Laici*.

The restoration of monarchy gives its name to the period between 1660 and 1700 – "Restoration" – since it means restoration and revival of arts and literature as well leading to a further advancement and eventual victory of neoclassicism which would come to emphasise and prescribe the power of reason, empiricism, science, rationality, urbanity, clarity, regularity, order, common sense, normative restraint, rules, elegance, decorum, stylized poetic diction, poetic diction, faithfulness to genre, and so on, of which many are urged as normative rules to be followed by authors in their literary activity. Like on the Continent, English neoclassicism owes much of its theoretical effort to both empiricists and rationalists, namely John Locke's *Essay Concerning the Human Understanding* and Rene Descartes's *Discourse on Method, Meditations on First Philosophy*, and *Principles of Philosophy*, both philosophical trends being extremely important for the foundation of the modern, Western philosophical thought which would achieve its climax in the system of the eighteenth-century Enlightenment.

But unlike in the seventeenth century, in which innovation co-existed with tradition, which are involved in a "battle of the books", in the eighteenth century, neoclassicism, having institutionalized the revived in Renaissance ancient classical tradition, dominates the literary scene for more the one hundred years prompting a linear course to literary advancement through history.

In English literature, neoclassicism is a period of literary history covering the last part of the seventeenth century throughout the eighteenth century; neoclassicism is a movement in literature with its poetic works and a strongly normative and prescriptive doctrine; and, also, neoclassicism is the creator of a particular trend in poetry, philosophical and satirical.

English literature of the last decades of the seventeenth century and most of the eighteenth century, or, more precisely, the period from 1660s to 1780s (that is, from Restoration to the rise of romanticism), was dominated by the classical doctrine which continued and institutionalised the revival of ancient classical tradition which had started in Renaissance.

The new classical doctrine – which is referred to as "neoclassicism" – prescribed styles and rules of writing to writers and ways of critical thinking to literary scholars of the period, thus promoting the dependence of literature upon the ancient models. The leading country in Europe, both politically and culturally, France became the source of spreading the classical ideas to other countries, including Britain, pleading for what is natural and reasonable, and for rules, order, clarity, measure, sense of proportion, and good taste. On the general social level, following the "Glorious Revolution" of 1688 and the 1707 "Act for a Union of the Two Kingdoms of England and Scotland", Britain steadily embarked on the path of progress and prosperity based on the idea of order and proportion. The nation acquired a sense of stability and self-confidence, where

> an ideal of providential harmony, of co-operation, and of a political order reflecting that of nature seemed to many to be realized in the triumph of practical reason, liberal religion, and impartial law. Temperate kings would reign over a united nation in which individual liberty would be constitutionally guaranteed. (Sanders 277)

Based on ancient tradition and classical values, neoclassicism is the dominant theory of the period, whose corresponding literary practice includes satirical and philosophical poetry. It would influence not only the contemporary poetry and the consolidation of the novel writing tradition in the eighteenth century, but also the later Victorian realism with its novels of the socially concerned, realistic, traditional, normative, and moral type.

Coinciding with and corresponding to the general European "Age of Enlightenment", neoclassicism, its literary version in English cultural background, is considered as a period of literary history dating from the 1660s to the 1780s and as consisting of three parts: (1) the "Restoration Age" (1660-1700), or the "Age of Dryden", followed by (2) the "Augustan Age" (1700-1750s), or the "Age of Pope", and by (3) the "Age of Johnson" (1750s-1780s) which coincides with the "Age of Sensibility" reflecting the decline of the neoclassical period.

Starting with the weakening of neoclassicism by the mid-eighteenth century, pre-romanticism would mark the transition of literature from the neoclassical to the romantic period. The rise of the novel (with its realistic element, moral didacticism, and comic features) would signify the consolidation of an almost entirely new genre in English literature, that of imaginative prose, as well as the later flourishing of fiction, both novel and short story, in Victorian and later periods. Pre-romanticism was a trend in poetry ("primitive" and "mournfully reflective") which manifested as an alternative to neoclassical poetry and as a precursor to romanticism, without developing important critical theories. On the contrary, neoclassicism embraced both theory and literary practice, and many of the founders of the English novel expressed critical views on the newly rising genre.

Challenged by the poetic experimentation of the pre-romanticism, which emerged with its weakening in the 1750s, neoclassicism seizes to exist as a regular period and movement by the 1780s, being rejected and eventually replaced by romanticism.

The romantic doctrine, art and literature would break the linearity of literary development dominated by classical principles, rules and tradition, producing new views and rejecting tradition and rules, and reviving instead the innovative spirit in art, originality in literature, and proclaiming the freedom of artistic expression, which resulted again in the co-existence of both innovative and traditional trends in the Victorian epoch, the twentieth century, and contemporary period, therefore stimulating new, attractive to the scholar of literary studies, "battles of the books", as we shall see in the next books in our series on the advancement of English literature through history.

REFERENCES AND SUGGESTIONS FOR FURTHER READING

References

Abrams, M. H. *The Mirror and the Lamp: Romantic Theory and the Critical Tradition*. Oxford: Oxford University Press, 1953.
Abrams, M. H., and G. G. Harpham. *A Glossary of Literary Terms* (9th Ed.). Belmont: Wadsworth Publishing Company, 2009.
Auerbach, E. *Mimesis: The Representation of Reality in Western Literature*. New York: Anchor Doubleday, 1957.
Bakhtin, M. M. "Forms of Time and of the Chronotope in the Novel". *The Dialogic Imagination: Four Essays*. Ed. Michael Holquist. Austin: University of Texas Press, 1981. 84-258.
Bakhtin, M. M. "The Bildungsroman and Its Significance in the History of Realism: Toward a Historical Typology of the Novel". *Speech Genres and Other Late Essays*. Ed. Caryl Emerson and Michael Holquist. Austin: University of Texas Press, 1986. 10-59.
Baldick, C. *The Oxford English Literary History, Volume 10. 1910-1940: The Modern Movement*. Oxford: Oxford University Press, 2005.
Barry, P. *Beginning Theory: An Introduction to Literary and Cultural Theory*. Manchester: Manchester University Press, 2009.
Barthes, R. *Mythologies*. New York: The Noonday Press, 1970.
Bennett, J. *Five Metaphysical Poets*. Cambridge: Cambridge University Press, 1964.
Bjornson, R. *The Picaresque Hero in European Fiction*. Wisconsin: The University of Wisconsin Press, 1977.
Blamires, H. *A History of Literary Criticism*. London: Macmillan, 1991.
Bomher, N. *Initieri in teoria literaturii*. Iasi: Editura Fundatiei Chemarea, 1994.
Bressler, C. E. *Literary Criticism: An Introduction to Theory and Practice*. Englewood Cliffs: Prentice-Hall Inc., 2007.
Castle, G. *The Blackwell Guide to Literary Theory*. Oxford: Blackwell Publishing, 2007.
Ceuca, J. *Evoluția formelor dramatice*. Cluj-Napoca: Dacia, 2002.
Clement, B. *Tragedia clasică*. Iași: Institutul European, 2000.
Collini, S. "Introduction: Interpretation terminable and interminable". *Interpretation and Overinterpretation: Umberto Eco with Richard Rorty, Jonathan Culler, Christine Brooke-Rose*. Ed. S. Collini. Cambridge: Cambridge University Press, 1992. 1-21.
Cook, Guy. *Discourse and Literature: The Interplay of Form and Mind*. Oxford: Oxford University Press, 1995.
Cuddon, J. A. *The Penguin Dictionary of Literary Terms and Literary Theory*. London: Penguin Books Ltd, 1992.
Culler, J. *Structuralist Poetics: Structuralism, Linguistics and the Study of Literature*. London: Routledge and Kegan Paul, 1980.
Culler, J. *Literary Theory*. New York: Sterling Publishing Co., Inc., 2009.

Daiches, D. *Critical Approach to Literature*. London: Longman, 1982.
Ducrot, O., and J.-M. Schaeffer. *Noul dictionar enciclopedic al stiintelor limbajului*. Bucuresti: Editura Babel, 1996.
Dunn, Peter N. *Spanish Picaresque Fiction: A New Literary History*. Ithaca: Cornell University Press, 1993.
Dutton, R. *An Introduction to Literary Criticism*. London: Longman, 1984.
Eagleton, T. *Literary Theory: An Introduction*. Oxford: Blackwell Publishing, 2008.
Eco, U. "Overinterpreting texts". *Interpretation and Overinterpretation: Umberto Eco with Richard Rorty, Jonathan Culler, Christine Brooke-Rose*. Ed. S. Collini. Cambridge: Cambridge University Press, 1992. 45-66.
Eco, U. "Between author and text". *Interpretation and Overinterpretation: Umberto Eco with Richard Rorty, Jonathan Culler, Christine Brooke-Rose*. Ed. S. Collini. Cambridge: Cambridge University Press, 1992. 67-88.
Eco, U. "Interpretation and History". *Interpretation and Overinterpretation: Umberto Eco with Richard Rorty, Jonathan Culler, Christine Brooke-Rose*. Ed. S. Collini. Cambridge: Cambridge University Press, 1992. 23-43
Eco, U. *Apocalypse Postponed*. London: Flamingo, 1995.
Eliade, M. *Images et Symboles*. Gallimard, 1952.
Eliot, T. S. *The Sacred Wood: Essays on Poetry and Criticism*. New York: Alfred A. Knopf, 1921.
Fairley, I. R. "The reader's need for conventions". *The Taming of the Text: Explorations in Language, Literature and Culture*. Ed. W. Van Peer. London: Routledge, 1988. 292-316.
Fokkema, D., and E. Ibsch. *Theories of Literature in the Twentieth Century: Structuralism, Marxism, Aesthetics of Reception, Semiotics*. New York: St Martin's Press, 1995.
Fowler, R. "Literature". *Encyclopedia of Literature and Criticism*. Eds. M. Coyle, P. Garside, M. Kelsall, and J. Peck. London: Routledge, 2000. 3-26.
Frank, M. *Gender, Theatre, and the Origins of Criticism: From Dryden to Manley*. Port Chester: Cambridge University Press, 2002.
Frye, Northrop. *Anatomy of Criticism: Four Essays*. London: Penguin Books, 1990.
Galperin, I. R. *Stylistics*. Moscow: Higher School Publishing House, 1971.
Gardner, H. *The Business of Criticism*. Oxford: Oxford University Press, 1970.
Gengembre, G. *Marile curente ale criticii literare*, Iasi: Institutul European, 2000.
Graf, A. *Marile curente ale filosofiei moderne*. Iași: Institutul European, 1997.
Gray, F. "The essay as criticism". *The Cambridge History of Literary Criticism, Volume 3: The Renaissance*. Ed. G. P. Norton. Cambridge: Cambridge University Press, 2001. 271-277.
Hampshire, S. (Ed.). *The Age of Reason: The 17th Century Philosophers*. New York: The New American Library, 1956.
Harland, R. *Literary Theory from Plato to Barthes: An Introductory History*. New York: Palgrave Macmillan, 1999.
Heidegger, M. *Poetry, Language, Thought*. New York: Harper and Row, 1971.
Highet, G. *The Classical Tradition: Greek and Roman Influences on Western Literature*. Oxford: Oxford University Press, 1976.
Holman, C. H., and W. A. Harmon. *A Handbook to Literature*. New York: Macmillan, 1992.
Hutcheon, Linda. *A Poetics of Postmodernism: History, Theory, Fiction*. London, Routledge, 1988.
Jakobson, R. "Linguistics and Poetics". *Modern Criticism and Theory*. Ed. D. Lodge.

London: Longman, 2000. 30-55.

Jauss, H. R. "Literary History as a Challenge to Literary Theory". *New Directions in Literary History*. Ed. R. Cohen. Baltimore: The Johns Hopkins University Press, 1974. 11-41.

Jauss, H. R. *Toward an Aesthetic of Reception*. Minneapolis: University of Minnesota Press, 1982.

Kirkpatrick, D. L. (Ed.). *Reference Guide to English Literature*. London: St. James Press, 1991.

Leech, G. N. *A Linguistic Guide to English Poetry*. London: Longman, 1979.

Lodge, David. *The Novelist at the Crossroads and Other Essays on Fiction and Criticism*. Ithaca: Cornell University Press, 1971.

Machor, J. L., and P. Goldstein. *Reception Study: From Literary Theory to Cultural Studies*. London: Routledge, 2001.

Munteanu, R. *Metamorfozele criticii europene*. Bucuresti: Univers, 1988.

Munteanu, R. *Farsa tragica*. București: Univers, 1989.

Munteanu, R. *Introducere in literatura europeana moderna*. Bucuresti: ALLFA, 1996.

Nicol, Bran. *The Cambridge Introduction to Postmodern Fiction*. Cambridge: Cambridge University Press, 2009.

Peck, J., and M. Coyle. *Literary Terms and Criticism* (3rd Ed.). New York: Palgrave Macmillan, 2002.

Perkins, D. "Literary history and historicism". *The Cambridge History of Literary Criticism, Volume 5: Romanticism*. Ed. M. Brown. Cambridge: Cambridge University Press, 2000. 338-361.

Ricoeur, P. *Eseuri de hermeneutica*. Bucuresti: Humanitas, 1995.

Sambrook, J. "Poetry, 1660-1740". *The Cambridge History of Literary Criticism, Volume 4: The Eighteenth Century*. Eds. H. B. Nisbet and C. Rawson. Cambridge: Cambridge University Press, 2005. 75-116.

Sanders, A. *The Short Oxford History of English Literature*. Oxford: Clarendon Press, 1994.

Scholes, R. *Semiotics and Interpretation*. New Haven: Yale University Press, 1982.

Selden, R. *A Reader's Guide to Contemporary Literary Theory*. New York: Harvester Wheatsheaf, 1989.

Selden, R. "Introduction". *The Cambridge History of Literary Criticism, Volume 8: From Formalism to Poststructuralism*. Ed. R. Selden. Cambridge: Cambridge University Press, 1995. 1-10.

Shklovsky, V. "Art as Technique". *The Critical Tradition: Classic Texts and Contemporary Trends*. Ed. David H. Richter. New York: Bedford/St. Martin's, 1997. 774-784.

Shusterman, R. *The Object of Literary Criticism*. Amsterdam: Rodopi, 1984.

Stephen, M. *An Introductory Guide to English Literature*. London: Longman, 1984.

Stevenson, R. *The Oxford English Literary History, Volume 12. 1960-2000: The Last of England?*. Oxford: Oxford University Press. 2004.

Tynyanov, Y. N. "Literaturnyi fakt". *Poetika. Istoria literaturi. Kino*. Moscva: Nauka, 1977. 255-270.

Tynyanov, Y. N. "O literaturnoi evolutii". *Poetika. Istoria literaturi. Kino*. Moscva: Nauka, 1977. 270-281.

Urnov, D. M. (Ed.). *The Idea of Literature: The Foundations of English Criticism*. Moscow: Progress Publishers, 1979.

Van Emden, J. *The Metaphysical Poets*, London: Macmillan, 1986.

Vickers, B. "The Seventeenth Century". *The Oxford Illustrated History of English*

Literature. Ed. P. Rogers. Oxford: Oxford University Press, 1996. 160 – 213.
Webster, R. *Studying Literary Theory: An Introduction*. London: Edward Arnold. 1993.
Wellek, R., and A. Warren. *Theory of Literature*. New York: Harcourt, 1962.

Suggestions for Further Reading

General Literary History and Criticism

Abrams, M. H. (Ed.). *The Norton Anthology of English Literature*. New York: Norton, 1986.
Allen, W. *The English Novel: A Short Critical History*, London: Penguin Books Ltd., 1954.
Baker, E. A. *The History of the English Novel*, London: Witherby, 1969.
Bakhtin, M. M. *The Dialogic Imagination: Four Essays*. Austin: University of Texas Press, 1981.
Bakhtin, M. M. *Rabelais and His World*. Bloomington: Indiana University Press, 1984.
Bakhtin, M. M. *Problems of Dostoevsky's Poetics*. Minneapolis: University of Minnesota Press, 1984.
Bakhtin, M. M. *Speech Genres and Other Late Essays*. Austin: University of Texas Press, 1986.
Bateson, F. W., and H. T. Meserole. *A Guide to English and American Literature*. London: Longman, 1976.
Beachcroft, T. O. *The English Short Story*, London: Longman, 1964.
Belsey, C. *Critical Practice*. London: Routledge, 1980.
Bernard, R. *A Short History of English Literature*. Oxford: Blackwell Publishing, 1995.
Bjornson, R. *The Picaresque Hero in European Fiction*. Wisconsin: The University of Wisconsin Press, 1977.
Blamires, H. *A Short History of English Literature*. London: Routledge, 1984.
Blamires, H. *A History of Literary Criticism*. London: Macmillan, 1991.
Bressler, C. E. *Literary Criticism: An Introduction to Theory and Practice*. Englewood Cliffs: Prentice-Hall Inc, 2007.
Cartianu, A., and I. A. Preda. *Dictionar al literaturii engleze*. Bucuresti: Editura Stiintifica, 1970.
Ceuca, J. *Evoluția formelor dramatice*. Cluj-Napoca: Dacia, 2002.
Clement, B. *Tragedia clasică*. Iași: Institutul European, 2000.
Conrad, P. *The Everyman History of English Literature*. London: J. M. Dent and Sons Ltd., 1985.
Cuddon, J. A. *The Penguin Dictionary of Literary Terms and Literary Theory*. London: Penguin Books Ltd, 1992.
Cusset, C. *Tragedia greaca*. Iasi: Institutul European, 1999.
Daiches, D. *English Literature*. Englewood Cliffs: Prentice-Hall Inc., 1964.
Daiches, D. *A Critical History of English Literature*. New York: The Ronald Press Company, 1970.
Daiches, D. *The Penguin Companion to English Literature*. New York: McGraw-Hill, 1971.
Day, G. *Literary Criticism: A New History*. Edinburgh: Edinburgh University Press, 2008.

Day, M. S. *History of English Literature to Sixteen Sixty.* New York: Doubleday Books, 1963.
Drabble, M. (Ed.). *The Oxford Companion to English Literature.* Oxford: Oxford University Press, 2000.
Dunn, Peter N. *Spanish Picaresque Fiction: A New Literary History.* Ithaca: Cornell University Press, 1993.
Dutton, R. *An Introduction to Literary Criticism.* London: Longman, 1984.
Eagle, D. *The Concise Oxford Dictionary of English Literature.* Oxford: Oxford University Press, 1987.
Eagleton, T. *The English Novel: An Introduction,* Oxford: Blackwell Publishing, 2005.
Eliade, M. *Images et Symboles.* Gallimard, 1952.
Eliade, M. *Aspecte ale mitului.* București: Editura Univers, 1978.
Ford, B. (Ed.). *The New Pelican Guide to English Literature.* London: Penguin Books Ltd., 1982.
Fowler, A. *Kinds of Literature: An Introduction to the Theory of Genres and Modes.* Oxford: Clarendon Press, 1987.
Fowler, A. *A History of English Literature.* Cambridge: Harvard University Press, 1991.
Frank, M. *Gender, Theatre, and the Origins of Criticism: From Dryden to Manley.* Port Chester: Cambridge University Press, 2002.
Freidenberg, O. *Image and Concept: Mythopoetic Roots of Literature,* Amsterdam: Harwood Academic Publishers, 1997.
Frevert, U., and H.-G. Haupt. *Omul secolului al XIX-lea.* Bucuresti: Polirom, 2002.
Frye, N. *Anatomy of Criticism: Four Essays.* London: Penguin Books, 1990.
Galperin, I. R. *Stylistics.* Moscow: Higher School Publishing House, 1971.
Graf, A. *Marile curente ale filosofiei moderne.* Iasi: Institutul European, 1997.
Hall, V. *A Short History of Literary Criticism.* London: The Merlin Press, 1964.
Heidegger, M. *Poetry, Language, Thought.* New York: Harper and Row, 1971.
Highet, G. *The Classical Tradition: Greek and Roman Influences on Western Literature.* Oxford: Oxford University Press, 1976.
Holman, C. H., and W. A. Harmon. *A Handbook to Literature.* New York: Macmillan, 1992.
Jauss, H. R. *Aesthetic Experience and Literary Hermeneutics.* Minneapolis: University of Minnesota Press, 1982.
Jauss, H. R. *Question and Answer: Forms of Dialogic Understanding.* Minneapolis: University of Minnesota Press, 1989.
Kirkpatrick, D. L. (Ed.). *Reference Guide to English Literature.* London: St James Press, 1991.
Knellwolf, C., and C. Norris. (Eds.). *The Cambridge History of Literary Criticism, Volume 9: Twentieth Century Historical, Philosophical and Psychological Perspectives.* Cambridge: Cambridge University Press, 2001.
Lawrence, K. *The McGraw-Hill Guide to English Literature.* New York: McGraw-Hill, 1985.
Leech, C. *Tragedy.* London: Methuen, 1969.
Leech, G. N. *A Linguistic Guide to English Poetry.* London: Longman, 1979.
Legonis, E., and L. Cazamian. *History of English Literature.* London: J. M. Dent and Sons Ltd., 1971.
Lotman, Y. M. "Lektsii po strukturalinoi poetike". *Y. M. Lotman i tartusko-moskovskaya semioticeskaia shkola.* Moskva: Gnozis, 1994. 10-257.
Magill, F. N. (Ed.). *Cyclopedia of Literary Characters.* New York: Harper and Row, 1963.

Minnis, A., and I. Johnson. (Eds.). *The Cambridge History of Literary Criticism, Volume 2: The Middle Ages*. Cambridge: Cambridge University Press, 2005.

Munteanu, R. *Farsa tragica*. București: Univers, 1989.

Nisbet, H. B., and C. Rawson. (Eds.). *The Cambridge History of Literary Criticism, Volume 4: The Eighteenth Century*. Cambridge: Cambridge University Press, 2005.

Norton, G. P. (Ed.). *The Cambridge History of Literary Criticism, Volume 3: The Renaissance*. Cambridge: Cambridge University Press, 2001.

Ousby, I. (Ed.). *The Cambridge Guide to English Literature*. Cambridge: Cambridge University Press, 1993.

Parrinder, P. *Nation and Novel: The English Novel from its Origins to the Present Day*. Oxford: Oxford University Press, 2006.

Richter, D. H. *The Critical Tradition: Classic Texts and Contemporary Trends*. New York: St Martin's Press. 1989

Ricoeur, Paul. *Eseuri de hermeneutica*. Bucuresti: Humanitas, 1995.

Robert, M. *Romanul inceputurilor si inceputurile romanului*. Bucuresti: Editura Univers, 1983.

Rogers, P. (Ed.). *The Oxford Illustrated History of English Literature*. Oxford: Oxford University Press, 1990.

Sampson, G. *The Concise Cambridge History of English Literature*. Cambridge: Cambridge University Press, 1970.

Sanders, A. *The Short Oxford History of English Literature*. Oxford: Oxford University Press, 1994.

Shklovsky, Viktor. *O teorii prozy*. Moskva: Federatia, 1929.

Stapleton, M. *The Cambridge Guide to English Literature*. Cambridge: Cambridge University Press, 1983.

Stephen, M. *An Introductory Guide to English Literature*. London: Longman, 1984.

Thornley, G. C., and G. Roberts. *An Outline of English Literature*. London: Longman, 1995.

Ubersfeld, A. *Termenii cheie ai analizei teatrului*. Iasi: Institutul European, 1999.

Urnov, D. M. (Ed.). *The Idea of Literature: The Foundations of English Criticism*. Moscow: Progress Publishers, 1979.

Van Boheemen-Saaf, C. *Between Sacred and Profane: Narrative Design and the Logic of Myth from Chaucer to Coover*, Amsterdam: Rodopi, 1987.

Ward, A. C. *Illustrated History of English Literature*. London: Longman, 1960.

Ward, A. W., and A. R. Waller. *The Cambridge History of English Literature*. Cambridge: Cambridge University Press, 1953.

Waugh, P. (Ed.). *Literary Theory and Criticism: An Oxford Guide*. Oxford: Oxford University Press, 2006.

Wynne-Davis, M. (Ed.). *The Bloomsbury Guide to English Literature*. London: Bloomsburg Publishing Ltd., 1960.

Seventeenth-Century Literature

Alvarez, A. *The School of Donne*. New York: Pantheon Books, 1962.

Bald, R. C. *John Donne: A Life*. Oxford: Clarendon Press, 1986.

Bennett, J. *Five Metaphysical Poets*. Cambridge: Cambridge University Press, 1964.

Bloom, H. (Ed.). *John Donne and the Seventeenth-Century Metaphysical Poets*. New York:

Chelsea House, 1986.

Bredvold, L. I. *The Literature of the Restoration and the Eighteenth Century: 1660-1798*. New York: Collier Books, 1962.

Bush, D. *English Literature in the Earlier Seventeenth Century 1600-1660*. Oxford: Clarendon Press, 1962.

Duncan, J. E. *The Revival of Metaphysical Poetry: The History of Style, 1800 to the Present*. University of Minnesota Press, 1959.

Eliot, T.S. *The Varieties of Metaphysical Poetry*. London: Harvest Books, 1996.

Ferry, A. *All in War with Time: Love Poetry of Shakespeare, Donne, Jonson, Marvell*. Cambridge: Cambridge University Press, 1975.

Fish, S. E. (Ed.). *Seventeenth Century Prose: Modern Essays in Criticism*. Oxford: Oxford University Press, 1971.

Griffin, D. *Regaining Paradise: Milton and the Eighteenth Century*. Cambridge: Cambridge University Press, 1986.

Hammond, P. *John Dryden: A Literary Life*. London: Palgrave Macmillan, 1991.

Hampshire, S. *The Age of Reason: The 17th Century Philosophers*. New York: The New American Library, 1956.

Hill, C. *The Century of Revolution: 1603-1714*. London: Routledge, 1991.

Holland, P. *The Ornament of Action: Text and Performance in Restoration Comedy*. Cambridge: Cambridge University Press, 1979.

Hopkins, D. *John Dryden*. Cambridge: Cambridge University Press, 1986.

Hunt, C. *Donne's Poetry: Essays in Literary Analysis*. New Haven: Yale University Press, 1954.

Hunter, G. K. *Paradise Lost*. London: Allen and Unwin, 1980.

Hyman, L. *Andrew Marvell*. New York: Twayne Publishers Inc., 1964.

Jones, R. F. *The Seventeenth Century: Studies in the History of English Thought and Literature from Bacon to Pope*. Stanford: Stanford University Press, 1951.

Keast, W. R. (Ed.). *Seventeenth Century English Poetry: Modern Essays in Criticism*. Oxford: Oxford University Press, 1962.

Legouis, P. *Andrew Marvel: Poet, Puritan, Patriot*. Oxford: Oxford University Press, 1968.

Osgood, C. G. *The Classical Mythology of Milton's English Poems*. New York: Gordian Press, 1964.

Rajan, B. *The Lofty Rhyme: A Study of Milton's Major Poetry*. Coral Gables: University of Miami Press, 1970.

Sambrook, J. "Poetry, 1660-1740". *The Cambridge History of Literary Criticism, Volume 4: The Eighteenth Century*. Eds. H. B. Nisbet and C. Rawson. Cambridge: Cambridge University Press, 2005. 75-116.

Stein, A. *The Art of Presence: The Poet and the Paradise Lost*. Berkeley: University of California Press, 1977.

Van Doren, M. *John Dryden: A Study of His Poetry*. Bloomington: Indiana University Press, 1960.

Van Emden, J. *The Metaphysical Poets*. London: Macmillan, 1986.

Vendler, H. *The Poetry of George Herbert*. Cambridge: Harvard University Press, 1975.

Vickers, B. "The Seventeenth Century". *The Oxford Illustrated History of English Literature*. Ed. P. Rogers. Oxford: Oxford University Press, 1996. 160-213.

Wallerstein, R. *Studies in Seventeenth Century Poetic*. Madison: University of Wisconsin Press, 1950.

Walton, G. *Metaphysical to Augustan: Studies in Tone and Sensibility in the Seventeenth Century*.

London: Bowes and Bowes, 1955.
Weston, P. *John Milton: Paradise Lost*. London: Penguin Books Ltd., 1987.
Williamson, G. *Seventeenth Century Contexts*. Chicago: University of Chicago Press, 1961.
Wilson, A. N. *The Life of John Milton*. Oxford: Oxford University Press, 1983.

INDEX

Abrams, M. H., 22, 23
Ackroyd, Peter, 35, 38
Ali, Monica, 35
Amis, K., 35
Apollinaire, G., 35
Aragon, L., 35
Aristotle, 22, 23, 65, 80, 89, 90, 91, 93, 97, 105, 106, 140
Arnold, Matthew, 2, 11, 14, 34, 38, 66, 78, 84
Astell, Mary, 123
Auden, W. H., 69
Auerbach, Erich, 18
Austen, Jane, 1, 33

Bacon, Francis, 12, 32, 85, 87, 89-90, 93, 97, 99, 103, 119, 131, 144, 175
Bakhtin, Mikhail, 1, 4, 10, 24, 41, 42, 45, 46, 50, 53, 56, 71, 130
Barnes, Julian, 35, 38, 41, 59, 60
Barrett Browning, E., 9
Barthes, Roland, 21
Beardsley, M. C., 51
Beaumont, Francis, 99, 104, 105, 111, 112, 124
Beckett, Samuel, 35, 38
Bede, 32
Behn, Aphra, 123
Bergerac, Cyrano de, 94
Berkeley, George, 96, 97
Bhabha, Homi, 55
Birkenhead, John, 122
Blake, William, 33, 37, 41, 69, 78, 84, 119, 164, 176
Bloom, Harold, 46
Boccaccio, G., 165
Boileau-Despreaux, Nicolas, 90, 91, 92, 99, 100, 101, 128
Braine, John, 35
Brontë, Charlotte, 34, 38
Brontë, Emily, 34, 38
Brooke, Christopher, 134
Browne, Thomas, 111
Browne, William, 111

Browning, Robert, 34, 38, 69, 70, 84
Bunyan, John, 88, 110, 111, 120, 121, 122, 129, 131, 176, 177
Burns, Robert, 34
Burton, Robert, 110
Butler, Samuel, 99, 112, 163, 178
Byron, G. G., 33, 34, 37, 70, 160, 164

Caedmon, 32
Calderon de la Barca, Pedro, 124
Calinescu, George, 19
Campion, Thomas, 111
Carew, Thomas, 112
Carroll, Lewis, 34
Carlyle, Thomas, 38, 64
Carter, Angela, 35, 54
Catullus, 150
Cazamian, Louis, 37
Cervantes, Miguel de, 1
Chapelain, Jean, 90
Chapman, George, 87, 111, 175
Chateaubriand, 12
Chaucer, Geoffrey, 31, 32, 37, 70, 74, 84, 165
Churchill, Caryl, 35
Cicero, 89, 91, 175v
Coelho, P., 54
Coleridge, S. T., 2, 28, 33, 34, 37, 41, 44, 66, 70, 71, 78, 84, 95, 114, 146, 173
Comte, A., 34, 89
Congreve, William, 88, 107, 125
Conrad, Joseph, 34
Cook, Guy, 10, 23, 24, 42, 57
Copernicus, Nicolaus, 93
Corneille, Pierre, 90, 91, 92, 124
Coward, Noel, 127
Cowley, Abraham, 88, 102, 104, 112, 113, 120
Crashaw, Richard, 112, 113, 118, 172
Cromwell, Oliver, 33, 86, 88, 109, 119, 120, 147, 148, 152, 158, 165, 177, 178
Curtius, E. R., 18
Cynewulf, 32

Daiches, David, 51, 106
Dante, Alighieri, 1, 34, 69, 162
Darwin, Charles, 34
Defoe, Daniel, 33, 37, 107
Dennis, John, 99, 100, 107
Derrida, Jacques, 12, 89
Descartes, Rene, 85, 89, 93, 96, 97, 98, 99, 103, 128, 179
Dickens, Charles, 1, 7, 34, 37
Dickinson, Emily, 84
Donne, John, 1, 33, 37, 72, 84, 87, 109, 110, 111, 112, 113, 114, 115, 117, 118, 119, 133-144, 151, 152, 171, 172, 173, 174, 175, 177, 186, 187
  The Good-Morrow, 135-136,
  The Ecstasy, 136-137,
  The Canonization, 137-139,
  A Valediction: Forbidding Mourning, 140-142, 172-173,
  Holy Sonnets, 142-143,
Doolittle, Hilda, 35
Dostoyevsky, F., 1
Doyle, A. C., 34
Drabble, M., 35
Drayton, Michael, 102, 111
Dryden, John, 2, 33, 37, 39, 64, 65, 84, 88, 92, 100, 102, 103, 104-108, 112, 114, 115, 122, 123, 125, 126, 128, 133, 164-170, 171, 178, 180, 182, 185
  An Essay of Dramatic Poesie, 104-108, 168-170,
Drummond, William, 111

Eagleton, T., 39
Eco, Umberto, 7, 12, 17, 20
Eliade, Mircea, 54, 79
Eliot, George, 34, 37
Eliot, T. S., 1, 2, 13, 35, 37, 38, 41, 42, 45, 46, 47, 64, 69, 84, 106, 116, 118, 144, 151, 163, 172, 173
Etherege, George, 103, 125, 126
Euripides, 1, 91
Even-Zohar, I., 55

Faulkner, W., 35
Fenelon, Francois de, 129, 130
Fielding, Henry, 2, 33, 37, 39, 65, 107
Fish, Stanley, 13
Flecknoe, Richard, 103, 167
Fletcher, John, 99, 104, 105, 112, 124, 168
Fowles, John, 35, 38
Freud, Sigmund, 3, 34
Frost, Robert, 66, 84
Frye, Northrop, 14, 16, 20, 65

Galilei, Galileo, 93, 96, 152
Galsworthy, John, 14, 35
Goethe, J. W., 44, 45, 47, 56, 91
Golding, William, 35, 38
Goldsmith, Oliver, 127
Gongora, Luis de, 143, 171
Gower, John, 32, 37
Gray, Thomas, 54, 68, 78, 80
Greene, Graham, 35
Greene, Robert, 32, 33
Grierson, Herbert J. C., 151
Grimmelshausen, Hans Iacob von, 129, 130
Guevara, Velez de, 128, 130

Heaney, S., 35, 84
Hegel, G. W. H., 89
Heidegger, Martin, 98
Herbert, George, 87, 111, 113, 118, 119, 133, 134, 144-146, 172
  The Altar, 145-146
Herder, G. H., 1, 12
Herrick, Robert, 112
Heywood, John, 133
Hill, G., 69
Hobbes, Thomas, 85, 88, 93, 94-96, 97, 99, 102, 110, 120, 121
Hoccleve, Thomas, 32
Homer, 1, 69, 105, 157, 159, 163, 169
Hopkins, G. M., 34, 37
Howard, Henry, 32
Howard, Robert, 103, 105, 126
Horace, 22, 34, 93, 100, 105, 106, 112, 115, 148
Hughes, Ted, 35, 38
Hume, David, 89, 96, 97, 107
Husserl, Edmund, 89
Hutcheon, Linda, 4, 54, 55
Huxley, Aldous, 35

Ionesco, E., 54

Jakobson, Roman, 9, 10, 14, 23, 25, 42, 55
James, Henry, 2, 47, 112
Jauss, Hans Robert, 18, 19, 20
Johnson, Samuel, 1, 2, 33, 96, 104, 106, 107, 108, 114, 115, 128, 163, 176, 180
Jonson, Ben, 2, 33, 39, 54, 87, 102, 104, 105, 106, 107, 110, 111, 112, 119, 123, 124, 126, 128, 134, 168, 169, 170, 174, 175
Joyce, James, 1, 28, 29, 35, 37, 38, 64, 77
Jung, Carl, 96

Kafka, Franz, 35
Kant, Immanuel, 89
Keats, John, 34, 37, 68, 164
Killigrew, Anne, 123
Killigrew, Thomas, 123, 164,
Killigrew, William, 123
Kipling, R., 34
Kis, Danilo, 54
Kristeva, Julia, 46, 55
Kundera, Milan, 54
Kyd, Thomas, 32

La Fontaine, Jean de, 91, 92
La Mesnardière, Hippolyte Jules Pilet de, 91
Langland, William, 32
Larkin, Philip, 35, 38, 84
Lawrence, D. H., 14, 35, , 37, 38
Lee, Nathaniel, 164
Legouis, Emile, 37
Leibniz, Gottfried Wilhelm von, 93, 97, 97, 99
Lessing, G. E., 1
Leavis, F. R., 13, 18
Locke, John, 85, 88, 89, 96, 97, 99, 103, 122, 128
Lodge, David, 2, 15, 17, 35, 38, 64
Lorca, Garcia, 35
Lotman, Yuri, 42
Lovelace, Richard, 112
Lowth, Robert, 12, 107

Lubbock, Percy, 1
Lydgate, John, 32
Lyly, John, 32, 33
Lyotard, Jean François, 89

Macpherson, James, 33
Madame de Stael, 12
Malory, Thomas, 32, 70
Mandeville, Sir John, 32
Marino, Giovan Battista, 114, 143, 171
Marlowe, Christopher, 33, 37
Marquez, G. G., 54
Marvell, Andrew, 33, 37, 109, 110, 112, 113, 118, 120, 133, 146-151, 153, 172, 177
An Horatian Ode, 148
The Garden, 149-150
To His Coy Mistress, 150-151
Marx, Carl, 34
Maugham, W. S., 35
McEwan, Ian, 35, 38, 54
Milton, John, 33, 37, 68, 69, 84, 87, 88, 102, 109, 110, 112, 119, 120, 121, 122, 133, 146, 147, 151-164, 165, 171, 175, 176
L'Allegro and *Il Penseroso*, 153-155
Sonnets, 156-157,
Paradise Lost, 157-164
Mitchell, Margaret, 38
Moliere (Jean-Baptiste Poquelin), 91, 92, 124, 126
Montaigne, Michel de, 89, 90, 113
More, Thomas, 32, 133
Morris, William, 34
Muddiman, Henry, 122
Munteanu, Romul, 19, 94
Murdoch, Iris, 35, 38

Nashe, Thomas, 32, 129
Needham, Marchamont, 122
Nicol, Bran, 4, 54, 55
Newton, Isaac, 34, 96, 97, 103, 149

Orwell, George, 35, 76
Osborne, John, 35

Pascal, Blaise, 93, 96, 98
Pater, Walter, 1, 2, 28, 38, 47, 66

Percy, Thomas, 12
Perrault, Charles, 101
Philips, Katherine, 123
Pinter, Harold, 35, 38
Plato, 22, 104, 136, 142, 144, 149, 168, 182
Plautus, 126
Plutarch, 89
Pope, Alexander, 2, 33, 37, 54, 84, 89, 96, 100, 104, 107, 108, 128, 134, 158, 164, 168, 173, 176, 177, 180
Pound, Ezra, 35, 118
Proust, Marcel, 1, 29, 35

Quarles, Francis, 119
Quevedo, Francisco de, 128, 130
Quinault, Philippe, 124, 165

Racine, Jean, 91, 92, 101, 124
Radcliffe, Ann, 34
Raleigh, Walter, 175
Rapin, Rene, 90, 92, 99, 100, 128
Reeve, Clara, 34
Richards, I. A., 13, 18
Richardson, Samuel, 33, 37, 107
Ricoeur, Paul, 58
Rossetti, D. G., 34, 69
Rushdie, Salman, 35
Ruskin, John, 2, 38
Rymer, Thomas, 99

Sackville, Charles, 105, 124
Safak, Elif, 54
Sanders, Andrew, 31, 85, 123
Sarasin, J. F., 1, 91
Saussure, Ferdinand de, 12
Scarron, Paul, 129, 130
Scholes, R., 25
Scott, Walter, 34, 44, 178
Sedley, Charles, 105, 124
Selden, R., 14, 25
Seneca, 89, 175
Shadwell, Thomas, 103, 167, 178
Shakespeare, William, 1, 32, 33, 37, 39, 41, 54, 64, 69, 70, 76, 84, 87, 99, 102, 104, 105, 106, 107, 110, 111, 112, 115, 120, 123, 124, 126, 151, 157, 162, 165, 168, 169, 170
Shaw, George Bernard, 35, 38

Sheffield, John, 124
Shelley, Percy Bysshe, 2, 33, 34, 37, 47, 66, 68, 70
Sheridan, Richard, 127
Shklovsky, V., 1, 42, 45, 46, 47, 50
Schlegel, Friedrich, 14, 20
Schleiermacher, Friedrich, 12
Sidney, Sir Philip, 2, 32, 37, 38, 84, 102, 106, 107, 111, 157, 168, 174
Sillitoe, Alan, 35
Snow, C. P., 35
Sophocles, 91
Sorel, Charles, 120, 130
Southey, Robert, 34
Spark, Muriel, 35, 38
Spenser, Edmund, 32, 37, 111, 115, 152, 157
Spinoza, Baruch de, 93, 97, 98, 99
Stein, G., 35
Stendhal (Marie-Henri Beyle), 91
Sterne, Laurence, 33, 37, 64
Stevenson, R. L., 34
Stoppard, Tom, 35
Suckling, John, 112
Swift, Graham, 35
Swift, Jonathan, 28, 33, 37, 101, 107
Swinburne, C. A., 34, 38

Tacitus, 89
Taine, H., 1, 20, 34
Taylor, Jeremy, 110
Temple, William, 100, 107
Tennyson, Alfred, 34, 38, 69, 70, 84
Terence, 91, 126
Thackeray, W. M., 34, 121
Thomas, Dylan, 35
Tolkien, J. R. R., 164
Traherne, Thomas, 112
Tynyanov, Yuri, 1, 4, 6, 9, 18, 20, 23, 39-55
Tzara, T., 35

Valery, Paul, 35
Vaughan, Henry, 113, 118, 119, 172
Vega, Lope de, 124
Viau, Theophile de, 143
Villiers, George, 127, 168
Virgil, 157, 163, 165, 178

Wain, John, 35
Waller, Edmund, 112, 177
Walpole, Horace, 34
Walton, Izaak, 111, 135
Warren, Austen, 14, 18, 52
Warton, Thomas, 12, 107
Waugh, Evelyn, 35
Wellek, Rene, 14, 18, 52
Wells, H. G., 34
Whitman, Walt, 84
Wieland, C. M., 44
Wilde, Oscar, 2, 14, 34, 38, 66, 127
Williams, W. C., 35, 80
Willy, Margaret, 114, 137
Wilmot, John, 125
Wimsatt, W. K., 51
Wither, George, 112

Woolf, Virginia, 2, 13, 28, 35, 38
Wordsworth, William, 2, 28, 33, 37, 41, 47, 64, 65, 69, 96, 114, 173
Wotton, William, 100
Wyatt, Thomas, 32, 69, 115
Wycherley, William, 125

Yeats, W. B., 35, 69, 75, 118

www.ingramcontent.com/pod-product-compliance
Lightning Source LLC
Chambersburg PA
CBHW071741150426
43191CB00010B/1654